JAPANESE TEMPLE BUDDHISM

Topics in Contemporary Buddhism
GEORGE J. TANABE JR., EDITOR

Establishing a Pure Land on Earth: The Foguang Buddhist Perspective on Modernization and Globalization
STUART CHANDLER

Buddhist Missionaries in the Era of Globalization
LINDA LEARMAN, EDITOR

Being Benevolence: The Social Ethics of Engaged Buddhism
SALLIE B. KING

Japanese Temple Buddhism: Worldliness in a Religion of Renunciation
STEPHEN G. COVELL

TOPICS IN
CONTEMPORARY
BUDDHISM

JAPANESE TEMPLE BUDDHISM

Worldliness in a Religion of Renunciation

STEPHEN G. COVELL

University of Hawai'i Press
Honolulu

© 2005 University of Hawai'i Press
All rights reserved
Printed in the United States of America
10 09 08   6 5 4 3 2

Library of Congress Cataloging-in-Publication Data
Covell, Stephen Grover.
Japanese temple Buddhism : worldliness in a religion
of renunciation / Stephen G. Covell.
    p.   cm.—(Topics in contemporary Buddhism)
Includes bibliographical references and index.
ISBN-13: 978-0-8248-2856-1 (hardcover : alk. paper)
ISBN-13: 978-0-8248-2967-4 (pbk.: alk. paper)
1. Buddhism—Japan—1945–   2. Priests, Buddhist—
Japan—Office.   I. Title.   II. Series.
BQ697.C67 2006
294.3'65'0952—dc22
                                        2005008002

University of Hawai'i Press books are printed
on acid-free paper and meet the guidelines for
permanence and durability of the Council on
Library Resources.

Printed by The Maple-Vail Book Manufacturing Group

For my brother John,
who was always there for me

and

for Iwasaki Takako,
who will be remembered for her loving-kindness
during our seven years in Tokyo

Contents

Series Editor's Preface   ix

Acknowledgments   xi

Reign Periods   xiii

Introduction: Snapshots of Buddhism in Today's Japan   1

1   Temple Buddhism Today: Scholarly and Popular Images of Corruption   11

2   Laity and the Temple: Past and Present   23

3   Trying to Have It Both Ways: The Laity in a World-Renouncer Organization   43

4   The Contemporary Priesthood: Images of Identity Crisis   62

5   New Priests for New Times?   90

6   Coming to Terms: Temple Wives and World-Renouncers   109

7   Money and the Temple: Law, Taxes, and the Image of Buddhism   140

8   The Price of Naming the Dead: Funerals, Posthumous Precept Names, and Changing Views of the Afterlife   165

Epilogue: The World of Householding World-Renouncers   191

Notes   199

Sources Cited   239

Index   251

Series Editor's Preface

As the basic social unit of Buddhism in Japan, temples are the sites where priests and laypersons attempt to live worldly lives according to teachings of renunciation. This is a certain recipe for failure, the story of which is bound to be fascinating. What is remarkable about institutional Buddhism in Japan, however, is not its much-criticized decline into meaningless customs and pecuniary interests, but its struggles to keep alive ancient religious ideals and practices in one of the most technologically advanced nations in the world. "Funeral Buddhism," for instance, is a pejorative term that describes highly profitable rituals that few understand. At the same time, postmortem rites, whether people realize it or not, speak explicitly about the classical objective of achieving enlightenment.

Not surprisingly, the clash between worldliness and renunciation produces ironic relationships between magic and science, priests and their wives, professed poverty and accumulated wealth, secularization and sanctity, social involvement and withdrawal, real religion and its counterfeits. These are grand themes in the study of Buddhism, but few have centered their examinations in the real life of temples. Stephen Covell gives us a rare view from within a temple, offering detailed accounts of what it is like to be a priest, wife, and parishioner. He also presents views from a larger institutional platform and looks at sectarian attempts to make temples and the priesthood viable in a rapidly changing society. The story is compelling in its twists and turns about a religion that is as threatened as it is secure, and Covell's telling raises intriguing questions about what will happen next.

George J. Tanabe Jr.
SERIES EDITOR

Acknowledgments

Were it not for the help, encouragement, assistance, and generosity of many people, this book would never have come to be. I am indebted to the faculty and graduate students at the Religion Department at Princeton University, where I completed my dissertation, upon which this work is based. Jacqueline Stone, my advisor, read through many early drafts, made sure I always had funding during my initial fieldwork, and kept my ever-wandering writings on track. Stephen Teiser offered insightful guidance and much-needed words of encouragement. Sheldon Garon helped focus my interest on state and religion, and the advice of Martin Collcutt helped make my fieldwork possible. Also, Mark Rowe provided many insightful comments on later drafts.

In Japan, Ichishima Shōshin of Taishō University introduced the world of living Buddhism to me. Without his kindness, advice, and help, this project would never even have begun. Saitō Enshin, also of Taishō University, made time in his busy schedule to discuss sources and critique my ideas. Shimazono Susumu of Tokyo University talked through chapter outlines and pointed the way for further development. And the support of William Steele and the staff of the Institute for Asian Cultural Studies at International Christian University made writing in Japan possible. I would also like to thank the faculty and staff of the Sōgō Bukkyō Kenkyūjo at Taishō University for their advice over the many years this project took to come to fruition. Kawahashi Noriko, of Nagoya Kōgyō Daigaku, also gave extensive advice regarding the chapter on temple wives.

Of course, nothing would have been possible without the warmhearted help and patience of the many priests, temple wives, and *danka* members I met during my time in Japan. Special thanks must be given to Midorigawa Myōse for her friendship, support, and gentle guidance, and to Hayashida Yoriko for teaching me about the life of temple wives. Many thanks are also due to the priests and temple families of Kimyōji, Zenshōji, Jindaiji, Gionji, Saikōji, Fugenji, and Kannonin, and to the Tendai sect administration.

Funding for fieldwork, research, and writing was made possible by a number of organizations: the Harold W. Dodds Honorific Fellowship, the Center for the Study of Religion at Princeton University, the Japan Foundation, the Japanese Ministry of Education, and the Council on Regional Studies at Princeton University.

Finally, the encouragement of my parents made possible my many years as a graduate student. Also, my wife's patience and help were invaluable. She read through every chapter several times, even while suffering morning sickness when pregnant with our son. And I wish to thank my daughter, who scribbled on drafts and climbed on my back as I tried to type, taking joy in all; she helped to keep everything in perspective.

While I wish to share the credit for this project, any and all errors are my own.

Reign Periods

Heisei period (1989–present)	Contemporary (*gendai-genzai*)
Shōwa period (1926–1988) Taishō period (1912–1926) Meiji period (1868–1912)	Modern (*kindai-gendai*)
Edo period (Tokugawa period) (1603–1868)	Early Modern (*kinsei*)
Azuchi/Momoyama period (1568–1602) Muromachi period (1333–1568) Kamakura period (1185–1333)	Medieval (*chūsei*)
Heian period (794–1185) Nara Period (710-794)	Ancient (*kodai*)

Introduction
Snapshots of Buddhism in Today's Japan

A NEIGHBORHOOD TEMPLE, KANSAI AREA, FALL 1989

Shōshin and I sat on the floor in his room at the temple. Records were scattered all about, guitars leaned against the walls, and books cluttered the desktops. Coltrane played through old speakers as we sat working our way through a bottle of Japanese vodka (*shōchū*) and discussed Amida Buddha's vow to save sentient beings. We talked through the night. Shōshin earnestly strove to teach me about the truth of Amida's vow. In the morning, we made our way downstairs to have breakfast. Shōshin's young son greeted us loudly. Shōshin's father, the head priest of the temple, and mother were there as well, and his wife was finishing breakfast preparations in the kitchen. His wife's chores—caring for her children, helping Shōshin's mother manage the temple schedule, meeting with the laity, and cleaning—would keep her busy all day.

Shōshin, also a priest, helped his father with rituals held at the temple and taught children at the temple's Sunday school. He put his love of music to use by teaching the children different songs while instructing them in stories about Buddhism. He was also a full-time music teacher at a local junior high school, a job that allowed him to take days off when his ritual duties called. His father was often busy with a full schedule of memorial services. Weekends were an especially demanding time, as services had to be conducted for one family after another.

This is life as usual at most temples. The primary work of the priest is performing funeral and memorial services. Moreover, the priest does not live apart from the world, but is fully enmeshed in it. He is married, has children, eats meat, drinks alcohol, and usually has a full-time job outside the temple, such as teaching. This is not the Buddhism I came to expect through my studies at college and through my own reading. Like many others, I suppose I expected mountain temples, meditating priests, and beautiful works of art. At the same time, having lived in Japan and having talked with many people about Buddhism, I had also come to believe that contemporary Japanese Buddhism is no more than a corruption of "real" Buddhism, whatever that might be. Therefore, if I could not find meditating priests on mountaintops, I expected disaffected, business-oriented priests. Shōshin was neither. Certainly he was not sitting meditation with a shaved head in a mountain temple, but neither was he disaffected. As a matter of fact, when I first met him, he was in the midst of deep soul-searching, seeking for Amida with all his might and reflecting on what his future as the son of a temple priest would be.

In this sense, it was Shōshin's dilemma that first inspired me to further investigate contemporary Japanese Buddhism.

A LARGE TEMPLE IN THE KANTŌ AREA, NEW YEAR'S 1999

The temple had been busy with preparations for more than two weeks leading up to the New Year festival. For three days I had sat on the floor of the main hall assembling protective talismans (fuda) with three high school girls who had been hired as part-time help for the New Year's rush. Intermittently, a priest would walk over from the fire ritual hall after performing that day's ceremony and bless the thousands of items packed in boxes stacked three rows deep all around us. Meanwhile, the head priest and managing priest set about arranging for extra priestly help. Area temples sent their priests to help on New Year's Eve and the days that followed.

The ritual celebrations began at midnight on New Year's Eve. Temple lay members, local community members, and others lined up to ring the temple bell following a short ceremony led by the head priest. Meanwhile, across the compound, in the hall dedicated to the fire ritual (goma), priests began a near round-the-clock series of fire rituals. For the next week, in a display of austere practice that taxed their physical strength, ten to twelve priests would work in shifts performing the fire ceremony on two daises.

The hall at midnight on New Year's Eve was packed with temple members, the faithful, members of the local community, and others. Many had to stand outside the hall for want of space. Nearly all in attendance had given money in exchange for a talisman that would be empowered during the ceremony. Behind them thousands of visitors poured in a steady stream through the temple grounds.

As those in attendance sat shoulder to shoulder in the crowded hall fidgeting uncomfortably in the traditional seiza sitting posture (sitting on one's heels, legs folded under oneself), the priests filed in. The lead priest was clad in magnificent embroidered silk robes. The other senior priests wore similarly impressive robes. The two priests assigned to perform the fire ritual wore the white robes of Japanese Buddhist ascetics. The ceremony began with the sharp sound of a conch shell (horagai) blown by a priest who stood on the far side of the hall. A second priest began to play a strong and steady rhythm on a large drum (taiko). When the other priests began chanting, the drumming increased in strength so that the hall itself felt as though it was vibrating with life. As the ceremony progressed, flames began to leap from the center of the two daises, the fire stoked by the white-clad priests sitting before them. The room filled with the smell of burning wood and incense, and the sound of chanting and drumming. Those in attendance sat silently. When the ceremony ended, one of the two white-clad priests came forward to bless the audience. He repeated prayers in a loud voice while rubbing his prayer beads in palms pressed together to form a mudra (ritual hand gesture).

Anyone in attendance could not help but be impressed with the power and majesty of this performance. This ceremony and ones like it performed at temples of the Tendai sect across Japan communicate to all who attend the religious authority and otherworldliness of priests.[1]

In this impressive ceremony, I had at last found the Buddhism of renunciation and austerity I had come to expect based on my readings. It was experiences such as this that led me to question further contemporary critiques of Japanese Buddhism as corrupt. If corruption meant lack of sincerity or commitment, here were priests utterly dedicated to the task at hand and sincerely working to bring benefit to the laity.

At the same time, having witnessed the events from behind the scenes, I was impressed by the rapid change that took place as the priests prepared for each successive ceremony. After completing the rite with a bow to each other and the lead priest, those filing out of the hall would immediately seek out a seat in the cramped changing room and light up a cigarette or sift through the bags of donated sweets set out for them. Most would sip tea or coffee and strike up conversation about the latest news or soccer score, or gossip. Some caught a quick nap, while others watched whatever variety show happened to be on the small TV set in one corner. This rapid shift from sacred to profane and from austerity to prosperity, which for some reveals the hypocrisy of a disengaged, businesslike priesthood, only served to demonstrate for me the humanness of the priests. As Robert Buswell makes clear in his insightful work on contemporary Buddhist practice in Korea, "Monks are, in short, perfectly ordinary people."[2] They, like anyone else, are capable of pursuing seemingly contradictory goals simultaneously: in Japan, at least, they live as both world-renouncer and householder.

TEMPLE BUDDHISM IN CONTEMPORARY JAPAN: ISSUES AND IMAGES

According to government statistics, ninety-five million (75 percent) of all Japanese are Buddhist. Fifty-six million of these are members of a recognized Buddhist religious organization, of which approximately forty-three million claim membership in a sect or branch of Temple Buddhism (the others are members of Buddhist new religions).[3] And yet, despite the fact that Temple Buddhism is the largest form of organized religion in contemporary Japan, scholars have all but ignored it.

Scholars of postwar Japanese religion have tended to focus their attention on the new religions (shin shūkyō), such as Reiyūkai, and the new new religions (shin shin shūkyō), such as Agonshū.[4] These new religious movements exist alongside and in interaction with Temple Buddhism, and they form an integral part of the web of religious life in Japan. Their explosive growth in the postwar period attracted the attention of religious studies scholars and anthropologists. But just as Temple Buddhism cannot be understood apart from the rise of the new religions, they cannot be understood apart from Temple Buddhism. Nevertheless, most works on the new religions fail to discuss their relationship with Temple Buddhism, unless to dismiss Temple Buddhism as an antiquated and corrupt religion that no longer meets the needs of the people.

Buddhist Studies scholars, on the other hand, have focused largely on the medieval period. Sharing the same view of Temple Buddhism that plagues works on the new religions, Buddhist Studies scholars tend to locate "real" Buddhism—taken to emphasize monasticism, upholding of the precepts, and doctrinal debate—in the remote past. This study seeks to redress the lack of serious scholarly study on Temple Buddhism as lived today.

Funerals, families, ritual, salvation, money, married clergy, and community involvement are all aspects of Temple Buddhism in Japan today. Moreover, there are 157 sects, subsects, and branches; two hundred thousand priests; and more than seventy thousand temples (tables 1 and 2).[5] Given this wide array of activities, people, and institutions, there is no easy way to frame the world of contemporary Temple Buddhism. This study will focus primarily on the institutions of Temple Buddhism and on the responses of Temple Buddhism at the institutional level to changes in contemporary Japanese society.

To what does the term "Temple Buddhism" refer? It refers to the Buddhism as lived by the members of those sects of Japanese Buddhism that were founded before the 1600s.[6] The terms most frequently used to describe these sects are "established Buddhism" (kisei bukkyō) and "traditional Buddhism" (dentō bukkyō). Both terms are problematic. Many members of the sects of Temple Buddhism consider "established Buddhism" a derogatory term. They equate "established" with "old" or "ossified" or take the term as an indictment of unity with state interests. To some it is an indictment of their alleged corruption. Since this term is also used comparatively, placing the sects against the "newly arisen" (shinkō),

TABLE 1
Numbers of Temples

LINEAGES (COMBINES RELATED SECTS AND BRANCHES) AND SECTS	RELIGIOUS ORGANIZATIONS (NUMBER REGISTERED AS RELIGIOUS JURIDICAL PERSON)					
	Shrines	Temples	Teaching centers (kyōkai)	Proselytizing centers (fukyōjō)	Others	Total
Tendai lineage	6 (5)	4,462 (4,053)	340 (146)	168 (10)	33 (—)	5,009 (4214)
Tendai sect	—	3,345 (3,095)	—	—	—	3,345 (3,095)
Shingon lineage	1 (1)	12,411 (11,991)	865 (297)	1,181 (4)	489 (41)	14,947 (12,334)
Buzan branch	—	2,636 (2,636)	14 (14)	—	—	2,650 (2,650)
Chizan branch	—	2,858 (2,844)	36 (36)	—	—	2,894 (2,880)
Jōdo lineage	—	29,628 (29,490)	259 (179)	93 (2)	287 (212)	30,267 (29,883)
Jōdo sect	—	6,932 (6,899)	57 (50)	—	92 (77)	7,081 (7,026)
Jōdo Shin Otani branch	—	8,698 (8,594)	124 (67)	—	52 (52)	8,874 (8,713)
Jōdo Shin Honganji branch	—	10,329 (10,329)	13 (4)	42 (—)	101 (70)	10,485 (10,403)
Zen lineage	—	20,968 (20,891)	21 (14)	4 (1)	22 (2)	21,015 (20,908)
Rinzai Myōshinji branch	—	3,396 (3,396)	5 (5)	—	—	3,401 (3,401)
Sōtō	—	14,688 (14,640)	—	1 (—)	—	14,689 (14,640)
Nichiren lineage	—	6,905 (6,764)	937 (497)	1,329 (20)	3,309 (12)	12,480 (7,293)
Nichiren sect	—	4,636 (4.636)	327 (327)	265 (—)	—	5,228 (4,963)
Nichiren Shōshū	—	661 (574)	34 (30)	—	15 (—)	710 (604)
Nara lineage	—	230 (229)	39 (9)	59 (—)	—	328 (238)

Source: Bunkachō (1999)

TABLE 2
Numbers of Priests and Adherents

| | PRIESTS (KYŌSHI) | | | ADHERENTS (SHINJA) |
	Male	Female	Total*	
Tendai lineage	10,770	8,074	18,844	3,498,861
Tendai sect	3,919	528	4,447	1,531,498
Shingon lineage	28,668	33,705	63,483	12,737,382
Buzan branch	2,777	222	2,999	1,207,346
Chizan branch	4,092	89	4,181	1,512,488
Jōdo lineage	50,969	11,674	62,643	19,312,659
Jōdo sect	9,368	765	10,133	6,032,798
Jōdo Shin Otani branch	14,746	1,988	16,734	5,533,146
Jōdo Shin Honganji branch	21,562	8,309	29,871	6,940,681
Zen lineage	5,975	593	23,211	3,287,511
Rinzai Myōshinji branch	3,305	171	3,476	329,101
Sōtō	—	—	16,643	1,579,301
Nichiren lineage	18,828	9,974	51,644**	17,499,373
Nichiren sect	7,077	974	8,051	3,580,901
Nichiren Shōshū	734	—	734	283,354
Nara lineage	548	723	—	199,606
Others	70	91	1	10,079

Source: Bunkachō (1999).
*Some sects do not provide male/female numbers. Therefore, the total can appear much larger than the combination of male and female numbers given.
**This number includes 22,842 for Rishō Kōseikai.

"new" (*shin*), or "new new" (*shin shin*) religions (*shūkyō*), it is also disliked by some members of these new religious groups because it places them in the rhetorically inferior position of being "new," that is, less legitimate, or lacking the authority of established tradition. Members of the sects of Temple Buddhism often prefer the term "traditional Buddhism," and it is seen frequently in their literature. However, this term, too, places the new religions in a rhetorically inferior position (i.e., they lack a time-tested tradition). Both sets of terms, "established" and "new" and "traditional" and "nontraditional," assume that paradigm of corruption by which scholars and priests alike often view contemporary Japanese Buddhism. I have chosen, instead, the term "Temple Buddhism" to describe the type of Buddhism that is found in the tens of thousands of Buddhist temples scattered across Japan.

To be sure, Temple Buddhism includes a wide variety of sects and also considerable difference from sect to sect and from temple to temple, whether in doctrine, ritual, or priestly training. For example, the Tendai sect requires all priests (male or female) to attend a rigorous and grueling two-month retreat at the sect headquarters on Mt. Hiei, whereas the Nichiren sect requires an intensive thirty-five-day training retreat.[7] Rituals can also vary significantly from sect to sect. The funeral of the Sōtō sect, for example, is generally a far grander affair than that of the Tendai sect. Local obligations also shape temple activities and generate difference. Rural temples, for example, are more likely than their urban counterparts to have a wide variety of confraternities (e.g., women's groups, pilgrimage groups, chanting groups) that center on them as well as a wide variety of civic groups that avail themselves of the temple facilities (e.g., croquet clubs).

However, the sects of Temple Buddhism also share many things in common. Their doctrines and institutional structures have exerted influence on each other. The Tendai doctrine of original enlightenment, developed in the medieval period, for example, shaped nearly all later forms of Japanese Buddhism. Moreover, officiating at funerals and memorial services is the primary ritual role of priests today, as it has been for at least the last two centuries. Therefore, while rituals may vary in form, the priest's role as ritual specialist is common to nearly all sects. Furthermore, legal codes from the early modern period onward forced similar structural changes on all sects. The early modern temple registration system, discussed in chapter 2, was instrumental in creating the *danka* member system (*danka seido*, temple lay membership system) as it exists today, as well as the priest's position as caretaker of the dead. The postwar Religious Juridical Persons Law (*shūkyō hōjin hō*), though not as instrumental in shaping Temple Buddhism as the temple registration system, has been influential in constructing modern temple management structures and sect administration. Moreover, the problems that the sects of Temple Buddhism face in the postwar period have similar roots. Postwar land reform, for instance, changed the economic base of temples across the country. Furthermore, the changing nature of religious affiliation in contemporary Japan cuts across sectarian lines. Finally, the sects of Temple Buddhism have responded similarly to contemporary problems. Most sects, for example, began some form of social engagement campaign in the 1960s or 1970s. And all sects have begun to study methods for improving priestly recruitment and for coming to terms with open clerical marriage, which, as we shall see in chapter 6, represents a significant problem for the sects of Temple Buddhism today.

The Tendai sect, which has more than three thousand temples and four thousand priests, will serve as a representative example, though I will draw on evidence from a variety of sources, including many surveys based on other sects. Despite its relatively small size, I will focus on the Tendai sect for several reasons.[8] First, a growing body of scholarly work, especially that by sectarian scholars, exists on other sects, such as the Jōdo sect (one of the Pure Land sects) and the Sōtō sect (one of the Zen sects). This work consists of institutional histories, doctrinal and ritual studies, and essays on selected critical issues (funerals, discriminatory practices). The Sōtō sect, in particular, has drawn the attention of Western scholars[9] because it is one of the largest sects and Zen has proven to have a peculiar allure for Westerners.[10] By comparison, despite Tendai's pivotal role in the development of Japanese Buddhism in the medieval period and its still important role throughout the early modern and modern periods, there has been far less research conducted on Tendai overall, in Japanese or other languages, and almost none on modern Japanese Tendai.[11]

Second, some sects have unusual situations that make them less useful as examples. Nichiren Shōshū, for example, throughout the postwar period (until a schism in 1991), was structurally bound to the powerful new religion, Sōka Gakkai. The Jōdo Shin sect also has a unique history. Jōdo Shin was the first sect to openly recognize clerical marriage, centuries before other sects. Furthermore, it promoted itself as a lay-focused sect from its beginning. It has, therefore, openly forsaken portraying itself as primarily a world-renouncing organization, something the other sects of Temple Buddhism still claim to be.

There are also personal reasons for selecting the Tendai sect. I have long been interested in the doctrines of the Tendai sect, and my earlier work reflects this interest.[12] Moreover, my first introduction to Japanese Buddhist Studies scholars and the world of Temple Buddhism as it is practiced today was through Tendai scholars. Finally, as time progressed, I underwent ordination in the Tendai sect myself. For two years I was both participant and observer. I worked with a priest in the Kantō area helping him to perform funeral rituals and care for a temple left abandoned by its former priest. Like many other Buddhist scholars in Japan and the West, therefore, I have a personal interest in my topic.

Given the variety found within Temple Buddhism, the virtually complete absence of scholarly work on it, and the influence of the view that Temple Buddhism is corrupt, this study has one basic goal: to examine in depth the institutions and activities of contemporary Temple Buddhism in order to gain a more rounded understanding of contemporary Japanese religious practice and, thereby, to encourage others to begin their own research in this area.

In chapter 1, I seek to put to rest the "corruption" paradigm. As I will show, this model does not serve as a useful method for understanding Buddhism in Japan. It serves only to mask the varied and competing discourses that seek to define what Buddhism has been, is, and will be. I then seek to reexamine the many, often contradictory, facets of contemporary Japanese Buddhism. This examination reveals as a recurrent theme that Temple Buddhism at once renounces and confirms the world. Moreover, this apparently contradictory stance characterizes even the institutions and persons that seek to deny it. It is this conflict between a rhetoric of renunciation and the practices of clerical marriage and householding that characterizes much of contemporary Japanese Temple Buddhism and that serves as a constant basis of criticism. Unlike Shinran, the famous medieval Japanese monk who took a wife and proclaimed himself "neither monk nor layman," many contemporary priests identify themselves as renunciates and clearly distinguish themselves from the laity despite living lives mostly identical to those of the laity. They are both world-renouncers and laymen.

Chapters 2 and 3 take the state of the temple lay membership as their subject: contemporary temple *danka*, the historical roots of the conflicting views of the temple held by the temple and the *danka,* and the steps the sects of Temple Buddhism are taking to rectify these. In particular, chapter 3 analyzes the ways in which the Tendai sect seeks to change popular images of "funeral Buddhism," including efforts to redefine the roles of temple lay members in order to secure Tendai's place in contemporary Japanese society.

Chapters 4 and 5 take the priesthood of Temple Buddhism as their subject, examining the history of various negative images of the priesthood and the Tendai sect's efforts to create or re-create priestly roles that counter growing popular images of priests as funeral businessmen. Such efforts on the part of the Tendai sect, which are mirrored in other sects, bring to attention the manner in which sect leaders envision Buddhism and its place in contemporary society. Tendai efforts are placed in the context of currents within contemporary Japanese religion, such as competition from new religions and mail-order-priest companies.

Priests' wives are the subject of chapter 6. The wives of priests play a major role in temple management, and some are now seeking to overcome sex discrimination and to gain recognition of their critical role. Clerical marriage is the most obvious threat to the rhetoric of renunciation pursued by the sects of Temple Buddhism. In response, the Tendai sect, for example, has developed a special temple wife ordination (*jiteifujin tokudo*) ceremony in order to place temple wives within the religious and administrative structures of the sect. The efforts by temple wives to seek recognition reveal fractures in the world of Temple Buddhism that allow us the opportunity better to understand Temple Buddhism today, its history, and postwar Japanese religion in practice. Chapters 2–6 (temple lay members, priests, and temple wives) thus serve to introduce efforts by the sects of Temple Buddhism to maintain relevance in postwar Japanese society. They also bring to light sectarian, scholarly, and popular assumptions regarding Temple Buddhism.

Taxes and death are the subjects of chapters 7 and 8, which address the fiscal necessities of running a temple today and the practices priests engage in to meet needs. These chapters include an examination of how economic realities shape ritual practices as well as how such mundane factors as taxes shape the debate over Temple Buddhism's contemporary role in Japanese society. The taxation of temples and the practice of granting posthumous precept names in exchange for donations provide examples.

Focusing on the apparently self-contradictory character of contemporary Temple Buddhism makes it easier to understand its modern history and contemporary development.[13] By turning attention away from the corruption paradigm and the terminology of degeneration, I hope to overcome simplistic characterizations of old versus new, true versus corrupt, and philosophy (doctrine) versus practice. As many have already pointed out, it is imperative that we view religious practice as embedded and enmeshed within the social, economic, political, and other realms of quotidian life.[14] I will do just this for Temple Buddhism, and, in so doing, will highlight conflict and comprise between rhetoric and practice, between lofty ideals and practical needs, and between world-renouncers and householders.

1 Temple Buddhism Today
Scholarly and Popular Images of Corruption

Temple Buddhism has been described as a "corrupt" or "degenerate" form of Buddhism throughout the modern period. Most recently, priests have been portrayed in a negative light in popular films such as *Osōshiki* (The Funeral) and *Ohaka ga nai* (I Have No Grave). This image of Temple Buddhism as a degenerate form of Buddhism is by no means simply a popular construct. Scholars of Buddhism, Japanese and Western (many of whom are ordained as priests), have long painted a bleak picture of Temple Buddhism, as have many Buddhist priests. The corruption paradigm of interpretation can be seen in five areas: (1) the inclination to favor doctrine over practice, (2) the repudiation of "magic" by Weber (and Weberian scholars), (3) "corruption theory," (4) secularization theory, and (5) idealistic popular, scholarly, and priestly images of the priesthood.

First, there is the tendency of scholars of Buddhism, both those writing from within the tradition and from without, to stress the past, in particular classical written doctrine, over contemporary, lived practices and teachings. This tendency is the product of both the Western, Protestant-informed discipline of religious studies, which was introduced to Japan in the Meiji period (1868–1912), and the inherited tradition of sectarian doctrinal studies *(shūgaku)*. In particular, this tendency has led to an emphasis on the life and teachings of the sectarian founders (e.g., Saichō, Kūkai, Dōgen, Hōnen, Shinran, etc.). Indeed, during fieldwork priests and sectarian scholars told me on more than one occasion, "If you really want to study the teachings of Tendai, you have to study the writings of Saichō (767–822) or Chih-i (538–597)." Moreover, I was met with emotions bordering on shocked disbelief when I mentioned my interest in studying, as Tendai teachings, the writings, speeches, and videos of contemporary charismatic Tendai teachers such as Sakai Yūsai, Mitsunaga Kakudō, Hagami Shōchō, or Setouchi Jakuchō.[1] The implication of these responses is that the "real" teachings of Buddhism are those found in the classical texts and commentaries, and that "real" Buddhist teachings cannot be found in contemporary proclamations—especially those of popular preachers. This emphasis on past doctrine over contemporary teachings and practice has led to a large body of excellent scholarship on classical doctrine and a dearth of scholarship on Temple Buddhism today. Moreover, it has led to an emphasis on the past over the present, thereby reinforcing the impression that the practices of Temple Buddhism today do not reflect "real" Buddhism.

In addition to the influence of Western religious studies and sectarian doctrinal studies, turn-of-the-century sectarian scholars and Buddhist intellectuals, who had to battle severe ideological and physical attacks on the institutions of Temple Buddhism, were involved in a project of rehabilitation and survival. This battle led sectarian scholars in the late nineteenth and early twentieth centuries to emphasize the universal, cosmopolitan, and philosophical nature of Buddhism, which they believed could play an important role in the modernization of Japan.[2]

Anesaki Masaharu, concerning what he understood as a shift in emphasis from philosophical ("true") Buddhism to ritual ("degenerate") Buddhism, wrote in 1930 regarding the Tendai sect and the Buddhism of the Heian period (794–1185) that "the high ideals of Saichō's foundation were thus degraded by superstitious performances and his philosophy was abused in justifying the degeneration."[3] Although this critique is limited to the Heian period, Anesaki offers little evidence elsewhere to show that the degenerate Tendai ever recovered. This is often the case. Modern Temple Buddhism is simply set aside, with the assumption that it is a long since corrupted form of Buddhism. Yet ritual practices represented in the Heian period remain today the mainstay of temple activity; moreover, they were (and are) indispensable to doctrinal formulation and debate. Recent scholarship points out the limitations of viewing Buddhism as primarily a philosophy and the dangers of reading contemporary devaluation of practice into the past.

THE REJECTION OF MAGIC

Related to the emphasis on doctrinal studies as the best way to approach Buddhism is the repudiation of "magic," a concept that was introduced to Japan with Western scholarship, especially that of Weber, in the modern period and that played a role in constructing a picture of Temple Buddhism as moribund or degenerate. Magic is understood here to mean the utilization of supernatural entities or powers to bring about an effect, or the belief systems associated with such acts.[4]

Hayashi Makoto and Yamanaka Hiroshi succinctly outlined the development of Weberian scholarship in Japan and its effect on scholarly views of religion.[5] They showed that the scholar Ōtsuka Hisao stressed the importance of modern ethos for Japan's own modernization, located it, as did Weber, in

Protestantism, and dismissed Japanese religions as deficient. In a similar vein, Ienaga Saburō, in an early postwar article, attacked Temple Buddhism for its inability to modernize: "What is diagnosed as being difficult to maintain with the progress of modernization is the way of the Buddhist sects whose only social function is holding ritualistic funeral rites. If Buddhism gives up such premodern forms and finds a way out of its difficulties, the progress of modernization will never endanger the future life of Buddhism."[6]

Advancing on the work of Ōtsuka, later scholars emphasized the need to study Japanese religions and not discount them out of hand. However, they still argued that Japanese religions were a reflection of the magic-oriented nature of Japanese society, which made the Japanese susceptible to the worship of authority figures—a susceptibility that, in turn, provided the fertile ground for the growth of the emperor system. The view that Japanese religion, especially the sects of Temple Buddhism, played a role in the widely denounced emperor system and Japan's militarism in the modern period contributes to the construction of the image of Temple Buddhism as corrupt.[7]

During the late 1960s and early 1970s, scholars such as Yasumaru Yoshio attacked the bias of earlier scholarship against Japanese religions.[8] They also began to unearth the roots of Japan's own ethos for modernity in Japanese popular morality. However, for them, modernity was still connected to a rejection of magic. Hayashi and Yamanaka show that Shimazono Susumu was the first to overcome this attitude. Shimazono positively evaluated the role of magic through the concept of "vitalistic salvation" (seimeishugi).[9] The vitalistic concept of salvation is a life-affirming worldview with its roots in certain aspects of Japanese popular morality and an acceptance of magic. According to Shimazono, Japan's modernization was enabled not only by a popular ethos, but also by the vitalistic concept of salvation, which he and Tsushima Michihito claim is common to all new religions and to some extent to Temple Buddhism.

The work of recent scholars such as Shimazono and Winston Davis pushed the study of new religions even further to the forefront.[10] From stumbling blocks to modernization, new religions came to be recognized as enablers of modernization. The sects of Temple Buddhism, however, continued to be overlooked. First characterized as providing the doctrinal backing for magic, which, in turn, provided the framework for the emperor system, the sects of Temple Buddhism were the subject of critique once again with the valorization of magic. Unlike the new religions, which scholars found to play a positive role in modernization, Temple Buddhism was described as backward. In comparison with the rapidly expanding new religions and their modernization-enabling worldviews, the sects of Temple Buddhism appeared to be shrinking in size and to offer little to meet the spiritual or other needs of contemporary Japanese.

In *Practically Religious: Worldly Benefits and the Common Religion of Japan*, George Tanabe and Ian Reader go a long way toward shattering the view that Temple Buddhism is secularized or corrupt. Tanabe and Reader show that through the provision of means (rituals, sale of amulets, etc.) to obtain worldly benefits (safe childbirth, success in exams, travel safety, etc.), Temple Buddhism plays a vital role in the everyday life of most Japanese. However, they fail to address the fact that it is because of Temple Buddhism's critical role in the provision of this-worldly benefits and next-worldly care that critics see Temple Buddhism as corrupt. The roots of these negative images are found in the "corruption theory" of Japanese Buddhism (*daraku setsu*).

"CORRUPTION THEORY"

Critiques of Japanese Temple Buddhism are in no way limited to the contemporary setting nor are they limited to scholars. However, the work of scholars contributes to and reflects the greater negative image of Temple Buddhism in contemporary Japan. The most influential modern author in this vein was the prewar scholar Tsuji Zennosuke.[11] Tsuji made popular the term "corruption theory" in his *Studies on the History of Buddhism in Japan (Nihon Bukkyōshi no kenkyū)*. In describing what he calls "the origins of early modern Buddhist decline" (*kinsei bukkyō suibi no yūrai*), Tsuji points to two factors: the corruption of the Buddhist priesthood (*sōryo no daraku*) and the formalization (*keishikika*) of Buddhism. Tsuji traces the beginnings of the corruption of the Buddhist priesthood to at least the medieval period. He lists five sources of that corruption. First, he cites evidence to show that by politically challenging secular authorities, priests had become no different from ordinary secular individuals. Major temples, for example, held political, economic, and military might. In short, priestly interests had become thoroughly secular. Second, priests failed to maintain their strict codes of conduct. They engaged in illicit affairs with women, drank alcohol, and ate meat. Third, Tsuji claims that homosexuality was not uncommon among priests and was a clear sign of their corruption. Fourth, priestly status could be bought and sold and, therefore, held little legitimacy. Finally, priests were engaged in moneymaking ventures, such as money lending.[12] With the exception of homosexuality, each of the above critiques continues to be pursued in scholarly and popular and internal and external assessments of Temple Buddhism today.

Tsuji attributes the formalization of Buddhism to three factors. First, he cites the cessation of the development of new doctrine. Doctrinal debate, he argues, was frozen in the early modern period (1603–1868) and later devolved into merely sectarian sniping.[13] The second factor is the advent in the same early modern period of the *danka* membership system. Under this system, Tsuji asserts, temple priests became lax because their temples were under the protection of the government. This, he argues, "was the basis for temples divorcing themselves from the hearts and minds of the people" and led to the gentrification (*kizokuka*) of temples. The third factor is the further gentrification of the temples through both the government-enforced temple system (*honmatsu seido*), in which temples were required to organize within clear hierarchies, and the status system (*kaikyū seido*),[14] in which the people of Japan were classified into one of four status groups (samurai, farmer, artisan, and merchant). Government control and the status system combined to shackle the freedom of the temples and led to their becoming gentrified. Gentrification of the priesthood, he argues, led priests to forget the needs of the masses.[15] Just as the critiques of a corrupt priesthood remain strong today, so, too, do the critiques of formalization. This, indeed, is one reason why the sects of Temple Buddhism shy away from using the term "established Buddhism" when referring to themselves.

Tsuji's assumptions about Buddhist corruption, from which he cites no signs of recovery, have been widely extended by other scholars to include the modern and contemporary periods as well. For example, Ōno Tatsunosuke paraphrases Tsuji regarding the degeneration of Buddhism.

> The various sects of Buddhism in the Edo period were organized under the government's anti-Christian campaign, the danka membership system. And, because temples attained financial stability, the priests went along with the flow, and did *nothing more than* memorial services and funerals. The people saw and heard about the corruption of priests on a daily basis and in time lost interest in Buddhism.[16]

In short, according to Ōno, by accepting state backing and the financial stability it brought, Buddhists allowed themselves to become "mere" ritual performers. Similarly, Watanabe Shōkō wrote in 1958 regarding contemporary Temple Buddhism that

> one might say that Japanese Buddhism has fallen into formalism, and that its true nature has been forgotten. The Indian Buddhist Order revered a

simple way of life.... Since they did not perform rituals in order to be observed by others they were not concerned with putting on an appearance.... In Japan... the temples and monasteries just became places of entertainment for sightseers rather than places of discipline for monks.... With such an attitude it is natural that religious activity was completely degraded simply to recreation having no spiritual meaning.[17]

Watanabe claimed that Buddhism came to lack meaningful content—that is, form dominated over "true nature" and performance over practice. Today, according to Watanabe, temples have become "places of entertainment" and priests performers for an audience.

In 1963 Tamamuro Taijō, a renowned scholar of Japanese Buddhism, published his now classic work, *Funeral Buddhism (Sōshiki Bukkyō)*. While this work examined the history of Japanese Buddhism from its earliest stages to the Meiji period (1868–1912), it is clear that, for Tamamuro, the label "funeral Buddhism" applied to contemporary Buddhism as well. In the preface he states, "In contemporary Buddhism the aspects of healing and bringing of good fortune have grown comparatively weak. It would not be an overstatement to say that [Buddhism today] is solely about mortuary rituals."[18] Moreover, it is clear that the term "funeral Buddhism" is not complimentary, but rather a critique of the direction Temple Buddhism took from the early modern period onward. Tamamuro explains that

> Buddhists use the popular explanation that temple-danka relations were fixed by the Edo Bakufu [Edo period government] and led to the corruption of Buddhism. However, the Bakufu did nothing more than systematize temple-danka relations, which were already nearly complete. Moreover, the manner in which priests sought to ingratiate themselves with government officials is problematic. To say that [corruption] was the system's fault is not always appropriate.[19]

Here Tamamuro discredits the common attempt by many Buddhist priests in the modern period to deflect criticism of their current system of temple-*danka* relations by shifting the blame to the early modern government-enforced temple registration system. Far from dispelling critiques of corruption, Tamamuro makes it clear that the priests themselves, not the government, were to blame for the corrupt state of Buddhism.

In a similar vein, Tamura Yoshirō commented: "Buddhist temples were meant to be halls of truth, places where the Buddha's teachings are imparted and practiced and centers where those whose lives are sustained by that truth can gather. But, . . . Buddhist temples in Japan are now primarily cemeteries. The resident priests are custodians of the dead."[20]

Claims of Buddhist corruption, many tied to Buddhist reliance on post-mortem care roles—to Buddhists' perceived role as "custodians of the dead" rather than renunciates in search of enlightenment—are so widespread that degeneration is taken as fact. For example, Nakamura Hajime, one of Japan's most renowned scholars of religion, and the other editors of *Modern Buddhism* (*Gendai Bukkyō*) remark that the new religions flourished in postwar Japan because of the degenerate state of Temple Buddhism. "So why did the new religions proliferate in the postwar period? . . . First, established Buddhism was corrupted and no longer able to meet the needs of the people."[21]

More recently (1999), Tamamuro Fumio, the preeminent scholar of early modern Japanese Buddhism, has painted a very negative image of early modern (and by implication modern) Temple Buddhism. Although he avoids the term "degenerate," he clearly believes Temple Buddhism is corrupt. Tamamuro writes, "Our ancestors had to carry money to the temples even if that meant less food for them to eat. If they refused to donate, they suffered status and religious discrimination."[22] In his prologue Tamamuro states, "In short, *danka* [today] only understand the temple as a funeral parlor where funerals and memorial services are performed; they have no connection to the sect or to the ideals of the sect. I will examine just why it was that [Temple Buddhism] fell into this state of affairs (*naze sōnatte shimattaka*)."[23] Tamamuro's work fits well into a small boom in books by scholars and others that debate the *danka* system in contemporary Japan and, in particular, the dominant role of funeral and memorial services in Temple Buddhism.

Arguments such as this shed light by contrast on what many believe is "true" Buddhism. First, Buddhism should be a philosophy and not be corrupted by magic rituals. Second, temples should be a place of discipline for monks, not tourist sites or funeral parlors. Third, priests should not be concerned with matters economic. As I will show in the following chapters, these images still serve to shape scholarly, sectarian, and popular critiques of Temple Buddhism today, as well as the responses of Temple Buddhist sects to those critiques.

Tsuji backed his claims of corruption in the early modern period with extensive evidence of poor priestly behavior. The fact that there were priests who broke monastic codes of conduct and that temples came to play major bureaucratic roles for the government in early modern Japan is without doubt.

Assertions that such evidence can be equated with "degeneration," however, are more difficult to defend. The greatest weakness is that such assertions assume a pristine state from whence the corruption began. Finding such a state is primarily a matter of subjective assumption. Sectarian scholars of the early modern period might place the pristine beginnings at the time their respective founders lived. Modern sectarian and lay scholars might place it at the time of the historical Buddha. Others might place "pure" Buddhism solely within textual (doctrinal) evidence, to the exclusion of ritual practices. Still others might limit "true" Buddhism to that of the elite temple and disregard popular forms of practice as corrupt. All of these assumptions have been adequately critiqued over the years and need not be discussed at length here. For example, Jacqueline Stone and Rubin Habito have brought to light the intimate relationship between practice and doctrine in Heian period Buddhism, Nam-lin Hur has described the vibrant ritual life of Edo period Buddhism (1603–1868), and Gregory Schopen has exploded any pretensions that early Indian Buddhism was purely a philosophical teaching devoid of ritual practices or money making ventures.[24]

SECULARIZATION, MODERNIZATION, AND DEGENERATION

Critiques of secularization are related to corruption theory. Secularization theory generally holds that religion will eventually be eliminated as modernization and rationalization advance or that religious expression will continue but in a more diffuse form such as civil religion.[25] Treatments of the postwar experience of Temple Buddhism tend to be couched in terms of secularization. Regarding Temple Buddhism's response to the perceived usurpation of traditionally religious social roles by secular institutions, Gerald Cooke wrote in 1974 that the search was on for "signs of life" in the sects of Temple Buddhism and that there was "general agreement about Buddhism's approaching demise."[26] As with many authors writing in this period, he overlooked the religious nature of the search for this-worldly benefits that characterizes much of Japanese religious life, especially the religious life of temples. He also failed to challenge the discourses of degeneration and modernization and the negative views of ritual services, such as funerals, that are integral to them. Cooke, however, is not alone. Many critics of Temple Buddhism see funerals as contrary to the "true" or "proper" religious role of Buddhists and as a reflection of the professionalization (i.e., secularization) of Buddhist priests into ritual businessmen.[27]

A similar bias can be seen in the writings of Ienaga Saburō regarding the failure of modern Buddhist reform movements (collectively called New Buddhism [shinbukkyō]), which challenged established ritual roles and promoted philosophical engagement in the late Meiji and early Taishō periods. Ienaga writes,

> The New Buddhism did not last long and the leaders successively fell from the first line of the thinking world while the premodern ecclesiastical authority of the Buddhist sects they wanted to reform remained intact. This was a result of the fact that, while the Buddhist sects were deeply entrenched amid the backward farmers occupying the base of society, support for the idealism and the "New Buddhism" came only from a small number of urban intellectuals.[28]

In short, according to this view, there was no intellectual vitality among the "premodern" ecclesiastics who controlled Temple Buddhism. Similarly, noted Max Eger in 1980, "Buddhism had no vitality to lose to modernization."[29] In 1995, in an article discussing the dominant role that pursuit of this-worldly benefit has come to play in Japanese religious praxis today, Iijima Yoshihara found that religious practice in Japan has become secularized or commodified, which he associates with a decline or degeneration of practice.[30]

POPULAR IMAGES OF THE PRIESTHOOD

> Before the problem of whether a priest is single, or whether a priest marries or not, there is the problem of whether a priest has the consciousness to lead an outstanding lifestyle, the sort that makes others say, "It's no wonder that person's a priest."[31]

Not only scholars, but also priests themselves and society at large perpetuate the view that Japanese Buddhist priests fail to live up to an ideal image of what a Buddhist priest should be. The mass media (both print and film) have likewise come to portray priests as practitioners of degenerate Buddhism or as secularized ritual professionals. However, the rhetoric of renunciation remains vital to the religious legitimation of the sects of Temple Buddhism. Therefore, most sects strive to put forward an image of Temple Buddhist priests as world-renouncers engaged in meditative practice. At the same time, this rhetoric of renunciation is increasingly at odds with the daily reality of temple life. One of the greatest difficulties the sects of Temple Buddhism face today is that of bridging the gap between rhetoric and reality.

The image of what an ideal Buddhist priest is supposed to be and do has, no doubt, shifted with time and place, but there remain a few key building blocks from which to make some general suppositions. The most prominent image of a "proper" Buddhist priest is that of a world-renouncer (*shukkesha*). The basic distinction between one who is and one who is not a priest has been whether or not one has renounced the secular world and sought refuge in the teachings of the Buddha, thereby foregoing the pursuit of a worldly career. The position of world-renouncer, by definition, is juxtaposed to that of one who remains in the world, that is, a householder (*zaike*). There are a number of choices concerning how one lives that distinguish one who has left the world from one who remains in it. Most basic of these is the code of conduct by which the world-renouncer lives. This code of conduct, made clear in the precepts a priest must uphold, distinguishes the world-renouncer from the householder.

World-renouncers are set apart by their way of life. Regarding the Buddhist community in Sri Lanka, Richard Gombrich and Gananath Obeyesekere remark, "The integrity of the sangha [community of priests] is conceived to rest not so much on its orthodoxy as its orthopraxy."[32] First, the ideal Buddhist priest has been marked across the ages by celibacy. "Celibacy is essential to the homeless life of poverty and freedom from social obligations praised by the Buddha and his early followers."[33] Celibacy represents the complete denial of the householder's way of life. "In contrast to the secular world which placed supreme value on progeny, the ascetic renounced the possibility for sons, not to mention sexual pleasure, by living a life of sexual abstinence."[34] Second, the world-renouncer was marked by his or her place of residence. In his meditation manual (*Xiaozhiguan*, Jpn. *Shōshikan*), Chih-i, the sixth-century founder of Tiantai (the Chinese antecedent of Tendai), writes that one must live at peace in a quiet place.

> Here living at peace means no worldly activities. Quiet also means the absence of accustomed noise. This is divided into three types of place where meditation can be practiced. The first is deep in the mountains where people cannot disturb one. The second is a hermitage for austerities that should be separated from towns and villages by at least three *li* [several kilometers] and where there should be no sounds from pastures or other disturbances. The third type of place is within a monastery far from the homes of people. All of these are called peacefully living in a quiet place.[35]

Inasmuch as Buddhist priests relied on householders for their sustenance, they could not live far from towns and cities; but to decrease the likelihood that their practice would be destabilized by worldly interference, they were supposed to remain as far away as feasible. Third, the world-renouncer was marked by his or her dress. In early Buddhism, this was said to be a plain robe, perhaps made of collected rags sewn together.[36] In later Buddhism, and in Japanese Buddhism in particular, priestly costume remained different from that of the householder, though the variety of materials used for robes expanded greatly. Fourth, the world-renouncer shaved his or her head. This has been perhaps one of the most obvious marks of difference between priest and laity throughout history. Fifth, the world-renouncer maintained a diet very different from that of the average householder. In early Buddhism, priests relied on begging for their daily sustenance and were required (with some restrictions) to eat whatever was given them. In East Asian Buddhism, vegetarianism became the norm. Sixth, as just noted, the world-renouncer lived by means different from those of the householder. A world-renouncer was expected to rely on the donations of householders and was not expected to work at other jobs. Work, including farming, became part of priestly routine in many schools of East Asian Buddhism, but this generally did not entail taking on a full-time worldly career. Seventh, the world-renouncer was expected to maintain a certain deportment. He or she was expected to live by a strict set of manners that were prescribed in the priestly codes of conduct.[37] These seven factors served to distinguish the world-renouncer from the householder.

Finally, there are certain role expectations that serve to distinguish the world-renouncer from the householder. In his work on Chinese Buddhist hagiographies, John Kieschnick notes three types of ideal priest, and evidence suggests that this typology applies to the Japanese milieu as well. These categories—the priest as ascetic, as thaumaturge, and as scholar—describe the ideal Buddhist world-renouncer in the East Asian setting. Kieschnick notes, "The basic forms of asceticism required of all monks separated them from society, marking them as a fundamentally different category of person."[38] Regarding the thaumaturge he writes, "The accomplished monk was expected to have mastered a series of techniques—fortune-telling skills, spell-casting, meditation—and a body of knowledge, especially knowledge about the spirit world." Such abilities were linked to the "alien character of the monk." This, in turn, granted the Buddhist world-renouncer an "air of distinctiveness."[39] Finally, the scholar-monk is described as "an erudite master of the written word...a fierce debater; who, through swift rhetoric and wit, humiliated his opponents before crowds of admiring students...[and, he] was a great teacher who gathered together hundreds of disciples to absorb and carry on his teachings after his death."[40] These three categories clearly show that the priest was supposed to be a person apart from the ordinary. He or she possessed skills, and was capable of actions, that the ordinary, worldly person, as a householder, was incapable of possessing or doing.

The distinctive lifestyle and character of the priests as outlined in the seven distinctions and three categories described above enable him or her to function as provider of this- and next-worldly benefits to the laity.[41] The sects of Temple Buddhism in Japan today rely on the images of a world-renouncer just described to maintain their legitimacy and authority as representatives of the Buddhist religion. For this reason, sectarian public relations efforts are dedicated to countering images of degeneration (through engaging in outreach programs and seeking means to break free of the funeral Buddhism image) and promoting images of traditional Buddhist practice (through posters of contemporary ascetics engaged in practice, short-term meditation sessions in which laity can participate in meditation with priests and view their monastic lifestyle, etc.). Each sect maintains some form of publicly displayed austerity (such as the Tendai sect's *kaihōgyō*, the Nichiren sect's *daiaragyō*, the Hōsso sect's *mizutori*, and the winter *sesshin* practice of the Zen sects) that serves to demonstrate dedication to the ideal types. Furthermore, sects such as Tendai have removed their head temples from hereditary succession, thus placing them outside the realm of the householder.[42] Most sects also continue to require some form of basic training, during which time celibacy and asceticism are the norm. The sects of Temple Buddhism hope thereby to combat charges of corruption. Ironically, however, their emphasis on a priestly ideal type only serves to highlight the critiques of secularization and corruption by drawing attention to the contrasting lifestyle of the average contemporary temple priest.

2 Laity and the Temple
Past and Present

One often hears the phrase "The temple costs a lot [to support]," but the actual annual expenditure per household is 33,828 yen. Assuming four people to a household that is 8,457 yen each. Calculated on a monthly basis that is just 705 yen.[1]

I just cannot accept that the *danka* representatives ignored the decision of the sect head office and brought the question before the courts. That temple is a Sōtō school temple; therefore the *danka* representatives should follow the orders of the sect. That the *danka* would try to put in place someone they brought in as their own as head priest is an act that shakes the very roots and branches of the Sōtō sect![2]

The bedrock of Temple Buddhism is the *danka*.[3] Some temples survive with small lay memberships, or even none at all (large prayer temples, major pilgrimage or tourist sites), but the majority of temples in Japan fall into the *danka* temple (*dankadera*, lay-member-supported temple) category. It takes approximately two hundred to three hundred households to support a temple, the head priest, and his family; any less than that and the income from temple-related duties alone (primarily funerals and memorial services) will not suffice.[4] Just as few young doctors in the United States opt for a career in rural areas where there are too few patients to support a comfortable lifestyle, few priests in Japan relish the opportunity to work part-time jobs in order to support a rural temple with a small *danka* member base. As the *danka* member base in rural areas shrinks (for reasons discussed below), more and more temples are abandoned. Remaining *danka* member households are left to seek the services of the priests of neighboring temples. In this way, rural priests often slowly acquire responsibility for several temples, building their overall *danka* member base to a sustainable level. At the same time, however, *danka* members who have lost their head priest become further distanced from Temple Buddhism.

Rural temples have been the hardest hit by shrinking *danka* member numbers, but urban temples have been faced with their own financial and membership problems in recent years. The overall picture painted in newspapers, sectarian publications, and the like is of bedrock turned to quicksand, the world of Temple Buddhism built atop it slowly sinking to its demise.

This chapter examines the historical development of the *danka* temple and the problems related to the *danka* membership system facing contemporary Temple Buddhism. A study of the *danka* membership system demonstrates the pivotal place of the local *danka* temple in Temple Buddhism. It also makes clear a variety of interests in temple life today: sect interests, priestly interests, *danka* interests, and the interests of the local community.

EDO BEGINNINGS

The beginnings of the *danka* member system can be traced to the Edo period. In the early 1600s, the government *(bakufu)* began a campaign to eradicate Christianity. Some perceived Christianity as linked to European aspirations of conquest. The government exaggerated the threat Christianity posed to the country as a pretext for implementing measures of social control. The centerpiece of the campaign to eradicate Christianity was the temple registration system *(terauke seido)*. At first (1613), this applied specifically to so-called fallen Christians *(korobi kirishitan)*, those who were forced to apostatize. They were required to register at local temples, which allowed their ready control. Once registered, ex-Christians were also required to have all religious needs serviced by the temple as a demonstration of their newfound "faith." The government quickly found the registration system to be an extremely useful method for overseeing the general populace. By 1635, the registration system began to be applied to all Japanese, and in 1638, the government issued guidelines officially requiring compliance by all. Later, circa 1688, the systematized demonstrations of faith were expanded to all registered at the temple.[5] This requirement laid the foundation for the development of the *danka* membership system as described below. The *danka* membership system, in turn, came to dominate the ritual, social, and economic life of Japanese Buddhism. Indeed, this near total domination is one reason to speak of "Temple" Buddhism rather than of "traditional" or "established" Buddhism. The influence of the *danka* membership system, incorporating many aspects of its pre-Edo incarnations, makes Buddhism of the Edo period and later markedly different in organization and outlook from its past, despite the incorporation of many pre-Edo traits.

Buddhist sects were not slow to take advantage of the enormous power granted by the state, and the result was the *danka* membership system *(danka seido, literally donor-household system)*. The appearance in 1700 of the Regulations for Danka Members of the Sect (*shūmon danna ukeai no okite*) is evidence of the full-fledged development of the danka system. According to these regulations:

(1) Those who do not support the temple shall not be allowed as *danka* members.

(2) All *danka* members, even leading *danka* members, are duty-bound to visit the temple on the following occasions: the sect founder's memorial day, the Buddha's memorial day, the summer ancestral festival, the Spring and Autumn equinox, and the memorial days of one's ancestors. If [this is not observed], the temple seal will not be stamped on the Registry of Religious Affiliation Review, unless urgent reasons are reported to the office of religious affairs.

(3) On the memorial day of one's ancestors, one must invite the priest over to the house and treat him with generosity. Attempts to conduct a funeral by oneself, or to ask anyone other than one's *danka* temple [to perform the service], will be taken as a sign of belief in heretical religions and will be reported. Further, one must make donations to the temple in accordance with one's standing. And, one must financially support temple construction and repairs. Ancestral rites shall not be performed at the temples of other sects. One must obey temple edicts.[6]

This document, written to appear as a legal order, was the creation of Buddhists. Relying on the coercive legal authority of the official temple registration system, the *danka* system required all those registered at temples to fulfill all religious service needs at the temple and threatened striking *danka* member names from the registers for failure to comply. If one's name was struck from the register, a series of government penalties ranging from loss of status, to fines, to death awaited.

The above citation highlights the primary role of priests and their temples by the mid-Edo period—the provision of funerals and services to venerate ancestors. However, temples in the Edo period played a greater variety of roles as well.[7] They were local market centers, pilgrimage sites, festival sites, pharmacies, and schools. Yet the vast majority of small, local temples relied on income derived from the performance of funerals and memorial services. Prior to the temple registration and *danka* membership systems, most local temples relied primarily on agriculture for their support. The priest often plowed his own land.[8] The temple registration and *danka* membership systems provided a dramatic opportunity to shift the funding base. However, land ownership also remained an important source of income for temples. Land donated, or purchased through donations, was worked by tenant farmers and provided a steady source of income for temples until such lands were stripped away in later periods.

The temple registration system and its outgrowth, the *danka* membership system, developed into the cornerstone of Buddhist organizational structure and characterized the *danka*-temple relationship throughout the remainder of the Edo period and into the Meiji, Taishō (1912–1926), and Shōwa (1926–1989) periods. All along, *danka* members played a critical role in financing the temple and, through it, the sect. The temple registration system was repealed in the Meiji period when the government, as part of its efforts to eliminate the vestiges of the previous government, sheared away all Buddhist involvement in governing. Legally, registration switched from temple registration to family registration at the local government office, or the *koseki* system.[9] But the *danka* membership system, even when shorn of legal authority, lasted. Its roots in local culture and family religion had been firmly planted by the Meiji period. Few families opted out of the relationship with their family temple *(bodaiji)*. And despite many drastic measures against Buddhist sects and temples in the early Meiji period in which properties were seized or destroyed, the *danka* membership system, by then a part of everyday life, continued, and through it, temples and sects remained financially solvent and retained their religious role within family and community life.[10]

While the above discussion paints a one-sided picture of *danka*-temple relations, the evidence concerning the near total power of the temple over the life and death of its *danka* members is mountainous. *Danka* members met swift punishment for failing to support the temple.[11] Tamamuro Fumio concludes his work on the relationship between funerals and *danka* members with a bitter remark to the effect that temples have a long history of coercing funding from *danka* members, even threatening discrimination against those who failed to properly contribute to temple coffers.[12]

All the same, *danka* members were not completely without power or representation in the management of their local temple. It is likely that influential local families, generally the largest contributors to temple coffers, held some sway over the priest who received their largesse. Furthermore, the social role of funerals in confirming a family's status within a community often led to competition among leading families to hold lavish funerals.[13] Frequent notices from the government calling for austerity in conducting funerals attest to the investments some were making in death as an occasion to display wealth and status.[14] In short, the past is not simply a story of extortionist temples using their authority to force funeral services upon unwilling *danka* members. At least some *danka* members sought out the services of the temple and willingly—or at least more through social obligation than through fear of temple retribution—supported their temples financially.

In addition to being the primary source of funding for *danka* temples, *danka* members also came to play administrative roles. *Danka* representatives (*sōdai*) often functioned as assistants to the head priest. In some cases the *sōdai* played an active role in administering temple finances and even in selecting the head priest.[15]

This administrative role continued in a legally recognized (and, therefore, enforceable) form until the promulgation of the Religious Juridical Persons Law in 1951. For example, during the Meiji period *sōdai* were mentioned in government regulations concerning religious organizations, such as Ministry of Home Affairs directives.[16] These directives prescribed the boundaries of *sōdai* rights and duties vis-à-vis the temple and the head priest. The 1927 Religions Bill (*shūkyōhōan*) also clearly mentioned the *sōdai*, requiring their role to be written into temple bylaws and requiring a unanimous *sōdai* vote before temple assets could be dispersed.[17] Legal recognition of *sōdai* continued in the 1939 Religious Organizations Law (*shūkyōdantai hō*). It was not until the promulgation of the Religious Juridical Persons Law in 1951 that *sōdai* lost legal standing. Article 12 of the Religious Juridical Persons Law, however, stipulates that where there had been functionary offices other than those covered by the new law, the role of those offices must be defined in the temple's bylaws. The result was that *sōdai* generally remained in an advisory role to the head priest and that *sōdai* status was often made a prerequisite for membership on the temple's board of directors.[18]

DANKA TEMPLES DURING THE MEIJI THROUGH SHŌWA PERIODS

The *danka* membership system matured during the Edo period and, as we have seen, *danka* member roles in temple management continued to the present period. Nonetheless, the *danka* membership system was buffeted by waves of change following the Edo period. New religions, lay Buddhist societies, and constitutional provisions for freedom of belief threatened the *danka* membership system.

The Meiji Constitution's provision for freedom of belief highlights the new government's desire to demonstrate its "modern" outlook on religion.[19] The works of scholars such as Tamamuro give the impression that the *danka* membership system was one-sided and oppressive. Given this, one might expect that with both the permission freely to choose one's faith and the repeal of the temple registration system, *danka* members would have thrown off the oppressive yoke of their local temples and sought out new ways to meet their religious needs. To a limited extent, this did happen. During the closing years of the Edo period and again during the vibrant Taishō period, new religious movements came into being one after the other.

Moreover, nonsectarian lay Buddhist societies also became popular during the Meiji and Taishō periods. For example, Ikeda Eishun claims that lay Buddhist associations (*kessha*) originated at this time in the desire both of some *danka* members to break free of the restriction of the traditional *danka* and of some priests to create, with the laity, a modern Buddhism.[20] Ikeda also notes that the Taishō period witnessed a boom in the popularity of books on the lives of famous Buddhist figures. These books, some of which were serialized novels, enjoyed popularity among the new urban middle class and were the product not of Buddhist sects, but of secular writers or individual priests.[21] This boom demonstrates that the laity, or at least a certain portion of it, was beginning to enjoy access to Buddhism through new nonsectarian channels by the Taishō period. This trend continues today.

Despite these changes, however, the *danka* membership system survived. There are several possible reasons for its survival. Regarding the threat of the new religions, though they were growing in number, they were not as widespread during this period as they would become in the postwar period. Also, new religions were considered outside the mainstream. During the Edo period, religions not officially recognized were strictly controlled. They continued to be seen as a threat to the state throughout the Meiji, Taishō, and Shōwa periods. For example, the state forcibly disbanded Ōmotokyō, a new religion that garnered much attention during the Taishō period. Ōmotokyō's headquarters were dynamited, so that it might never rise again.[22]

Lay Buddhist societies appear to have been strongest in urban areas and among the middle class. The *danka* membership system was strongest, however, in rural areas and among agricultural workers. Thus, the urban movements may not have significantly influenced the rural temple-*danka* relationship.

However, the *danka* membership system, continued to thrive in urban areas as well. One reason lies in the temple's role in death and ancestor-related rituals. *Danka* members developed strong ties with the temple as an extension of their family through the pivotal role it played in ancestor-related rituals. That is, the temple became home to the family's ancestors, and the priest their caretaker. Abandoning the temple meant abandoning the ancestors.[23] Moreover, the community role of proper ancestor veneration (and especially the funeral rite itself), through which status within the community was demarcated, meant that failure to perform the proper rites for one's ancestors was socially unacceptable. Thus, the temple's role in ritual care for the ancestors helped to ensure the continuation of the *danka* membership system.

These observations point to the fact that the temple was in many ways situated within a prescribed community. As noted above, temple affiliation was initially a local affair. After an early burst of expansion, in which the teachings or specific rituals offered by certain schools of Buddhism helped to attract new *danka* members in the early Edo period, affiliation had much less to do with what form of Buddhism was taught than with family tradition, local community structure, the physical location of the temple, and the particular qualities of a specific temple (e.g., deities enshrined there, unique services offered there).[24] The temple was woven into the fabric of everyday life; local gatherings, community festivals, and the like all revolved around the temple. Moreover, service to the temple as a *sōdai* or other functionary often reflected one's status within the local community. In this sense, the temple was as much a community space as a space strictly for ritual or meditative practices. *Danka* members regarded support for the temple as more than simply supporting a site of priestly religious practice or even a priest and his family: they saw it as supporting a space central to community life.[25]

In a related matter, another explanation for the continuance of the *danka* membership system is that new religions rarely offered funeral services and often encouraged use of temple services for this purpose. New religions, which in general were concerned more actively with this-worldly problems, appear to have been willing to entrust the problem of the next world to the temples. Moreover, while many new religions were less concerned with funeral rituals, most were very concerned with care for the ancestors. Abandoned or improperly cared for ancestors were linked to many this-worldly problems such as illness and job loss. This veneration of ancestors served to complement the *danka* temple, which derived its existence from care for the ancestors.

Nevertheless, although new religions such as Risshō Kōseikai encouraged harmonious relations with temples regarding death rituals, some, such as Sōka Gakkai, were fiercely independent. Sōka Gakkai worked in harmony with the Nichiren Shōshū sect until a schism in 1991 but was stridently sectarian in its relationships with other sects of Temple Buddhism. This sectarianism earned Sōka Gakkai the lasting distrust of temple priests. One priest recalled in conversation that when Sōka Gakkai became popular in the area in which he resides, the river was awash in home Buddhist altars (*butsudan*) thrown out by converts to Sōka Gakkai to make way for proper Nichiren Shōshū altars. In general, however, it was possible for a *danka* member to join a new religion and still maintain affiliation with his or her local family temple. Multiple religious affiliations have been a hallmark of Japanese religiosity.[26] Surveys of Japanese religious affiliation conducted by the Ministry of Education in the postwar period have consistently shown that total membership in the various religions (new religions, Temple Buddhism, Christianity, etc.) is larger than the total population of Japan.

THREATS TO THE *DANKA* TODAY

The *danka* membership system managed to survive from its Edo beginnings as a partner in coercive state administration to become the center of family religion and community life and to last through Buddhist persecution in the Meiji period, constitutional freedom of belief, and the challenge of the new religions. The social and legal changes of the postwar period, however, may finally bring about the demise of the *danka* membership system. That certainly has been the constant fear of the leaders of the sects of Temple Buddhism since at least the 1960s. In the postwar period the *danka* membership system has been threatened by land reform, urbanization, changing family structures, the Religious Juridical Persons Law, changes in local community organization, a booming secular funeral industry, changing patterns of religious affiliation, and competing opportunities for religious expression.

LAND REFORM AND TEMPLE ECONOMICS

Shortly after the end of World War II, the Occupation authorities began land reform measures.[27] The result for temples was the loss of much of their landholdings. Under the 1946 law, temple land once leased to tenant farmers was purchased by the state and sold to the farmers. All other agricultural lands owned by temples were also purchased by the state and sold to third parties. Temples were generally allowed to keep forest and mountain properties, but at the time this often seemed more of a burden than anything else, and many temples sold such properties.[28] In one swift move, land reform eliminated a major source of income for temples, forcing an even greater reliance on income from ritual services or the development of other revenue streams. This development can be linked to increases in the fees charged for ritual services, especially for funerals and the granting of posthumous Buddhist names (*kaimyō*). This in turn led to growing discontent with temples, as their image shifted from one of caretaker of the ancestors to price gouger.[29] At the same time, these critiques were nothing new: critiques of ritual service fees have been around since the Edo period. This time, however, temples did not enjoy state support and therefore had to find alternative sources for meeting financial needs. Remaining temple properties were often converted into parking lots or apartment buildings, and new forms of memorial services were developed (pet memorials, memorials for aborted fetuses).[30] These ventures served over time to further the image of the temple as a money-making business and contributed to *danka* member discontent and to a general decline in the image of Temple Buddhism.

The heart of the problem facing Temple Buddhism today is, therefore, its ability to meet the needs of its primary constituents—the *danka* members—while simultaneously generating enough income to survive yet avoiding the appearance of greed and corruption. This problem has left many temples caught in a vicious circle: the loss of properties to land reform has led to increased reliance on funerals and memorial services for income, but increasing reliance on such sources, coupled with people's decreasing relations with the temple resulting from changing family structure and urbanization, have created the image of the temple as a place for only funeral rituals, thus limiting the ability of Temple Buddhism to re-create itself to meet contemporary needs.

Buddhist sects have also helped to create stereotyped images of "real" Buddhism that plague contemporary Temple Buddhism. Beginning in the Meiji period, Buddhist intellectuals realized that they had to create a new Japanese Buddhism in order to survive state persecution and potential competition from "modern" Western religions, primarily Protestantism. Following the views of their Western contemporaries, they criticized reliance on "superstitious" practices and ritual as part of a concerted effort to demonstrate to the West and, most important, to fellow Japanese, that Buddhism was every bit as modern as Christianity or Western philosophy. Thus was born the lasting view of "true" Buddhism as a rational philosophy that does not engage in ritual practices and other "premodern" activities. This view, of course, denied the Buddhism that was practiced by the majority of Japanese and at all Japanese temples. Funerals and other rituals conducted by priests came to be seen as embarrassing vestiges of a less-than-pure Buddhism. Priests were left bearing a "complex."[31] True Buddhists engaged in high philosophy, not funeral ritual. "Am I then," priests wondered, "a true Buddhist?"

Funerals were their bread and butter, but true Buddhism was supposed to be their calling.[32] This debate over true Buddhism spilled out of priestly and intellectual confines and into the popular realm, further contributing to the image of

Temple Buddhism as degenerate and in turn weakening the relationship between temples and their *danka* members.[33] For example, many popular books have appeared critiquing the Buddhism practiced in temples today, and newspapers often report on the high prices charged for funeral services by priests. The portrayal of priests as ritual professionals in films such as *I Have No Grave* is another example of how Temple Buddhist priests are portrayed as out for money. Finally, the view that true Buddhism cannot be found in local *danka* temples is reflected in the popular interest in books on Tibetan Buddhism (which, as in the West, is highly romanticized) and books on the lives of Japanese Buddhist practitioners of austerities.

URBANIZATION AND THE DEPOPULATION OF RURAL TEMPLES

Simultaneous with the changes in temple income were those brought about by urbanization. As Japan recovered from defeat, its cities began to prosper. Urban prosperity enticed ever-increasing numbers of rural Japanese to the cities. Rural temple *danka* size shrank concomitantly with rural depopulation. Because many families at first attempted to continue the relationship with their distant family temple, the effect on temples probably did not correlate directly with rural depopulation, but as time went on, urban family members began to seek the services of temples closer to their new home. Second- and later-generation urbanites are more likely to cut relations with their ancestral temples. Once their parents, for whom the connection to the hometown is still strong, have passed away, some now opt to move the family grave to a closer location to facilitate visits.[34]

As the number of *danka* members decreased, temple priests found it difficult to support their families. Some continued on, but encouraging sons to take over or hunting for an outside successor became an increasingly difficult task.[35] The result was a growing number of rural temples without a head priest.[36] In many such cases, *danka* members who rarely desired to relinquish power to a new head priest dominated the temple board of directors. Few priests were willing to take over an abandoned temple or to work under the temple board of directors.[37] With no priest present with whom to associate, the relationship between *danka* member and temple weakened.

Urbanization contributed to a decrease in the number of actively attended rural temples. However, the flow of people to the cities created a bonanza for urban temples. Many managed to maximize their *danka* size, allowing the priest a comfortable lifestyle without having to take on outside work. Also, urbanization led to an increase in urban property values. Urban temples suddenly found themselves sitting atop astronomically priced land. Land could be put to use by renting it out or selling it off, or as collateral for loans. Therefore, while urbanization can help explain the decline in rural Temple Buddhism, it fails to explain the difficulties faced by urban Temple Buddhism and why the sects of Temple Buddhism perceive their overall existence as threatened.

CHANGING FAMILY STRUCTURES

The *danka* temple in Japan is almost completely reliant on *danka* member families. Any change in family structure will almost certainly affect the *danka* temple. The number of traditional multigenerational households decreased as families moved to urban areas. As they decreased, the passing on of family religion through imitation of the older generation became nearly impossible. Furthermore, the carrying on of household rites, particularly the daily worship before a family household altar, became increasingly difficult in small urban apartments designed for nuclear families. There was simply no place to put the altar. This meant that families had no opportunity to reflect on religious matters related to a *danka* temple until a death in the family. Only with death were they forced to seek out the services of a temple. The connection to a family temple is often so thin by that point that surviving family members struggle even to remember what sect of Buddhism they used to belong to when they search for a new temple to fill their needs. In such cases, donations and how they are explained come to play a critical role in creating an impression of specific priests and of Temple Buddhism in general.

LEGAL REFORMS AND THE TEMPLE

The Religious Juridical Persons Law further altered the relationship between *danka* members and the temple. Before its promulgation in 1951, *danka* members had enjoyed a modicum of legal representation at the temple. They were specifically mentioned within previous laws governing religious organizations. The *danka* representatives had held legally recognized administrative positions within temple management. The extent of their actual power in the prewar period is not easy to determine, but it appears that they did play roles in the distribution of temple assets and, depending on the sect and the temple in question, in the selection of the head priest. The Religious Juridical Persons Law, however, was designed to establish secular management for religious organizations that chose to incorporate as juridical persons in order to qualify for tax and other benefits. Ideally, the creation of such a management position allowed legal oversight of religious organizations without interference in specifically religious functions.

Such a naive secular-religious division, of course, is virtually impossible to maintain in actual practice. The law became the source of numerous lawsuits as traditional religious actions were read as secular and vice versa.[38]

The *sōdai* were defined as religious functionaries and, under the new law, no longer recognized as managers accountable for incorporated temples. In their place the new law created the position of responsible officer *(sekinin yakuin)*. In most cases, temple bylaws require *sōdai* status for responsible officers. The Religious Juridical Persons Law thus created a double management layer—the traditional *sōdai* and the new responsible officers. According to that law, there must be at least three responsible officers, one of whom is to be the chief responsible officer. Responsible officers are legally accountable for all secular temple affairs, the most important being management of temple funds and assets. The vast majority of temple bylaws require that the chief responsible officer be the head priest.[39] Most often the head priest's son and wife are installed as the two other responsible officers. In this fashion, the role of *sōdai* in assisting in the daily management of temples has been severely weakened and so, along with it, has their investment in the temple.

Under the Religious Juridical Persons Law, *danka* members have been ruled to have very little say in temple affairs.[40] This lack of authority has been an ongoing source of conflict in the postwar period as *danka* members, who had grown to see the temple as "their" temple, find they have little legal recourse in determining how the temple is run or how temple assets are disposed of. What legal status they do have is determined by the type of relationship they have with the temple. The tighter the bonds, the more likely they are to have their status recognized by the courts. In certain circumstances, generally those having to do with temple assets, the courts have ruled that *danka* members possess legal standing vis-à-vis the temple. For example, if *danka* members financially support the temple, use its services exclusively, and participate through the *sōdai* and responsible officer positions in its administration, they are taken to have legal standing. But their legal status is severely limited. *Danka* members cannot make claims on the assets of the temple, and where their claims are based on "religious" grounds, which is often ruled to be the case, they have no standing in court.[41]

It is certain that (considered alongside the trend toward inheritance of the head priest position) changes in *danka* members' legal rights vis-à-vis the temple have contributed to the privatization of the temple by temple families.[42] The temple has come to be seen by priests and their families as "their" property, a trend that has further contributed to *danka* member alienation.

CIVIC AND TEMPLE COMMUNITIES

Compounding the above problems is the advent of civic centers. With the changes brought about by economic growth and urbanization, secular organizations have slowly encroached upon the role of temples as community centers. In particular, civic centers have taken over many of the roles once played by temples. Especially in urban areas, civic centers offer space for citizens to gather for meetings, club activities, and lessons in cultural activities such as ikebana and the tea ceremony, which had been seen as means to draw people to the temple as well as income sources for temples. Competition from the secular sector has thus decreased the ability of the temple to function as a community center, especially in urban areas where such civic facilities are abundant.

THE FUNERAL INDUSTRY AND GRAVE PLOTS

In the postwar period, the funeral industry has moved from the supporting role of providing the casket and labor for setting up the funeral to playing the lead role in funerals, pushing the priest into the background as an actor hired to chant at the appropriate times. This reversal in roles at the funeral has been brought about by the changing circumstances under which people die today. Until as recently as the 1970s, priests played an active role in the process of dying. Relatives of the dying *danka* member called upon the priest to conduct a short ritual at the time of death. From that moment on, the priest would guide the family through the death process—recommending a funeral company, answering questions on proper etiquette, and the like. Now, however, death has been removed from the hands of the family. An individual dies in the hospital, where nurses take care of the body.[43] Thereafter, funeral company officials handle the body. Traditional practices for confirming death through a slow process of bathing and staying with the corpse have mostly disappeared, as has the priest's presence at the time of death.[44] Instead, funeral company officials wait at the hospital, where they initiate contact with bereaved family members. It is often the funeral company that now calls the priest and that acts as advisor throughout the funeral.[45]

The weakening relationship between the temple and the *danka* members has created the greatest inroad into temple affairs for the funeral companies. Many people cannot recall the name of their family temple, and others struggle to remember to what sect of Buddhism their family traditionally belonged. Funeral company officials meet the needs of mourners by compiling their own list of priests. Since they no longer take an active a part in temple community life, people turn to the funeral company in their time of need. The priest and the temple, once a familiar part of everyday life, are thus further removed from the life of the *danka* members—cementing their image as paid actors at the funeral.

One such case occurred in a rural temple outside Tokyo during the course of my own fieldwork. A *danka* member lost her husband. In her grief she could not recall what sect of Buddhism she belonged to, despite the fact that she held a grave plot at her local temple, a temple whose head priest had fled to find a job in the city several years earlier. The funeral company that signed a contract with her at the hospital asked her what sect she preferred. When she could not respond, they selected a priest from their roster and had him conduct the funeral. In some ways, this particular case is extreme. The funeral company, which knew the location of the grave plot, should have contacted the temple representatives to ascertain whether a priest was serving the temple. The case shows that many people, even those affiliated with a temple through a grave plot, do not associate with the temple as active *danka* members and illustrates the effect the lack of a priest on hand can have. In this case, when the priest who was responsible for taking care of the needs of the woman (who was a *danka* member of a temple that was not his own but that had come into his care over time) found out, the woman was required to redo the graveside service and to change the grave marker she had purchased from the funeral company's priest.[46] The priest offered all his services free and sold her the grave marker at cost, saving the brunt of his anger for the funeral company director.

Drastic changes have also come about in the speed of the funeral. Most funerals take the following pattern: wake *(tsūya)*, held on the eve of the death or the next day; funeral, held on the day following the wake, unless that day falls on an inauspicious day; cremation, held within hours of the funeral; burial, held immediately after the cremation. Also, memorial services that were traditionally held on the seventh day and often the forty-ninth day after the funeral service are now often held at the end of the funeral service. The speed of this service leaves little time for healing. Furthermore, because the temple is no longer central to community life, the priest's relationship with the person who has died is minimized. For this reason, he is often unable effectively to tailor his sermon to the life of the deceased, limiting its impact.[47] Moreover, the relief that may have resulted from belief in the spiritual efficacy of the funeral ritual itself and in the capabilities of the priest as a ritual master have been diminished by the image of priests as not true Buddhist monks, by their businessman image, and by hereditary succession (which can call into question the faith of the priest). Healing, a traditional function of funerary rites, occurs after the priest has left the scene.

Such changes have come to call the value of having a funeral performed at a temple or by a priest into question.[48] Though still in the minority, some people now opt for "natural funerals" (shizensō). "Natural funeral" is a catchall term that generally applies to funerals that do not rely on a grave plot. Ashes are scattered at sea or in some instances in mountain reserves.[49]

Like changes in how the funeral is conducted and who conducts, changes in where one is buried also affect temple-danka relations. In the end, people return to the danka temple because that is where their family grave is. If at all possible, at least once a year during the obon season (summer festival for the dead), families visit their family grave. Take away the grave, and it appears unlikely that people will go to a danka temple. According to one survey, 82.8 percent of sōdai claimed that they go to the temple primarily for activities related to ancestor worship (this combines the totals for obon, higan [equinox festivals], haka mairi [grave visits], and nenki hōji [annual memorial services]).[50] All the same, temple graveyards, especially in urban areas, have not been able to meet the demand for space. Combined with the growth in public memorial parks, this space shortage has led to an increasing number of families owning grave plots off temple grounds. Although a priest will invariably officiate at the burial, it is less likely that one will be called out to accompany the family when it makes later visits. Even when a priest is called, association with the temple as a religious or communal space is minimized; the association is with the priest as a specialist hired per diem.

PATTERNS OF RELIGIOUS AFFILIATION

Underlying the threats from urbanization, changing family structure, and new funeral and burial options is the fact that, for many people, association with the temple is not based on personal choice. Tamamuro Fumio contends that association was from the start not a matter of individual choice but of obligation. Furthermore, as we have seen, the initial association with the temple was at the local level; there was no choice among schools of Buddhism. Over time, the obligatory relationship Tamamuro describes faded but loyalty to the temple continued—not out of faith in the teachings of the sect represented at the temple but because the temple was home to the ancestors. The survey cited above indicates that the majority of sōdai seek to pass on their position to their children not because of personal faith or even out of a desire to support the temple, but to carry on what has been inherited from their ancestors.[51]

This finding suggests another problem facing Temple Buddhism today. Even if religious affiliation can be assured at the local temple through ancestral bonds, can it be transferred to the sect? A 1975 survey conducted by the Sōtō sect was a wake-up call for the sects of Temple Buddhism.[52] The comprehensive survey of *danka* members revealed a near total lack of knowledge, and thus implied lack of interest, in the sect's history, practice, and major figures. Most respondents did not even know what deity was enshrined at their temple. For the average *danka* member, the temple appears to be the site of ancestor worship, nothing more. While individual priests may have been at ease about this, their role as caretakers of the ancestors apparently confirmed and secured, sect officials were horrified. The scare was twofold. On the one hand, it meant that temples were failing to be proselytizing centers. As noted above, the priesthood of contemporary Temple Buddhism worries about the perceived role of priests as funeral ritual professionals. The concern is based in part on the idea that true Buddhists must be actively engaged in the search for enlightenment and the salvation of others. A survey showing that not even their own *danka* members saw them in such a light was a shock to sect leaders. On the other hand, the survey awakened them to the fact that, given declining *danka* member numbers, even though some temples might survive as centers of ancestor worship, if better sect ("brand") recognition could not be obtained, the sect itself might not survive. Other data confirm these early Sōtō findings. A survey of Shingon sect *sōdai* found that while they willingly support the temple, few understand themselves as supporting the sect.[53] Such findings point out the sect-*danka* split that exists in most sects of Temple Buddhism. Sect ideals and *danka* needs are not necessarily the same. The need to negotiate tensions between the sects and the *danka* temples and to attract greater *danka* member support is among the pressing issues facing Temple Buddhism today.

Related to religious affiliation, Shimazono Susumu claims there has been a sea change in how people support religious organizations. The act of oblation, which he defines as "the act of giving up one's time and wealth or property in an attempt to consecrate oneself for the sake of God or Buddha, spiritual merit, and/or the religious community," is no longer the norm.[54] Shimazono demonstrates that Japanese have moved from a community-based form of religion and oblation to a personal-commodity-transfer-style religion. Commodified transactions can be conducted anywhere and with anyone who offers similar products. He goes on to note, "Such phenomena as hereditary clergy, funeral Buddhism, and the disappearance of traditional village ceremonies conspired early on to weaken the kind of voluntary communal oblation that forms the foundation of traditional religion. Today we see no indication of any reversal; the communal oblation sustaining traditional religious groups slips further and further into oblivion."[55] In short, changes in Buddhism that began in the Edo period and that led to the creation of funeral Buddhism, as well as changes in the modern period, such as the recognition of a married clergy and the inheritance of the position of head priest, altered traditional patterns of giving, which were based on a communal relation with the sacred. The captive market, which temples enjoyed throughout the Edo period, together with postwar social and economic changes, led to the commodification of services. The result was a shift to individual, non-communal relationships and onetime commodity transactions—for example, paying a set fee (still called a donation today despite its fixed, commodified nature) to have the priest perform a funeral (as a hired professional).[56] The demise of communal oblation, in turn, has led to further weakening of the relationship between *danka* member and temple. Thus, the position of the local *danka* temple is severely weakened.

The temples and sects of Temple Buddhism remain trapped between their past roles as caretakers of the ancestors and world-renouncing organizations and the realities of commodified religion and everyday financial demands at the present time. In particular, given the changing nature of religious affiliation, the sects are faced with the task of restructuring *danka*-temple-sect relationships. In short, sect officials are forced to define anew the place *danka* members will occupy in the religious and administrative structures of the sects of Temple Buddhism in the twenty-first century.

NEW TIME—NEW ALTERNATIVES?

If the link between *danka* members and the temple is weakening, are people seeking alternatives? In the early postwar period, the energetic new religions drew popular and scholarly attention because of their vibrant religious life and fervent followers. As Japan recovered from the war and entered a period of high economic growth, people's needs began to change. Especially following the burst of Japan's economic bubble in the 1990s, many Japanese raised in the postwar period of affluence, when life was supposed to be dedicated to the company in return for a comfortable and safe home life, were left with a feeling of emptiness. "What," they were left wondering, "is all of this for?" Again, Temple Buddhism was seen as failing to meet the needs of the people. The new religions, which had attracted so many in the early postwar period, were not seen to be of help either. They were too closely tied to the work ethos of the boom years. This conundrum led to the rise of the more personal, self-reflective, new new religions.[57]

Although the new new religions attracted a growing audience in the post-bubble years, the new religions continued to exist and to pose a threat to Temple

Buddhism. The new religions have an operational advantage over the sects of Temple Buddhism. They are centrally organized and thus able to react quickly and in a unified manner to new demands and also to disseminate a unified message. Sects of Temple Buddhism are far less centrally organized. For example, Tendai is perhaps best understood as a collection of separate temples, all of the Tendai "brand name," but each very much indebted to local customs, practices, and needs. The sect headquarters is rarely capable of one-sided administration.[58] Therefore, it is often difficult for the sect to respond rapidly to changes in society. It is also difficult for the sect to present a single message that is readily grasped and quickly of use to individuals in need of guidance. Thus, the new religions, which are generally more centrally organized, are better equipped to offer a recognizable brand image that is transferable and sought after from one area to another. The new new religions do not appear to have the same qualities of central organization that the new religions possess, and, in this sense, pose less of a threat to Temple Buddhism. However, like the new religions, or perhaps even more so, the new new religions possess a high degree of skill in advertising. They take advantage of new media sources such as the Internet and also publish numerous religious self-help books that serve to attract new followers.[59]

The new religions were not the only place people could turn to for knowledge of religion, and especially of Buddhism, in the postwar period. Just as in the Taishō period, many lay Buddhist study groups appeared.[60] Some even offered courses for becoming priests.[61] The temple, which has been seen as the place one goes to care for the dead rather than as a home to practicing world-renouncers, was not regarded as a source for knowledge about Buddhism. For example, when I asked a young priest if *danka* members consult the head priest of her temple about Buddhism, she restrained a laugh and replied that they do not, though they do consult regularly regarding funerals and memorial services. Individuals who wanted to learn more about Buddhism created their own opportunities to do so. In addition to lay societies and study groups, books on Buddhism have been enjoying an extended boom. Indeed, the current boom appears to be even more widespread than the boom in popular books on Buddhism during the Taishō period. Although the sects of Temple Buddhism participate in publishing texts on Buddhism, the majority of popular books are nonsectarian and discuss everything from Buddhist dieting to health techniques to Tibetan Buddhist ritual to oddities such as the medieval Tachikawa school of Buddhism that is said to have focused on enlightenment through sex. Also, the works of popular scholars such as Hiro Sachiya offer an introduction to many aspects of Buddhism.[62] In addition to traditional publications, recent years have seen a boom in religious Web sites.[63] Temples are participating in this new medium as well, but many sites are nondenominational. The accumulated effect may be to draw attention further away from the *danka* temple.

Critics claim that the preoccupation of the priests of Temple Buddhism with postmortem services is driving people to the new religions, the new new religions, and the bookstores to meet their religious needs. Moreover, even such care as is provided for the dead is seen as formalistic. Such claims are not altogether valid. Ian Reader and George Tanabe show that, despite images to the contrary, Japanese Buddhism is not simply about otherworldly matters. It plays a vital role in addressing people's everyday religious needs. Their work, *Practically Religious*, provides ample evidence for viewing Japanese Buddhism as concerned at least as much with this-worldly as with other-worldly matters. They present a powerful argument that Japanese religion is not "moribund."[64] But scholars and the popular press argue not so much that Japanese religion is moribund but that Japanese Temple Buddhism is moribund. The evidence Reader and Tanabe draw on—pilgrimages, talismans, and the like—does not apply to the vast majority of Buddhist temples. They recognize this and make note of it briefly as follows:

> The erosions of social support for Buddhism are, in effect, those that affect *danka* (parishioner) temples, which depend on danka membership structures... which are vulnerable to social change and shifting population structures. Buddhist sects, too, may be struggling to keep in touch with the changing patterns of religious behavior in contemporary society, especially as social ties weaken and people no longer feel the need to follow socially prescribed religious practices.[65]

Reader and Tanabe's suggestion that it is when Buddhists "departed from their central (and sūtra validated) dynamic of this-worldly benefits" that they ran into "problems of stagnation" hints at the deeper problem facing Temple Buddhism today.[66] Here Tanabe and Reader assert that *danka* temples, which rarely offer this-worldly benefits, are no longer attracting *danka* members because they fail to provide the benefits people have come to expect. The popular image, however, is that Temple Buddhism has departed not from a sutra-validated role as provider of worldly benefits, but from the quest for otherworldly enlightenment. Indeed, the sects of Temple Buddhism themselves put forward this image. The Tendai sect, for example, actively promotes itself as a world-renouncing sect. Promotional videos, posters (distributed from the sect to temples nationwide), and books frequently portray images of the famous *kaihōgyō* practitioners running through the deep forests of Mt. Hiei (headquarters of the Tendai sect), emerging from the practice hall after nine days without eating, sleeping, drinking, or lying down, or of priests performing the *goma* fire ritual.[67] However, these images are counterproductive because they promote an image of austere practices that cannot be readily encountered at local *danka* temples.

At present, Temple Buddhism finds itself in a quandary regarding its identity. As we have seen, developments in the *danka* membership system are in large part responsible for their quandary. The "return" to this-worldly Buddhism—which many individual temples are engaged in to remain religiously relevant and financially solvent—when placed against the images of austere practice put forward by sects such as Tendai to promote their legitimacy as "true" Buddhism, only feeds the larger image of Temple Buddhism as not simply moribund but corrupt. However, the sects and individual priests of Temple Buddhism are now involved in seeking ways to overcome their corrupt image while simultaneously recasting how this-worldly practices should be perceived.

3 Trying to Have It Both Ways
The Laity in a World-Renouncer Organization

Despite having other places to go for religious needs, most Japanese still turn to the temple for funeral and mortuary rituals. As we have seen, however, even the shelter of the funeral is being taken away from Temple Buddhism. What are the temples and the sects of Temple Buddhism doing to respond to new religious trends, new funeral options, and the effects of urbanization and changing family structures? The sects of Temple Buddhism have been very slowly reengineering their organizations and their practices to meet contemporary needs. Let us examine the Tendai sect's attempt to create new roles for the *danka* and thereby to invigorate Buddhist practice from the local temple level upward.

At the local level, many individual temples are aggressively engaged in seeking new sources of income as well as new ways to make themselves meaningful to their *danka* members and others. Most local efforts center on creating new versions of old ritual themes. *Mizuko kuyō* (memorial services for aborted fetuses), are one such example.[1] Other services include memorial services for pets (*petto kuyō*), blessings for cars, and the development of new trendy talismans, such as one with the "Hello Kitty" figure on it. (Hello Kitty is a hugely popular kitten character and is part of a major memorabilia industry).[2] Some temples have opened home pages that offer online graveyards, while others have begun online counseling. These and other developments figure more fully in the discussions in chapters 7 and 8. The move to cater to the this-worldly benefits so aggressively sought out by Japanese may serve to keep a small percentage of temples financially solvent, but it is doubtful that it will stanch the steady flow of potential *danka* members away from the sects of Temple Buddhism.[3] Without a large *danka* member base to support them, the sects that sit atop the Temple Buddhism pyramid will crumble over time. The leaders of the sects of Temple Buddhism are keenly aware of this and have initiated innovative ways of recreating their role in society and thus of appealing to *danka* members for continued support. The centerpiece of the Tendai sect's efforts has been an attempt to create a place within the renunciate organization for the laity to play an active role.

The Tendai sect's efforts to reestablish and redefine *danka*-temple and *danka*-sect bonds take place through the sect's Light Up Your Corner Movement (Ichigū Wo Terasu Undō). The movement seeks to address two issues critical to revitalizing relations with *danka* members (and to attracting new members).

First, it posits a values crisis as the reason for the decline in traditional family structure (which sect leaders blame for declining numbers of *danka* members). It then seeks to teach a Tendai way of life that is based on the family in order to reestablish and strengthen family values. Second, through teaching a Tendai way of life, it seeks to recreate the *danka* member's connection to the temple. The temple is no longer to be seen as simply a center for funerals and memorial services, but as the center for the family's engagement in society and the revitalization of Japan.

The Tendai sect is not alone in starting up a popularly focused movement. Between 1962 and 1971, most sects began similar movements aimed at refiguring themselves as people's organizations *(minshū kyōdan)*. These developments coincided with a boom in holding major memorial anniversaries for sect founders. The largest and most influential of these was the 1961 joint 750th anniversary for Hōnen (1132–1212, founder of the Jōdo sect) and 700th for Shinran (1173–1262, founder of the Jōdo Shin sect). As many as two million people are said to have participated in the various ceremonies held on this occasion.

The Tendai sect was comparatively late in organizing its own social engagement movement. For example, the Sōtō sect began its movement, the Danka Member and Faithful's Sect Support Association (Danshinto Shūmon Gojikai) in 1963, the Shingon sect Chizan branch began its Danka Member and Faithful's Cooperative Association (Danshinto Kyōgikai) in 1965, the Nichiren sect began the Defend the Dharma Movement (Gohō Undō) in 1966, and the Jōdo sect began its Hand in Hand Movement (Otetsugi Undō) in 1967. The appearance of such movements in this period can be linked to the threat sects felt from the boom in new religions. Indeed, during the same period many new religions were developing similar national movements. For example, Myōchikai Kyōdan began a national effort for local social improvement in 1967, and Risshō Kōseikai began its Brighter Society Movement (Akarui Shakai Zukuri Undō, commonly known as Meisha Undō) in 1969.

The sects of Temple Buddhism were also spurred on in the development of social engagement movements by the actions of their younger members. As in the United States and elsewhere, the 1960s and 1970s were a tumultuous period in Japan. There were protests against the Vietnam War, protests against U.S.-Japan security arrangements, and later environmental and antinuclear protests. Many of the young leaders of the sects of Temple Buddhism were actively involved in or influenced by these movements. The early leaders of Tendai's Light Up Your Corner Movement, for example, participated in protests against the war in Vietnam.

However, this period also represented a period of stability for the sects of Temple Buddhism. Economic recovery meant prosperity, which translated into increased donations to temples. With their immediate postwar economic worries in check (e.g., rebuilding of war-damaged structures, securing of income for priests), the sects were able to turn their efforts to preaching.[4] The Tendai sect's Light Up Your Corner Movement, like the movements of other sects, came to play an important role in the sect's efforts to recreate itself, just as Japan was rebuilding itself.

THE LIGHT UP YOUR CORNER MOVEMENT

"It seems that whenever you open the newspaper in the morning there is an article about crime committed by youth."[5] This is a quotation from one of the leaders of the Tendai sect in an article reflecting on the thirtieth anniversary of the 1969 founding of the Light Up Your Corner Movement. The Light Up Your Corner Movement is the Tendai sect's catchall campaign. It is at once a social welfare movement, an environmental movement, and a method for revitalizing *danka*-temple relations and reenvisioning the role of priests in contemporary Japan. Here, I focus on the movement as an effort to revitalize bonds with *danka* members. (In chapter 5 we will discuss the movement's role in recreating the role of priests.)

Books published by the priesthood of Temple Buddhism over the last thirty years seem invariably to mention how crime is on the rise, youth are out of control, and the country is in danger. The leader quoted above continues:

> Following the war, religion was barred from public education. Japan followed the constitution and, under the pretext of "freedom of religion," forced the freedom not to believe. As a result, ethics and morals were destroyed, and the Japan we see now was born. Ethics and morals without roots in religion are like cut flowers. They may be beautiful to look at, but they will soon wilt.[6]

This statement describes a common vision of contemporary Japan held by Tendai priests. However, this view is by no means limited to Tendai priests. It is a common conservative view. It is an image of a country floundering because it has no morals rooted in religion. The Light Up Your Corner Movement was founded thirty years ago in response to this image. At least, that is the view presented on the home page of the movement in 1999.

At the same time there exists another set of images of postwar Japan, the images described in the preceding chapter of Temple Buddhism in decline: pre-war traditions under question, new religions, urbanization devastating rural *danka* member support, and the derogatory label "funeral Buddhism." Tendai has been engaged in an uphill battle to create a positive image for itself while countering these negative trends. How could Tendai overcome negative images, strengthen *danka* member bonds, and recruit new *danka* members? In short, how could it continue to survive? It is arguable that it was in response to these pressures, just as it was in response to the vision of crumbling Japanese values, that the Tendai sect instituted the Light Up Your Corner Movement.

The Light Up Your Corner Movement began in 1969. It originated not from the sect headquarters but from the Tokyo Teaching District as part of the efforts of the Propagation Teachers Association of Western Japan (Fukyōshi Renmei Kanshinkyō). Efforts to spread the teachings of Tendai at the local level were focused on the slogan Light Up Your Corner, which is derived from one of Saichō's writings.[7] The movement was soon co-opted by the sect at large and organized on the national level. A considerable amount of tension has remained between local movement leaders, especially those in the Tokyo Teaching District, and the sect. For example, Tokyo movement leaders recall a period early on when there were frequent disagreements with the sect regarding the direction of the movement. Local leaders sought to focus on local needs; the sect, on the other hand, wanted to focus on using the movement to increase sect recognition among members. To that end, the sect used the movement to encourage members to purchase statues of Saichō to install in their home altars (and thus increase sect awareness) and to sing the sect song. One local leader went so far as to say that, once the sect took over, the movement underwent a period of institutionalization that ended in a hollowing out of the original principles.[8]

In addition to conflict between center and periphery, a scholarly debate raged for years around the very term "light up your corner."[9] Some scholars, such as Fukui Kōjun, hold the view that a character in the original text has been misread. They argue that what had been read as *sen* (one thousand) should be read as *wo* (a particle marking a verb). Reading the character as *wo* results in the phrase *"ichigū wo terasu"* (light up your corner) and supports the use of that phrase as the name of the movement. Okubo Ryōshun writes that this reading makes the most sense in classical Chinese, the written language used by Saichō. However, others argue that this is an incorrect reading and, therefore, an incorrect interpretation of Saichō's teaching. They argue that the character in question should be read as *sen* (one thousand). The meaning of the phrase would then be "light up one thousand, and defend and maintain your corner" (*sen wo*

terasu, ichigū wo mamoru). Fukui Fumimasa and Okubo Ryōshun also offer differing readings, and the debate continues today. This debate reveals divisions
within the sect between scholar-priests as well as divisions between scholar-
priests and activist-priests (though these are not always mutually exclusive categories). It also shows the manner in which Buddhist Studies in Japan has direct
relevance on the practice of Buddhism. In the end, it may little matter, as the
name for the movement has remained unchanged. As one priest told me, "What
does it matter? The point is to get people involved."

Perhaps because of these conflicts, the movement is now without a single
readily identifiable focus. On one level, it is a public relations movement. The
first convention (*taikai*) was held in a public hall. It was hoped that a public
space would attract people not already affiliated with Tendai and raise the public image of Tendai, or as one priest said, "image up" (*imeiji appu*) Tendai.[10]
Although the first such event was deemed a success, later public meetings ran
into trouble attracting crowds. After a dismal turnout at the 1976 Tokyo convention, sect leaders decided the movement should turn inward and focus on the
danka member base.[11] Once every several years, a large public convention is held
to appeal to a broader audience, but, in general, meetings are focused inward
with prayer services, dharma talks, and the like. Thus, a second way to view the
movement is as a method to strengthen *danka* member bonds to local temples
and the sect.

Danka members are not required to participate in the movement. However,
there is pressure on priests to increase local involvement, so some priests have
registered all of their *danka* members and paid the nominal annual fee themselves.[12] Thus, while the movement appears to be expanding and attracting large
numbers of *danka* members in support of it, in actuality it may not be growing
much at all. On the thirtieth anniversary of the first convention, a forum was
held in Tokyo to discuss the past and future of the movement. At this meeting
the lack of direct *danka* member participation in anything other than the conventions was lamented.

Future plans now call for increased *danka* member involvement in the
planning and implementation of activities. However, here, too, many problems
exist. *Danka* member leadership roles generally fall to *sōdai*. Because of their
position at the temple, *sōdai* would most likely be selected as representatives to
the movement. Yet because the *sōdai* position is often inherited, there is some
question as to whether any would actively participate. To expand the call to
service to include non-*sōdai* as representatives to the movement might ensure
active participation, but it would run the risk of upsetting traditional local tem-

ple power structures. Here the delicate sect-temple balance comes into play: How do sect and temple balance their own needs against those of the other? Furthermore, even if room is made for *danka* members within sect administrative hierarchies, exactly how are *danka* members to be incorporated into a sect that describes itself as a world-renouncer organization *(shukke shūdan)?*

Moreover, despite efforts to make *danka* members the focus of the movement, priests remain critical participants in the welfare, environmental, and aid activities conducted by the movement. The movement was initiated by priests and still exists as a platform from which priests may seek involvement in local, national, and international welfare and relief efforts, as well as in propagation. It is also a platform through which the sect encourages priests to increase their involvement in such issues. Thus, a third way of looking at the movement is as a platform for expanding or recreating the role of priests.[13] This aspect of the movement is dealt with in more detail in chapter 5.

A fourth way of viewing the movement is as a social welfare movement. Movement leaders advocate involvement in society to better self and society. The movement offers volunteer programs to build schools in Laos, to travel to slums in Thailand, to donate money to UNICEF, and to plant trees on Mt. Hiei. Also, regional conventions are held annually, permitting the sect an opportunity to bring *danka* members together to discuss the accomplishments of the various welfare activities.

Indeed, the aims of the movement are as varied as its beginnings as a local effort later co-opted by the sect. One leader wrote recently, "There is a lot of discussion as to what the movement is about. Is it a social service movement? Is it a Tendai sect faith movement? Is it a movement to develop individual character?"[14] The bylaws of the movement demonstrate the breadth of the movement's goals: everything from publishing a newsletter to creating a Pure Land. The bylaws read,

> Purpose: This movement takes as its purpose the actualization of the spirit of the founder Dengyō Daishi, to promote the Light Up Your Corner Movement, to broadly raise the spiritual life of society, and to build a Buddhist Pure Land. In order to realize its purpose the movement will undertake the following: (1) activities to proclaim broadly the spirit of Dengyō Daishi, (2) the publication of periodicals and other materials, (3) the holding of conventions, lectures, and study meetings, (4) granting recognition for those who are involved, (5) cooperation in world peace and environmental efforts, (6) aid for internal and foreign disaster and

conflict relief, and (7) other activities recognized as contributing to the aims of the movement.[15]

This broad definition is a source of weakness for the movement. Because sect leaders are unable to focus on a direct course of action, some participants, both priestly and lay, are often confused or apathetic. Despite this situation, efforts to reach out to and engage *danka* members in sect activities have been marginally successful.

FOCUSING ON THE DANKA MEMBERS

How did the sect respond to the vision of crumbling Japanese values and the declining future prospects of Temple Buddhism through the Light Up Your Corner Movement? The answer to these questions lies in the movement's role in strengthening *danka* member bonds with the sect and local temples by offering opportunities for *danka* member involvement in sect-sponsored activities for bettering society. In short, the movement created new religious and administrative roles for *danka* members within the sect. These activities allow *danka* members the opportunity to put into practice the teachings of the sect or, put another way, to learn a way of life based on Tendai teachings. *Danka* members are thereby drawn into a closer relationship with the sect.

The textual source for the movement is found in Saichō's *Regulations for Ordinands (Sangegakushōshiki)*,[16] which is cited on the movement's home page and elsewhere. It reads, "What is the nation's treasure? The will to enlightenment is the treasure, and one who possesses it is the nation's treasure. There is an old saying that a string of jewels is not the nation's treasure; the nation's treasure is one who lights up his corner." The movement's home page develops this as follows:

> Money and material assets, these are not the nation's treasure. The irreplaceable treasures of the nation are those who do their best and brighten the world around themselves, at home, at work, wherever they might be. Society as a whole is made a brighter place by [each persons] giving their all just where they are. Seek out joy for the entire human race, not just for yourself. "One who understands the pain of others," "one who can take pleasure in the joy of others," "one who is kind, thoughtful, and warmhearted" is the nation's treasure. This is what [Saichō] was saying. If warmhearted people gather we can create a brighter society (*akarui shakai*). The Light Up Your Corner Movement

seeks to bring the spirit of Dengyō Daishi [Saichō] alive today. It was
founded in 1969 to build a brighter society in which people lift up their
hearts and minds to become better human beings. Wherever you are,
whatever position you might hold, do your best and shine forth. If you
shine, your neighbors, your town, your society will shine, too. By
gathering together these points of light, Japan will shine, the world
will shine and the whole earth will shine. Light Up Your Corner![17]

Tendai *danka* members are asked to embody the founder's teachings by going out
and becoming the nation's treasures through lighting up the world around them.
The Light Up Your Corner Movement provides practical opportunities to do
this, as well as a wealth of material to support such a way of life, such as inspirational essays and sermons that delineate the Tendai way of life.

The Tendai way of viewing the world and acting properly within it are
brought together in the Three Practices for families. The Three Practices are
Living in Harmony, Service, and Life. The Three Practices slogan is a relatively
new development. It was created for the twenty-fifth anniversary of the movement.[18] The emphasis on the family reflects the desire to cure Japan's ailing value
system by enriching family life, thus saving the traditional family. The family
emphasis also reflects the desire to strengthen the bonds between families and
their temples, bonds that are the foundation of the *danka* system upon which
Temple Buddhism rests.

THE THREE PRACTICES

The first of the Three Practices is the practice of Living in Harmony, which
takes as its theme helping the environment and thus furthering awareness of the
co-dependent nature of existence. The core act is reducing the amount of
garbage produced at home. The home page notes,

> Fresh air and pure water, the nourishment and natural resources given
> by the earth, these blessings are the wellspring of life. But, they are not
> inexhaustible. The increase in waste, especially household waste, which
> is now more than can be disposed of, invites major environmental degra-
> dation. First, we must treat things preciously and decrease the amount of
> household waste. Then, we should recycle as much as possible.[19]

The theme of living in harmony with one's surroundings, of learning not to be
wasteful, is closely tied to the vision of postwar Japan as a consumer society run

amok. According to this view, the postwar period of high growth led Japanese to value consumption and comfort over anything else.[20] The view of Japan as a society that has forsaken its traditional moral values in the pursuit of personal monetary gain is common among the leaders of both Temple Buddhist sects and the new religions. For example, Niwano Nikkyō, the head of Risshō Kōseikai, noted in his speech at the first Brighter Society Movement convention (April 1969) that Japan was spiritually impoverished and that the Japanese, in their pursuit of money, had become self-centered.[21]

Through the Light Up Your Corner Movement, the Tendai sect seeks to put Japan's value system back on track. For example, Saichō's teaching that "within the will to enlightenment there is food and shelter, but the will to enlightenment does not exist within food and shelter" (*dōshin no naki ni ejiki ari, ejiki no naka ni dōshin nashi*) is often quoted. This statement teaches people today that their values are backwards. One can never find true happiness (enlightenment) within consumerism and mass consumption. However, within the search for true happiness, one's material needs will be met. The movement suggests that one way to realize this is to reduce wasteful consumption.[22]

From recycling at home, the practice points to getting involved in environmental protection projects. The headlines on the front page of a recent issue of the sect newspaper read, "Times That Question How We Live" and "Changing to a Recycling Society." The essays instruct the reader that the way to bring about a recycling society is through the efforts of individuals doing whatever they can within their own limits.[23]

Environmental protection became part of special Light Up Your Corner thirtieth-anniversary efforts.

> Today many of the earth's forests are sending out an SOS. Forests, the source of our water and air, are disappearing because of uncontrolled development and logging. As part of its thirtieth-anniversary efforts, the Light Up Your Corner Movement is adopting environmental protection as a theme. As the first step, a tree-planting effort was undertaken on Mt. Hiei to repair the damage caused in the Saitō area by last year's typhoon.

> Developing countries, including our own Japan, are practicing uncontrolled development and are harming the forests. With the loss of the forest comes loss of animals, loss of potential cancer-curing medicines, flooding, and a loss of soil nutrients. We Japanese are world-class wood

users. Thirty years ago, Tendai began stressing that we had forgotten what true wealth was during the high growth period and began the Light Up Your Corner Movement, recalling [Saichō's] call to forget self and benefit others.[24]

The focus of the Living in Harmony practice is to learn to recognize that one lives in a dependent relationship with nature. Understanding the dependent nature of one's existence is true wealth. This practice finds its foundation in the teaching that one is given life by all that surrounds one, a core teaching of contemporary Tendai that draws on the Buddhist concept of co-dependence. The broader Tendai teaching of Living in Harmony here has been harnessed to the popular contemporary interest in environmentalism to produce a practice that is meaningful to the members, teaches core Tendai concepts, and offers *danka* members a way to become involved in society through the Tendai sect.[25]

The second practice is Service. This practice centers on service to society, especially through, but not limited to, volunteer activities. The question is asked, "In this messed-up world, what can be done to make a bright and peaceful society?" The answer is found in Saichō's call to "forget self and benefit others" *(mōkorita)*.[26] The movement brochures continue, "Volunteering is putting into practice the Buddhist spirit of giving *(fuse)*. For the world to live in peace, we must think and act from the point of view of the meek. Compassion and thoughtfulness should be nurtured in the household. Let's put our hearts and minds together and volunteer as a family. Volunteering enriches the heart and mind of the volunteer."[27] The practice of Service is to engage society in an effort to better both self and society. An article in the sect newspaper states, "Try to do your best at those good works that you are able to do. If you fail, reflect on your mistakes and devise [a new approach]. This is the nature of the Light Up Your Corner Movement: individual activities link together to form a large ring. Lighting up a corner leads to lighting up a thousand miles."[28]

In addition to larger projects, such as participating in school-building efforts in Laos or aiding in disaster relief around Japan, many local activities are encouraged. Whatever the activity, the goal is to not only help others, but also to better one's character. For example, members are encouraged to skip meals occasionally and to donate the money saved to help others.[29] The emphasis, however, is not said to be the money, but the act of skipping a meal. Through fasting, one learns compassion for the hungry. One also learns discipline if fasting is made a regular practice.[30] As one priest notes, "The value of [the] Light Up Your Corner [Movement] is that it teaches us to build up good acts one at a time."

Social welfare cannot," he says, "simply be reduced to the giving of material items. It must include the giving of self." He adds that "Japanese give money easily, but must learn to give of themselves."[31]

The last of the Three Practices is Life. What is the practice of Life? The movement literature says the following: "Give thanks that you were born as a human, and realize that you were brought into this life-path passed down from your parents and ancestors. Know the importance of life. For the sake of the children of the future, pass on what our ancestors taught us of how to be virtuous, and rejoice at the birth of new life from the bottom of your heart."[32]

The head of Tendai's college at its headquarters on Mt. Hiei comments that an important part of one's character is the desire to give back the gift of life, "We must not forget the importance of giving back [the gift of life]. When we wake in the morning, we should face the family Buddhist altar, press our hands together, and call to mind the thought of returning the favor [of the gift of life]."[33] Of the three practices, this is perhaps the most fundamental. It calls for the revitalization of ancestor veneration at home—the cornerstone of family religion in Japan. The traditional family has fallen apart because "postwar education created a spirit of pillaging."[34] Traditional values were discarded in favor of mass consumerism. This "spirit of pillaging," in which individuals seek their own fulfillment without regard for those around them, is seen as lying at the heart of Japan's current values crisis.

At the same time, the movement leaders claim that the crisis can be overcome through a return to traditional Japanese values.[35] For example, one leader notes that he read a survey showing that multi-generational families in which the grandparents prayed regularly before the home Buddhist altar had less chance of producing problem children. Prayer, he added, is the foundation of the movement.[36] And the root of prayer, added another leader, is the ancestors.[37]

The Three Practices are grounded in the family, and on this account of the matter, the family is grounded in the ancestors. If the roots of the family tree are strong, the tree will survive even a typhoon, the family will prosper, and society will shine.[38] One learns to appreciate the gift of life through paying respect to one's ancestors; selfish individualism is replaced with the will to return the favor of the gift of life. Thus it is taught that one has the power to break the chain of individualism and consumerism, in which life is seen as something created by individuals like any other product and not understood as a precious gift.[39] That is the beginning of lighting up one's corner of the world, according to Tendai sect leaders. "Begin by cleaning the household Buddhist altar, returning the favor [of the gift of life] through offering thanks to your ancestors. That is the spirit of returning the favor, and the foundation of the Light Up Your Corner Movement."[40]

According to movement leaders, a return to the practice of ancestor veneration would solve not only Japan's current values crisis, but also the negative image of Temple Buddhism. The image of funeral Buddhism remains indelible. *Danka* members do not know about other temple activities. If *danka* members could be brought to the temple and the temple were made a part of everyday life once again, one Tendai leader argues, Tendai's image problems would disappear.[41] The way to do that is through encouraging respect for the ancestors, which in turn rebuilds the family, which serves to support the temple that brings the family back together and seeks to keep the family together by offering new activities for volunteering together to better society.

Taken together, the Three Practices form the foundation for a Tendai-based way of life centered on the family. They provide *danka* members the opportunity to become engaged in society and in the teachings to underpin such engagement. In her work on the worldview of new religions, Helen Hardacre comments that Temple Buddhism sects do not provide a systematized worldview for families.[42] Movements such as Tendai's Light Up Your Corner, however, demonstrate that the sects of Temple Buddhism do at times attempt to incorporate a systematized worldview into their teachings aimed at *danka* members. Such a systematized worldview attracts many to the new religions and keeps them there. It is perhaps no coincidence that Temple Buddhism sects began to develop programs such as the Light Up Your Corner Movement just as the new religions were soaring to new peaks in membership.

It is also striking how similar the worldview presented by Tendai's Light Up Your Corner Movement is to that of the new religions. The emphasis on giving thanks for one's life, for example, recalls to mind the worldview that Tsushima Michihito and Shimazono Susumu describe as central to the new religions.[43] The foundations of this worldview are found in Japanese folk religion and culture, as are the roots of Temple Buddhism's worldview as found in Tendai's Three Practices. Yasumaru Yoshio describes the base for this worldview as conventional morality (*tsūzoku dōtoku*). "Conventional morality" teaches loyalty, obedience, sincerity, and filial piety and is focused on the household (*ie*) as a social institution. Many of these aspects can be found in the rhetoric of the Light Up Your Corner Movement: loyalty to the sect, sincerity in one's actions, filial piety, and the desire to maintain the household as an institution. The sect, in turn, links these ideals to creating a better society and ending the moral malaise into which it takes Japan as having fallen. These goals are similar to the functions that

Yasumaru describes conventional morality as having played within Edo and Meiji society and also those that the vitalistic worldview, as described by Shima-zono, plays within postwar society.[44] It is a conservative rhetoric that especially supports the views of the prewar and transwar generations. As Winston Davis notes, this rhetoric works as a passive enabler of modernization by helping people cope with the changes modernity brings about and supports the state's aims at creating content workers to power the economy.[45] Indeed, the Japanese state is today calling for a return to moral education in order to instill these very values. The Ministry of Education's 2002 white paper states, "In order to nurture the rich humanity of our children, moral education is extremely important."[46] In this sense, Tendai's Light Up Your Corner Movement is clearly part of a larger, dominant, conservative worldview.

THE CONVENTIONS

The conventions that are held annually in most Tendai-sect teaching districts (kyōku) provide the sect an opportunity to gather in one place danka members, priests, temple families, and interested outsiders. We have seen that movement leaders originally saw the conventions as an opportunity to draw in people not already affiliated with Tendai. Even from the start, however, filling seats in a large public hall proved to be difficult. Danka members had to be bused in from a distance to guarantee a respectable turnout.[47] Although the original aim was to draw outsiders, in the end more than 90 percent of movement members were danka members.[48]

The large-scale involvement of danka members helped leaders realize that the movement could be used as a rallying point for the sect. Vertical integration is weak in the Tendai sect: it is more of a federation of individual temples sharing a common membership than an organization that leads from the center.[49] It was hoped that the movement would provide a way to integrate local efforts into the center and to disseminate the teachings and orders of the center to local temples. Furthermore, by linking the sect (center) to the temples (periphery), temples could share in the legitimating authority of the sect, which works assiduously to maintain an image of the sect headquarters on Mt. Hiei as a center for Buddhist austerities and traditional Japanese culture. The conventions became the centerpiece of such efforts. Through conventions, local members (danka members as well as priests) were given the opportunity to hear directly from sect leaders and to learn about the Tendai sect.

The conventions became arranged in what is called the dokujukai, or sutra-reading-group, format. Sutra reading groups are common to many temples.

Group members, primarily *danka* members or local faithful *(shinja)*, meet regularly (daily, weekly, or monthly) at local temples to chant Buddhist texts and to listen to a short sermon by the priest. By taking on the sutra-reading-group format, the conventions switched from being primarily outward, popularly focused events, to being focused inward on *danka* members. Initially, conventions were public events—taking place in public halls and emphasizing social welfare activities. Following the shift to the *danka* member focus and the sutra-reading-group format, the conventions came to be conducted as ceremonies. Even when conventions take place in public venues, the interior hall is decorated with distinctive Tendai accessories (images of Saichō, an altar, etc.). It was hoped that such an inward turn would make the conventions a vehicle for increasing *danka* member identification with the sect as well as with their local temples, many of which attempt to organize group attendance. To provide a sense of what a convention is like, I shall briefly describe one I attended.[50] Most conventions follow a similar pattern.

The venue is a public hall in downtown Tokyo. In the parking lot are parked several tour buses used to bring in *danka* member groups. At 12:30 the hall is nearly filled to capacity with more than 1,500 people in attendance. At 1:00 a professional announcer steps to the microphone to bring the meeting to order. It proceeds like a well-directed and well-rehearsed production. The first speaker is the Tokyo Teaching District assistant director. He introduces the day's events for ten minutes. His talk focuses on the increasing number of crimes committed by youth. The world today is "dark," he says, not "bright." People must, he continues, do everything they can to bring a little light to their corner of the world; in particular, they should begin their efforts at home. For example, mothers are no longer at home for their children. Children return to a dark house. Working is fine, but women must see to lighting up their house before they leave it.

After the speech, a few moments pass before the curtains are pulled back to reveal a wide stage. In the back center of the stage is a large altar, adorned with offerings of fruit, candles, and incense. Hanging from the ceiling above the altar is a sizeable painting of Saichō sitting in meditation. For the rest of the meeting, the painting hangs there facing out over the audience. Next, a procession of priests clad in purple, green, brown, and orange silk robes comes on stage. The priests enter as the Tokyo Teaching District Temple Wives Buddhist Hymn Group sings the Dengyō Daishi hymn off stage. Then the priests begin *shōmyō* chanting, a special kind of songlike chanting. Once they have finished, the audience members are asked to take out the Tendai liturgy booklet they were given as part of their package upon entrance. Together with the priests, they then chant the Heart Sutra and other portions of the liturgy. Half an hour later, when the liturgy has finished, the priests file offstage as the Tokyo Teaching District Temple Wives Buddhist Hymn Group sings the Mt. Hiei hymn.

Next, the opening ceremony is held. First, the author of the new Light Up Your Corner Movement theme song is introduced. He tells how he was inspired to write the song and then presents an award of thanks to the composer who wrote the music for him. The composer, in turn, presents the lyricist with a donation for the movement. Then the Tokyo Teaching District Temple Wives Chorus Group takes the stage and sings the new theme song.

Two leading priests from the sect headquarters are now introduced and give short speeches. Once again, the high rate of youth crime is mentioned. The source of the problem is identified as the corrupt values the young hold today, values that are said to be the fault of the education system and a lack of discipline at home.

Next an award ceremony is held in which three million yen is presented to the movement's sect headquarters for building schools in Laos. The head of the movement then gives a short speech discussing the accomplishments so far in Laos and what still needs to be done there.

Following a break, the entertainment portion of the convention begins. First up is the hugely popular writer of books on Buddhism, Hiro Sachiya. He gives an engaging one-hour talk on the importance of giving thanks. A Korean women's Buddhist choir that flew from Korea to give a special performance follows him.[51] The choir, in turn, is followed by a young blind *shamisen* (Japanese banjo) player who dazzles the audience with his virtuosic playing.[52] Finally, the Tokyo movement leader takes the stage to say farewell, and at shortly after 4:00 P.M., the convention ends.

The convention weaves between religious service, an appeal to traditional culture, general meeting (with award ceremonies and speeches on accomplishments), inspirational gathering (talks by well-known figures on inspirational themes), and entertainment (musical performances). The service conducted by the priests presents a positive image of priests sincerely engaging a nonfuneral-related ritual. The impact of the chanting and of a stage filled with priests in magnificent robes provides a powerful image of religious authority. The songs sung by the Tendai choir all appeal to the history and authority of the founders of Tendai.

The speeches by the Tendai priests are directed at the mostly female audience. As in the new religions, women, especially middle-aged and older, are the most active at their temples. Most temples offer instruction in Buddhist hymns (*goeika*). This instruction is popular among late-middle-age women, who attend (and sometimes perform at) the conventions. The message conveyed in the speeches, like that in the Three Practices, is conservative and gendered. Women, it is argued, have an important role to play in society—namely, to be good mothers and wives. If they maintain such roles, the family will not float away into a sea of moral crisis, and society will be a better place. The home, therefore, is the "corner" that the women are called upon at the conventions and elsewhere to "light up."[53] Women are thereby employed by the sect to rebuild the family, the base upon which Temple Buddhism rests.

As for the guest speakers, not all conventions have as famous a figure as Hiro Sachiya present, but most seek out a secular or religious celebrity as the key speaker. Another convention I attended featured Sakai Yūsai, a famous Tendai charismatic religious figure.[54] Of the convention speakers from 1999 and late 1998, eight of twenty-four were celebrities or well-known individuals from secular society, one was a religious celebrity, five were leading Tendai figures, and the remaining ten were local or national Tendai figures.

By making use of such well-known people, the conventions teach and entertain the *danka* members gathered. *Danka* members are kept informed about sect and movement activities and are made to feel a part of the efforts of the sect and the movement. In these ways, the bonds between individual *danka* members and the sect are strengthened.

LIGHT IN THE FUTURE?

The Light Up Your Corner Movement illuminates the many problems facing contemporary Temple Buddhism: waning *danka* member interest, local versus sect needs, and the changing nature of affiliation with the temple. The question of who participates in sect administration and planning exposes the divide at the center of contemporary Temple Buddhism between the laity and the priesthood. Recall that the movement was founded and is managed by priests. Priestly participation is virtually guaranteed. All Tendai-affiliated temples are registered as local offices of the movement, and the head priests are required to be the local office leaders. Thus, at least on a minimal level, all head priests are involved. Most of the international volunteer activities, such as building schools in Laos, are staffed not by *danka* members, but by priests. Involvement at the local level by *danka* members appears to depend significantly on the enthusiasm of the local temple priest. If the priest is able to communicate the need for becoming socially engaged and is able to develop local practices, *danka* member interest increases. However, even the most enthusiastic priests must counter images of the temple that have developed from the late 1600s onward as a place for death rituals and of the priest as interested only in funerals. One priest writes, for instance, that when he began a stamp-collecting drive, he met with many early difficulties. The purpose of stamp drives is twofold. On the one hand, the cutting and sorting of the stamps by *danka* members is supposed to be a form of practice (*gyō*). As they cut and sort, they reflect on their own fortunate circumstances and give rise to compassionate thoughts for those less fortunate. On the other hand, the stamps are collected at the temple and sent to the sect headquarters, where they are massed with others and sold. The proceeds are then used for various social welfare programs. The priest was dismayed when one *danka* member, missing the point of the stamp drive, returned from vacation in Germany with a package of stamps. The *danka* member said, "I hear you are collecting stamps and thought you might enjoy these."[55]

Another problem facing the movement is the gap between sect and local temple needs and expectations. For example, one local leader writes that too much energy is now focused on projects that send funding up the ladder to the sect to be used for international relief efforts.[56] He argues that the movement should focus on efforts closer to home.[57] It should also, he notes, better inform members concerning how their money is spent, so they do not see their donations as just one more time they have been squeezed for money by their temple.[58] The gap between sect and local temple needs—and the lack of ability to overcome that gap in a systematic, structured manner—makes clear differences between the efforts of sects of Temple Buddhism, such as Tendai, and those of new religions. The success of programs operated or sponsored by new religions, such as Risshō Kōseikai's Brighter Society Movement, is based in part upon strong centralized control combined with mechanisms for local leadership and also on an effort to enroll nonmembers in leading positions to increase the program's appeal to a broader, nonsectarian audience.[59]

Despite problems, however, there is some evidence that *danka* members are becoming more involved or at least that the movement has succeeded in raising *danka* member awareness of sect history and teachings and, thereby, has drawn *danka* members into a closer relationship with the sect. The primary evidence for this is the lasting appeal of the conventions. Regional conventions are held every year in most teaching districts. The conventions regularly bring together several hundred *danka* members as well as local temple priests and their wives. At the conventions, they sing the sect song and, since 2000, the new Light Up Your Corner theme song. They also listen to sermons on Saichō's teachings and to the speeches of invited guests.

It is arguable that the movement has been at least partially successful in encouraging new forms of *danka* member involvement in the sect and in deepening *danka* member ties with the sect through involving *danka* members in conventions and through teaching a Tendai way of life through the Three Practices. At the same time, its limited audience hinders the movement's effectiveness. In many ways, it is preaching to the choir. The majority of *danka* members who attend conventions are those already involved with their temples. In particular, a large portion of the audience appears to be women who are participating as members of their local temple's hymn group. Still, the fact that the conventions are "preaching to the choir" points out the peculiar situation of Temple Buddhism today. As we have seen, *danka* temples as presently structured initially developed under the temple registration system of the Edo period and came to provide primarily funeral and memorial services, which are becoming commodified. The sects of Temple Buddhism seek to hold at bay the gradual commodification of religious action and association by actively restructuring temple-*danka* bonds through efforts such as the Light Up Your Corner Movement.

Moreover, in the eyes of Tendai sect leadership, the *danka* members whose association with the temple have been based on the grave are in need of a kind of conversion. They must be converted from their reliance on the temple for funeral-specific needs to active participation in the programs of the sect and to active belief in the teachings of the sect. *Danka* members must also be converted from commodified religious affiliation to traditional affiliation. However, conversion efforts of the movement face difficulties because the sect is attempting to re-create *danka*-temple-sect bonds through a focus on the family and the traditional *danka*-temple relationship centered on paying respect to the ancestors. While the sect has offered new opportunities for acting on a Tendai worldview, such as those seen in the Three Practices, the underlying message is a conservative—even reactionary—one that may not appeal to younger generations, who are often blamed for Japan's perceived moral crisis. The conservative message may also not appeal to those women who seek to break free from traditional role restrictions and to those women who are forced by the extended recession of the 1990s to work outside the home and who seek less moralizing and more opportunities.

By way of contrast, the members of new religions (or at least first-generation members) are not in need of conversion. They chose to become members out of an interest in the teachings and benefits of the religion. Temple Buddhism members, on the other hand, generally enter the relationship through birth. Some also enter the relationship through death (e.g., in seeking a grave site and funeral service for a loved one), but most who do so appear to make their decisions based more on the practical need for a grave plot than on an interest in doctrine or worldview. Temple Buddhism members, therefore, remain in need of conversion to the teachings and potential benefits of membership. The new religions, which teach a conservative family-values-oriented worldview similar to that found in Temple Buddhism, also find it difficult to attract young recruits. However, new religions are much more aggressively engaged in establishing programs to incorporate their second- and third-generation members and in appealing to Japanese youth than are the sects of Temple Buddhism. Nevertheless, the success of the new new religions and the popularity of New Age goods suggests that the conservative agenda of both the new religions and Temple Buddhism lacks appeal to many Japanese youth.

From its beginnings in the Edo period, the *danka* system in Japan has strictly limited the roles open to *danka* members. Prior to the contemporary period and the creation of campaigns such as the Light Up Your Corner Movement, *danka* members were not called upon to perform active roles within the sect. Their place within the religious and administrative structures of the sect and temples was to support the sect and temples and to rely on them for the performance of rituals. Theirs was a passive role. The Tendai sect, like most other sects of Temple Buddhism, has sought to create a space within the sect for an active *danka* member role in order to strengthen the *danka* member base upon which the sects rely for their existence. At the same time, the Tendai sect has also sought to maintain the traditional passive role of its *danka* members. The inability of the Tendai sect to fully integrate *danka* members into active roles is due in part to the continued reliance on *danka* members as passive players, and this reliance, in turn, continues because sect officials still envision the sect as a world-renouncing organization. Within such an organization, *danka* members, who are by definition householders, can only play supportive roles. The persistence of traditional constructions of Tendai and other sects of Temple Buddhism as world-renouncing sects supported by lay households works against efforts to integrate lay practitioners into more active roles.

4 The Contemporary Priesthood
Images of Identity Crisis

(1) So long as I have not attained the stage where my six faculties are pure, I will not venture out into the world. (2) So long as I have not realized the absolute, I will not acquire any special skills or arts (such as medicine, divination, and calligraphy). (3) So long as I have not kept all the precepts purely, I will not participate in any lay donor's meeting. (4) So long as I have not attained wisdom, I will not participate in worldly affairs unless it be to benefit others. (5) May any merit from my past, present, and future be given not to me, but to all sentient beings so that they may attain supreme enlightenment.[1]
—Saichō, c. 785.

I am a priest.
Wearing my robes, my prayer beads in my left hand, I ride my bicycle.
I go from house to parishioner's house and chant sutra.
I am a priest.
I have a wife, I have a child.
I drink *sake*, I eat meat.
I eat fish, I lie.
And, still, I am a priest.
A dirty, too dirty, priest.
When I call upon parishioners and accept their donations,
is this not theft?
Oh, the five precepts that Shakyamuni kept,
I have broken them all.
But, yet, I am a bodhisattva.
I travel the path of the bodhisattva.
I have faith in the Dharma, I sit in the palm of the Law.
I live in the Dharma, I live amongst the people.
Within endless life, I practice the way.
Hand in hand with other practitioners, I proceed down
this peaceful path, this path without equal
the path of Truth, the bodhisattva path.

I am filthy, and I have broken all of the five precepts but,
but, because of the Dharma, all will become Buddhas.
That path, that bodhisattva path.
I am standing on that path.[2]
—Temple priest, c. 1980

Priests today live trapped between images of the ideal—"true Buddhism"—
and images of the corrupt—"funeral Buddhism"; between the fiscal and ritual
necessities of everyday temple life as it has developed since the early modern
period and popular dissatisfaction with that way of life; and between calls to
retain "tradition" and calls to address contemporary needs and demands.
Conflicts such as these are not new to the postwar period. They have existed in
various forms since premodern times. However, it is particularly in the modern,
and especially postwar, period that the images of "real" or "true" Buddhism have
come to clash with the images and realities of Buddhism as it developed under
the *danka* member system.

We have seen how the Tendai sect has engaged in efforts to re-create
temple-*danka* bonds as one way to remain relevant. But it is not only at the
danka level that efforts are being made to revitalize and re-create the sects of
Temple Buddhism. The priest, the most visible figure in Temple Buddhism, is
also the object of a concerted and multivalent effort by the sects to invigorate
and ensure the survival of Temple Buddhism through the twenty-first century.
This chapter and the next explore the Temple Buddhist priesthood today and
look at the Tendai sect's efforts to preserve tradition while also creating new
images through recruiting drives and new roles for priests.

Temple Buddhism sects face certain negative images regarding the priesthood. They also face a lack of interested successors to the priesthood. The two are
linked. The image problems are not contemporary in origin, though modern forms
of mass media have made their dissemination faster and more thorough than ever
before.[3] The primary problematic image is a sense that temple priests do not practice true Buddhism. The roots of this problem can be traced to the following factors: the long association of priests with the state (but especially in connection
with Buddhist institutional support of modern imperialism and war), the breaking down of boundaries between lay and professional members through the
relaxation of precept maintenance (especially so in the case of clerical marriage,
discussed in chapter 6), modern ideas concerning the proper roles of clergy, and
priestly involvement in moneymaking ventures (discussed in chapters 7 and 8).

MEMBERS OF THE STATE

One source of contemporary negative images of Temple Buddhism is its association with the wartime state. Buddhism in Japan has been intimately tied to the
state since its introduction in the sixth century, when it arrived as a powerful
state-protecting gift to the emperor of Japan from the king of Paekche on the
Korean peninsula. Kuroda Toshio notes,

> In Buddhism the most common term for ordination, *shukke*, refers to
> ridding oneself of all secular things, including authority, status, property,
> and family life, and turning to the true dharma. This, however, was not
> true of Japanese Buddhism in the medieval era. Under the Ritsuryō
> system of the ancient imperial state, the Buddhist clergy lived within
> the establishment, in institutions—temples—founded and authorized by
> state authority.[4]

The Tendai sect, which was founded in the Heian period is a particularly
good example of early state-religion relationships. According to legend, the
emperor moved his capital to Kyoto because Mt. Hiei, where Saichō practiced,
was to the northeast of the proposed capital. Northeast was the direction that
misfortune was said to come from; therefore, having a renowned Buddhist practicing there acted like a dam, keeping misfortune from spilling into the capital
environs. Moving beyond legend, it is clear that Saichō argued for the establishment of his school based on its ability to protect the state.[5] The concept of
state protecting (*chingo kokka*) espoused by Saichō centered on Buddhism's existing for the sake of the state. Rituals were performed to protect the emperor and
to secure the prosperity of the state.[6]

By the early Kamakura period (1185–1333), Buddhism's role in protecting
the state had become thoroughly integrated into both organizational and ideological structures through the concept of king's law–Buddha's law (*ōbō–buppō*).

> [Buddhism] actively embraced the role of ideological partner of the state,
> and generated much of the doctrinal rationale for it, as well as for the
> legitimation of imperial rule. . . . [It] functioned . . . not simply as a source
> of ideological justification, but also as one of the institutional pillars of
> society. . . . Hence, when the language of mutual dependence between *ōbō*
> and *buppō* was invoked, it reverberated not only at an abstract, doctrinal
> level but also at a concrete, institutional level."[7]

However, as seen in the previous chapter, full-scale incorporation of Buddhist priests into state administrative practices through the temple registration system occurred in the Edo period.

So thoroughly intertwined were state and Buddhist institutions that, when the new Meiji government came to power in 1868, it began a programmatic separation of Buddhism and state as part of its effort to dismantle the previous administration.[8] Separation took place on three levels: physical, organizational, and ideological. Physically, the state relieved many temples of properties bequeathed by the Edo government. Because the Tendai sect held many temples closely associated with the Tokugawa family, the rulers of the Edo-period government, Tendai suffered more acutely than the Jōdo Shin, Sōtō, and Nichiren sects, which relied more on *danka* and privately donated lands.[9]

Organizationally, Meiji government laws, including ones that repealed previous such as those forbidding clerical marriage, radically changed the status of priests.[10] Legal changes designed to eradicate the status structures of the Edo period reduced priests to professionals when the priestly class, understood as a separate category from ordinary individuals, was eliminated and priests joined the ranks of everyday citizens. The priesthood thereby became just one profession among many.[11]

On the view that a separation of secular and nonsecular realms did not exist as such prior to its introduction by the West, it is arguable that the concepts "secular" and "nonsecular" are not applicable to pre-Meiji Japan or, indeed, to modern Japan, either.[12] However, it is certain that both status and lay or religious distinctions did exist. The distinction between lay and religious was maintained through use of the ideal types of world-renouncer and householder. With the legalization of marriage and the eventual near-universal adoption of marriage by the clergy, the distinction between world-renouncer and householder lost practical meaning. The changes that removed legal coercion for maintenance of priestly codes of conduct led to significant changes in temple life and priestly image. For example, clerical marriage led to temple households. The creation of such households soon created an image problem for Temple Buddhism. How could it bridge the gap that existed between the world-renouncer ideal type, still espoused by most sects of Temple Buddhism, and the visible reality of temple households? Clerical marriage also led to such practical problems as how to define the relation between father (master) and son (disciple), as well as how to administer temple succession.

Nativist scholars and others who sought to push Buddhism out of the ruling ideological framework of the newly born Meiji Japan attacked Buddhist teachings concerning the importance of Buddhist law to king's law. Buddhists were later able to counter these attacks in part by demonstrating that Buddhist law still could support the king's law (imperial rule) and also by creating new theories as to how Buddhism could benefit the state. For example, Buddhists argued that Buddhist philosophy provided Japan with a native rational philosophy equal to, or better than, anything the Western powers had to offer.[13] Furthermore, from the Christians, Buddhists learned the value of social work, both to reach a broader audience and to prove themselves useful to the state.

In addition to direct state efforts to disentangle Buddhism from the mechanisms of the state, a semiofficial persecution took place. This, too, was a reaction against the position of political privilege held by Buddhism under the Edo government. The movement to destroy Buddhism and throw out Shakyamuni (*haibutsu kishaku*) of the early Meiji period enjoyed the implicit support of the state in its initial stages.[14] Under the banner of throwing out the Buddha, temples were ransacked, priests defrocked, and properties confiscated. The movement was stronger in some areas than others, leaving pockets of severe devastation contrasting with areas that suffered little or no effect.

Despite such aggressive anti-Buddhist campaigns, Buddhism survived. From being pariahs, Buddhists soon found themselves taking part in the state's nascent efforts to instill national values in the people to create citizens (*kokumin*) of a modern state. This relatively short-lived education campaign (1870–1884) allowed Buddhists the chance to demonstrate their value to the new state. However, as Ketelaar points out, Buddhists soon realized that the campaign was designed to create a national Shinto-based religion and eventually to erase or to absorb Buddhism and Christianity. Luckily for Buddhists, those in charge of the campaign began to prove themselves incompetent, earning their office the nicknames "Bureau of Indecision" and "Office of Naps."[15] Similarly, popular opinion began to turn against the extremist nature of the initial efforts. It was at this time, according to Ketelaar, that the state shifted the emphasis from teaching a national Shinto doctrine to "a concern for a national and social doctrine training *per se*."[16] Still seeking state support, Buddhists pushed this agenda, which centered on uniting Japanese hearts and minds and on building a wall against the incursion of Christianity, as the following letter signed by representatives of several sects, including Tendai, shows.

> Buddhism should be used to facilitate the hardening of the hearts of
> foolish men and women to prevent their being deceived by Protestant or
> Catholic teachings. If this is done, we priests, with over one thousand

years of devotion to our nation, will be able to continue our loyal
service. . . . All [Buddhist] sects uphold the Great Teaching of our
Imperial Nation; thus, without exception, the teaching of each
[Buddhist] sect should be used in the guidance of the people's hearts.[17]

Under the instructors in (national) doctrine (kyōdōshoku) system, begun in
1872, a nationwide network of instruction centers was developed. The headquarters was the greater learning center (daikyōin) located in Tokyo on the
grounds of Zōjōji, the temple once dedicated to the ancestors of the Tokugawa
family. A middle learning center (chūkyōin) was established in each prefecture,
and, at the bottom of the schema, local temples and shrines were made lesser
learning centers (shōkyōin). Buddhist priests, as well as others, could test for
ranking within the system. The decriminalization of marriage and meat eating
was promoted by some as a way to free Buddhist priests from outdated prohibitions and to let them aid the country to their fullest through what they did best,
preach.[18] Anyone without an official rank was not allowed to preach; thus there
was considerable pressure to take the test and to join the ranks. By 1880, some
81,000 of 103,000 instructors were Buddhist priests.[19] Thus, a few short years
after suffering drastic setbacks at the hands of the new government, Buddhist
priests once again had found roles serving the government.

By 1875, the kyōdōshoku system had changed and each sect had established
its own greater learning center and in its own middle learning center in each
prefecture. Tendai placed its greater learning center on the grounds of Sensōji, a
major temple in the Tokyo area.[20] These changes laid the groundwork for later
sect organizational structure. For example, in 1880, a Tendai sect general meeting (Tendaishū daikaigi) was held at Sensōji, and the Tendai sect organizational
outline (shūsei) was drawn up and put in place. The Tendai sect's greater learning center was designated the sect administrative headquarters (Tendaishū shūmuchō). In 1884, the kyōdōshoku system was abolished. In 1888, a sect meeting
was held at the religious headquarters of Tendai, Enryakuji on Mt. Hiei; at that
meeting it was decided to move the sect administrative headquarters from
Sensōji to Mt. Hiei, at Shigain. An administrative office was then established in
Tokyo.[21] In 1896, the Tendai sect constitution was promulgated, marking the
beginnings of a modern organizational structure.

With the end of the kyōdōshoku system, the active role of priests as the
nation's preachers, inculcating citizens into the moral code of the Meiji government, ended. However, the need felt by the Buddhist sects to demonstrate their
loyalty and usefulness to the state did not end with it. Sects such as Tendai had

yet to recoup lands lost during the early days of the Meiji period. Christianity, which intellectuals linked closely to the modern ideal of nationhood pursued by the state's leaders, also threatened them. Government leaders sought to learn from the West, and many Buddhist leaders feared they might equate Christianity with modernization. The influential intellectual civilization and enlightenment (bunmei kaika) movement, which sought to modernize Japan, included many Christians. Some, including Fukuzawa Yūkichi, thought Christianity would aid in Westernization efforts.[22] In addition to threats from Christianity, sect leaders feared defection of parishioners to new religious groups. Such fears were based on new realities. According to a 1924 survey, there were 918 new religions active by then. And a 1925 survey conducted among junior high school students in the Osaka region found that 90 percent responded that religious faith was necessary, but that only 35 percent responded that they would put their faith in Buddhism.[23] Buddhist sects also sought the implementation of laws so they could use legal coercive powers to centralize their organizational structures. Therefore, throughout the remainder of the Meiji period and well into the Taishō and Shōwa periods, Buddhists continued to court leaders of state in an aggressive way.

Buddhist sects, as well as popularly led Buddhist movements, emphasized Buddhism's usefulness to the state. This emphasis was not purely politically motivated; it reflected the nationalistic sentiments of many Buddhists. The historical role of Buddhism as protector of the state, which had developed since at least the Heian period, should not, such Buddhists argued, be forgotten.[24]

Imperial Japan's war with China (1894–1895) allowed Buddhists the opportunity to serve their fellow citizens and the state. In the Sino-Japanese War, Buddhist sects adopted a prowar stance. They comforted soldiers at home and abroad, worked to increase support for the state's efforts at home, took care of families whose men were at the front and of orphans, and held memorial services for those who died in the service of their nation. Japanese Buddhist priests, however, also gave sermons to Chinese prisoners of war and held memorials for non-Japanese dead.[25] This support of state efforts abroad through work at home and in the field continued when Japan went to war with Russia ten years later (Russo-Japanese War, 1904–1905).[26]

Buddhist priests thus continued to be associated with the state. Throughout the early twentieth century, Buddhist organizations petitioned the government to strengthen control over the new religions, to return nationalized lands, and to provide a legal framework for sect organization. In 1915, the Federation of Buddhist Schools (Bukkyō Kakushū Rengōkai) formed a committee to draft a religion bill for presentation to the government. The draft was completed in

1920. Government leaders interpreted the draft as, in part, a demand to be met before Buddhist cooperation in new government campaigns to inculcate good morals in the citizenry would be forthcoming. Among the Buddhist demands were a call for the return of land lost to the government in 1871, a strong centralized administrative *kanchō* system,[27] and government recognition only for temples that were affiliated with established sects. The Buddhist draft and the concerns of government officials regarding the burgeoning number of new religions led to a response by the government. The Religion Policy Investigative Committee (Shūkyō Seido Chōsa Kai) within the Ministry of Education (Monbushō) was not formed until May 12, 1926, but soon presented a draft bill (the 1927 Religions Bill) for consideration in the Diet.[28] Akazawa Shirō outlines eight main points found in the 130 articles of the bill. The bill established (1) a system for designating religions, (2) limitations on religious activities, (3) a hierarchy for the supervision of religious organizations not affiliated with recognized religious organizations, (4) rules concerning separately established churches and religious associations, (5) extensive powers of supervision for the Ministry of Education over religious organizations, (6) national standards for religion instructors, (7) a *kanchō* system and limitations on the rights of main temples, and (8) provisions for the return of land to temples. In addition, the bill called for treating Buddhism, Shinto, and Christianity as equals.[29] This bill went before the conservative House of Peers in 1927, where it was defeated after a fierce debate over freedom of religion. A similar bill was defeated in 1929.[30] However, government officials were able to implement many of the features of these bills by passing ordinances that did not require Diet approval. It was not until 1939 that a comprehensive religions law was passed. The Religious Organizations Law, which went into effect in 1940, included many of the features of the 1927 and 1929 bills, including centralization of sect authority.

Japan's long war in the Pacific had mixed results for the sects of Temple Buddhism. On the one hand, it represented an opportunity to serve the state and to expand the influence of Japanese Buddhism through missionary efforts in Korea and Manchuria. On the other hand, as the war lingered on and the Western powers were brought into the conflict, the situation on the home front deteriorated rapidly, and Buddhist activities were severely curtailed. The example of Taishō University, a Buddhist university jointly supported by the Tendai, Shingon (Buzan and Chizan branches), and Jōdo sects provides a window onto Buddhism in wartime Japan.

In 1939, the Ministry of Education ordered universities, including Buddhist universities, to conduct military drills. In 1940, the government ordered the creation of national devotion groups/national devotion armies (*hōkokudan/hōkokutai*) in universities. Taishō University's national devotion group was in place by 1941. In 1941, physical education classes became devoted to military training. Furthermore, Taishō students were sent to help in Manchuria in 1939, 1940, and 1941.[31]

Research on campus also began to change. In 1939, the Imperial Buddhist Research Institute (Kōdō Bukkyō Kenkyūjo) was founded, followed in 1942 by the East Asian Studies Division (Tōagakka), dedicated to studying the languages and cultures of Asian countries.[32] However, there was little time for students to conduct research. In 1941, the Ministry of Education ordered early graduation for students. In 1942, programs at Taishō were shortened to allow rapid graduation, which freed students for service in the war effort. Furthermore, from 1942 onward, students spent most of their time working in factories or in the fields. By 1943, Taishō students were involved almost full time in labor or military drilling. Finally, to increase student productivity, a factory was built on campus in 1944.[33] Faculty members were made factory floor overseers.

The sects that supported Taishō did little to protest the war or its effects on the home front. Rather, young Buddhist priests in training were organized to support the war effort through work in the fields and factories and through efforts in Manchuria.

Yamada Etai, the most influential head priest (*zasu*) of the Tendai sect in the postwar period, records the following conversation with his master. The conversation is that of a young priest worried about military service. (Yamada joined the military for one year prior to the outbreak of hostilities in the Pacific.) His master reassures him by explaining that killing is permissible, if it is done on orders and not out of one's own volition.

> YAMADA: I have two questions. First, if I am enlisted I may have to take up arms against the enemy. How should I respond if someone says, "You're a priest, you're not supposed to kill people"? And, second, if I go into the army I will have to eat meat [literally, food that smells]. If I am asked if it is O.K. to eat meat and fish, how should I answer?
>
> MASTER: Will you think the enemy is a hateful being and shoot him? Or will you think him bad and stab him with a sword?
>
> YAMADA: Since I won't be able to see him it won't occur to me one way or the other. If my officer orders me, I will shoot. When it is kill or be killed, I must kill or I will be the one killed.

MASTER: There are two kinds of Buddhist precepts, Hinayana and Mahayana. In the Hinayana precepts killing is forbidden no matter what the time or situation. That is why even if a bug is in the way they sweep them away and don't squash them. That's what the whisk [priests carry] is for. However, in the Mahayana precepts if the Dharma is being carried out properly and something gets in the way, then it is swept away as evil. If, when you see many people coming to harm, then you may be left with no choice but to kill. Inarguably, the one who does the killing will fall into hell and suffer, but because he takes on suffering for the many, his action is called "taking on suffering out of great compassion." If the war is a just fight, and if it is your duty as a citizen, you will have to shoot, and you will have to eat meat, but is this something you yourself asked for?

YAMADA: No, it was something chosen for me.

MASTER: To have something chosen for you, this is to receive a donation. When receiving a donation, if it is in a situation where you must do so in order to preserve life, then it is not considered breaking the precepts.[34]

Yamada's statement may be seen as passive acceptance of a role in war through twists of doctrinal interpretation. Support for the war was not limited to those sects backing Taishō University. The following comments by Harada Daiun Sōgaku, a renowned Sōtō Zen priest, make clear that some Buddhists were vocal proponents of the war. "If you see the enemy you must kill him; you must destroy the false and establish the true—these are the cardinal points of Zen.... Isn't the purpose of the sitting meditation (zazen) we have done in the past to be of assistance in an emergency like this?"[35]

This is not to say that Buddhists universally supported the imperial government or the war. Some priests protested; however, they were few in number; and, what is more relevant to the lingering image of Buddhism as once subservient to the state, Buddhist sects as a whole denounced members who stood against the war. For example, Mibu Shōjun, a Tendai priest, was arrested in 1937 and held for interrogation for one year because of his participation in the Youth Alliance for New Buddhism (Shinkōbukkyō Seinen Dōmei),[36] which had been founded in 1931 in Tokyo. Its leaders sought to re-create Buddhism for the modern world. Temple Buddhism, they felt, had become set in its ways and had strayed far from the teachings of Shakyamuni. They called for a return to the teachings of Shakyamuni.

Members began to be arrested in 1936, and the alliance eventually ceased to exist after all its leaders were jailed and many members arrested and interrogated. Their crime had been to call for the application of Buddhist teachings of equality to reform capitalist society. The police saw the alliance's call for equality as their greatest threat. It was interpreted as a direct attack on the divinity of the emperor. Mibu's name was stricken from the Tendai sect registry of priests at the request of his master, who had come under criticism from other priests and who wanted to spare the sect any further criticism. Mibu, however, was able to find support from within the sect. The head priest of Sensōji, a leading Tendai figure, together with the director-general of the Tendai sect (who was also a professor at Taishō University), testified on his behalf at his trial. Following Mibu's release from prison and the end of his probation, the Tendai sect reinstated him in the register of priests in 1943. The police continued to monitor his activities, to open his mail, and to interrogate him for the duration of the war.

More severe examples can be found. For example, the Sōtō sect of Zen quickly distanced itself from one priest who protested the war and was executed. He was defrocked and struck from the list of priests. It was not until 1993, forty-eight years after the end of the war but only one year after issuing a general apology for its war efforts, that the sect restored his name posthumously to the list of priests.[37]

In the postwar period, Buddhists have slowly come to recognize publicly the role they played in prewar and wartime Japan's imperialistic efforts. Sugitani Gijun wrote the following in 1995, when he was director-general of the Tendai sect:

> We Buddhists must not forget that we bear a heavy responsibility. It goes without saying that the first of the five precepts of Buddhism is "not to take life." Ghandi's nonviolent protest movement is famous for being based on this. To not take life means to respect life. No matter what the reason, Buddhists should always stand against supporting war. Yet whether one was wholeheartedly for the war or critical of it, at that time everyone was forced into fighting. In particular, from the Meiji period on, our founder Dengyō Daishi's *kokka chingo* [defend the nation] was interpreted as nationalistic thought. And I believe [*kokka chingo*] bears no small amount of responsibility for its use to support the war. This is something we should truly repent. Originally, the thinking of the founder was that first Mahayana bodhisattva priests were to be nurtured, and only then could the nation be protected.[38]

This was written to commemorate the fiftieth anniversary of the end of the war. The portion cited above appears in the context of an essay devoted primarily to discussing the damage caused to all nations by the war, the suffering caused by the atomic bomb in Japan, and questions regarding war reparations still being sought from Japan. Although the portion cited above recognizes the role played by Tendai teachings, it, and the following, are couched in terms of "being used" by the state or others. In that sense, the passages demonstrate that the sects of Temple Buddhism have yet to come to terms with the direct and often willful role of priests in the war. "Many priests were themselves used. Even though they were clerics they were sent to the battlegrounds without mercy. They had to take up arms."[39]

More recently, in September 2002, Nishioka Ryōkō, the director-general of the Tendai sect, made a personal apology for the sect's support of war efforts at a religion and peace summit sponsored by the Vatican. In a sign of the pressures he faces, it is also reported that a member of the ruling coalition of the national Diet has stated that, while personal apologies are fine, a sect-level apology is not necessary. To date, only the Ōtani and Honganji branches of the Jōdo Shin sect, the Myōshinji branch of the Rinzai sect, and the Sōtō sect have made formal sect-level apologies.[40]

The long and intimate relationship between Buddhism and the state in Japan casts a dark shadow over the image of Temple Buddhism. Despite the fact that the postwar constitution separates religion and state, and Buddhist sects, therefore, are no longer called openly to support the state,[41] the wartime and state-subservient image of Buddhism plays a part in how Buddhists are looked upon now. This image is linked to larger concerns regarding the proper role of a priest and the true teachings of Buddhism.

REAL PRIESTS AND TRUE BUDDHISM

Today many scholars, members of the mass media, and even priests question whether contemporary Temple Buddhism is true Buddhism. Two sets of issues shape the image of contemporary Temple Buddhism as falling short of the ideal. The first concerns maintaining a divide between secular and nonsecular, as this relates to the popular image of real priests. The divide between secular and non-secular has been blurred by changes in how priestly precepts are envisioned and maintained, and also by the professionalization of priestly labor. The image of real priests as world-renouncers stands in conflict with the lived reality of most priests of Temple Buddhism. Second, there remains a public debate as to whether the Buddhism practiced by contemporary Japanese Buddhists is "true" Buddhism.

This debate has left priests bearing what Yamaori Tetsuo calls a "complex" that shapes consciously and unconsciously how they view their role and how they act upon that vision.

REAL PRIESTS: PRECEPTS AND IMAGES

As we have seen, maintaining a divide between secular and nonsecular is critical to preserving a positive image for priests. Headlines such as "Buddhist Priest Nabbed for Bag-Snatching,"[42] "Priest Arrested for Sniffing Thinner,"[43] or "Priest Conducts Funeral for Own Traffic Victim" (in which a priest ran over a *danka* member, failed to stop, and later performed her funeral),[44] compete with claims such as "priests make money hand over fist" (*bozu marumōke*) in the mass media and contribute to an image of priests being all too human. One way to create and maintain the lay-clerical divide and to bolster the image of priests, it has been argued, is to strictly maintain the precepts, or priestly code of conduct.

The precepts that priests must follow have been debated throughout Buddhist history. In Japan, Saichō, the founder of Japanese Tendai, sits at the center of the debate. Saichō introduced the bodhisattva precepts, a list of ten major and forty-eight minor precepts derived from the *Brahma-Net Sūtra* (Bonmonkyō). Saichō introduced these out of concern that the full precepts (*shibunritsu*; 250 for monks and 348 for nuns) of the *Dharmagupta Vinaya* were for practitioners of Hinayana (literally "lesser-vehicle," a derogatory term for early Buddhism) and not for practitioners of Mahayana, the form of Buddhism transmitted to Japan.[45] The bodhisattva precepts he introduced went on to become the standard form of precepts in Japan. Although it is clear that Saichō did not advocate such an extreme, the full precepts of the Dharmagupta Vinaya fell out of use.[46] Over the centuries since their introduction, there have been repeated efforts to supplement the bodhisattva precepts and calls for a return to the full precepts.

Toward the end of the Edo period, precept reform was looked upon as a positive way to address the critics of Buddhism. Previous attempts to answer attacks on Buddhism centered on the theme of the unity of Confucianism, Shinto, and Buddhism, or on the king's law–Buddhist law theme. Compared to these, the precept revitalization movement (*kairitsu fukkō undō*) of the Edo period was a "quieter movement," but it spoke to the core issue of priestly identity.[47]

The precept reform movement began in the late 1600s. Priests representing different sects began various reform movements. Perhaps the most famous is that of Jiun Sonja (1718–1804) and the Ten Good Precepts (*jūzenkai*). Jiun promoted the Ten Good Precepts, long considered lay precepts, for priestly adoption as the foundation of the life of a world-renouncer. He also strongly urged the laity to take them in order to form a foundation for a proper moral life. Jiun's campaign to promote the Ten Good Precepts had a lasting effect on Buddhism, providing the basis for later developments in precepts rituals such as the temple wife precept ordination ceremony created by the Tendai sect in 1995.[48]

Within the Tendai sect, the move to reform precept adherence began with Jisan Myōryū (1636–1690), who studied the possibility of adding the full precepts of early Buddhism to the bodhisattva precepts commonly used in Japan. Jisan was followed by Kōgen Ryōkū (1653–1739). Because Kōgen lived at Anrakuin, the precepts he argued for became known as the *anraku* precepts (*anrakuritsu*). Keikō, who claimed they transgressed Saichō's instructions, later refuted these.[49]

In the modern era, the withdrawal of the government from precept enforcement in the early Meiji period through the "eat meat and marry" law reverberated for decades within Buddhist communities. Buddhist leaders pleaded with the government to reinstate legal requirements of precept maintenance for fear that without the coercive backing of the government they would lose control over their priests. Moreover, an 1872 petition to the government shows that Buddhist leaders claimed that

> the lifting of the ban against eating meat and marriage would only serve to confuse the traditional distinction between lay and clergy and would make a mockery of parishioners who had given donations to the temple for religious activities. In addition, the decriminalization of marriage would confuse the Buddhist clerical community by allowing married clerics to mix with celibate ones, thereby hindering the teaching of Buddhism.[50]

In short, without government support, Buddhist leaders feared the collapse of discipline, and with it, the collapse of Buddhism. About the same time that the Sōtō sect sent the above petition to the government, it distributed to doctrinal instructors a text that included the following statement:

> The Buddhist precepts are not the laws of the secular world. Since medieval times the precepts have become confused with the laws of the rulers, leading to a situation in which those who violate the precepts are punished in public courts of law. Today it is right and proper that the public authorities leave the handling of Buddhist precepts and their observance or nonobservance to the discretion of

the Buddhists themselves. However, if the rules adopted by the respective sections [of our school] are not strictly enforced, it will become difficult to promote our teachings.[51]

It appears that Sōtō leaders sought to instill a sense of duty to maintain precepts within the rank and file, while at the same time (as the 1872 petition described earlier shows) petitioning the government to restore coercive measures of enforcement to ensure compliance where willpower failed.

In many ways, the fears of Buddhist leaders at the turn of the century were confirmed. By 1875, more than 28 percent of priests were married. The rapid growth in married clergy shows that, in all likelihood, many priests previously had common-law wives.[52] An 1879 survey of priests in Yamagata prefecture found that 77.8 percent of Tendai sect priests were married. Morioka Kiyomi suggests that this high percentage reflected the relative wealth of the Tendai temples.[53] A 1994 Tendai sect survey found that 904 of 951 responding head priests were married.[54] In contemporary Japan there are very few priests who do not marry, eat meat, and drink alcohol. Not only has marriage become acceptable, but for most sects it has come to be seen as the best way to secure the next generation of priests. Suzuki Kōkan, a scholar at Komazawa University, a Buddhist university associated with the Sōtō sect, comments, "Today it's even come to the point where a priest who doesn't take a wife is looked at as odd, so I have the feeling that to ask 'What does it mean to leave home?' has become trite in this country."[55]

Today, priests must often choose either to cease such activities or to attempt to explain them away. Few choose the former path, in part because of the realities of temple life. For example, because temple priests are expected to take part in the meals that are given following funerals, memorial services, and local cultural events, it is often difficult for them to avoid alcohol and meat.[56] Without fail, leading *danka* members will walk to the head of the table to offer the priest a glass of *sake* or beer. The food served at these occasions, though once vegetarian, now often includes popular meat dishes including sushi and sashimi. Many priests informally asked about the eating of meat at such occasions responded, "In early Buddhism there were no restrictions against eating meat."[57] Unless the priest has abstained from alcohol from the start, any refusal might be interpreted as an insult and could damage priest-*danka* relations.[58] Priests live in a dependent relationship with their communities, and drinking is a major part of interaction in Japan.

The acceptance of marriage, meat eating, and the like do not mean that Buddhists today care little for the precepts. It means that they do not envision the precepts as they were envisioned in the past. According to literature produced by the Tendai sect in the postwar period, the precepts must be made the foundation of faith, and priests and *danka* members alike must hold to the precepts (*danka* members to the lay precepts, priests to the bodhisattva precepts).[59] Yamada Etai, the head priest of the Tendai sect from 1974 to 1994, argued that Tendai must distinguish itself by associating Tendai with the taking of precepts.[60]

The contemporary Tendai understanding of the precepts can be found in a book based on a lecture by Yamada Etai and in other literature produced by the Tendai sect Division of Doctrine (Kyōgakubu). Taking the precepts (lay or priestly) is described as the first step toward realizing that all sentient beings possess Buddha-nature and is the basis for becoming one who lights up his or her corner of the world. The precepts lead one to understand the relationship between cause and effect. This understanding in turn leads to the practice of the four limitless virtues: love, the basis for interaction with others; compassion, helping others unconditionally; joy, taking joy in the joy of others; letting go, not becoming attached to the first three and not engaging in them with the expectation of getting something in return. Next, Tendai practitioners (lay and professional) must take the bodhisattva vows, which are linked to the four limitless virtues: sentient beings are limitless, I vow to save them all; the passions are inexhaustible, I vow to extinguish them all; the teachings are limitless, I vow to master them all; enlightenment is unsurpassed, I vow to attain it.[61] The practitioner is encouraged to base his or her life on this understanding of the precepts. Precepts are taken in the presence of buddhas and bodhisattvas, who act as witnesses to the vows. They, in turn, it is explained, stand by those who have taken the precepts, lending them strength in times of need. Moreover, even if one falls into hell at death, those bodhisattvas and buddhas who witnessed the vows will appear in that person's defense. A far worse fate awaits those who have not taken the precepts, worse even than that of those who have broken their vows.[62]

Through publications aimed at the priesthood, lectures by prominent priests to the laity, and publications for the laity, the Tendai sect encourages people, priests, and laity alike to become people who light up their corners of the world through maintaining a way of life informed by the precepts.[63] Moreover, through maintenance of different sets of precepts, with different expectations, the sect seeks to manage and systematize the divide between lay and professional.[64]

The maintenance of different precepts by priests and laity is one way in which priests are distinguished from worldly individuals. However, the precepts are not the only distinction. Priests are supposed to be people who in word and deed demonstrate knowledge of the sacred. They must live a more austere, simple life and must possess spiritual abilities. And real priests are seen as working in a vocation. The priesthood is pictured as beginning with the will to enlightenment (bodaishin), a driving aspiration to seek enlightenment for oneself and salvation for others.

The practitioners of the kaihōgyō, a severe Tendai practice involving a seven-year retreat, are often used by sect officials to promote an image of Tendai priests as just such individuals: real priests focused on traditional practices and driven on by a sincere desire to attain enlightenment and to help others through compassionate acts. The example of Sakai Yūsai, the most famous of postwar kaihōgyō practitioners, is often raised. He leads a simple life on Mt. Hiei: eating a sparse vegetarian diet, practicing rituals daily, and meeting with devotees who regularly visit his temple for advice and blessings. Of course, the practice of putting forth living examples of real priests may backfire by only serving to demonstrate further how far from the ideal most priests fall. Only forty-eight individuals have successfully completed the kaihōgyō since 1585.[65]

Like the kaihōgyō practitioners, Buddhist priests are expected to possess something unique that sets their activities apart from those of their secular contemporaries. For example, some argue that priests should be true ritual masters, not ritual-performing professionals. Hasegawa Daishin, a priest of the Rinzai sect of Zen, uses the analogy of a carpenter to describe what sets the ritual performed by a priest apart from that performed by a lay practitioner. Anyone can learn to hammer a nail in straight, he states, but only a true carpenter can build a house that will last for generations. It is more than physical mastery of a skill that sets the carpenter apart: it is heart or spirit. That is what makes the nail driven by a carpenter different and the sutra chanted by a priest different.[66]

As the sparse number of kaihōgyō practitioners and their counterparts in other sects shows, few approach the ideal image in reality. In the end, most priests have been unable to meet the ideal image of a true Buddhist practitioner. The danka member system, with its peculiar demands, has contributed to this inability by fostering the development of a priesthood that is dedicated to serving the memorial needs of the laity and to the continued existence of a particular temple. For example, once economic stability was achieved in the postwar period, a hometown (furusato) nostalgia boom began among those who had moved to urban areas. This, in turn, led to a boom in ancestor veneration that brought many people to temples. While financially beneficial for the temples, it only served to emphasize the view of priests as specialized, wage-earning laborers. The image of real priests with which funeral priests are compared (by themselves and others) only came to stand out more.[67] The longer and more thorough the image of priests as worldly laborers remains, the more likely it is that the ceremonies they perform will come to be seen as staged sacred ceremonies. A recent survey of temple wives in which the question was asked "What kind of image do you have of the priest overall?" found that 18.5 percent said "highly respectful," while a full 29.1 percent said "average," and another 5 percent said they had "little" respect for them.[68] As one person commented regarding a popular "fake" priest who plies his trade offering fortune-telling and healing rituals at Shinjuku train station in Tokyo, "Being a priest is often just a 'job,' not a vocation; so as long as the rituals are done right, it shouldn't really matter."[69] The appearance of priest-robots points to the direction in which some priests and critics fear the priesthood of Temple Buddhism is heading. Some memorial parks have begun to employ these lifelike robots, programmed in the sutra and ceremonial protocol of all the sects, to chant sūtras on demand.[70]

As we have seen, the failure to address the precept issue in a public and decisive manner also contributes to the problem. Precept maintenance is one of the most publicly visible ways in which to demonstrate a clear barrier between secular and nonsecular. The relaxing of precepts leaves little to distinguish priest from laity. Furthermore, the moral authority derived from maintaining a strict code of conduct is lost. The contemporary situation appears to confirm the fears of Meiji Buddhist leaders that clerical marriage would cause irreparable harm to the legitimacy of the priesthood. Rather than entering the temple as an act of leaving home (renouncing the world), the priest now views the temple as his household.[71] This viewpoint leads to the conclusion that contemporary priests are not answering a higher calling but are simply born into a unique profession. One scholar comments, "I think it is necessary to explain to people why, even though they have families, [priests use] the term 'world-renouncer' and not 'householder.' If this question is not cleared up, young priests will always have an unsettled feeling."[72] Regarding the ideal image of the priesthood, another contemporary scholar argues, in a work titled *An Argument for the Reformation of Buddhism,* "So what is the role of a priest? If it is simply having no faith or interest in Buddhism, holding the title of priest, and performing funerals, then it is no more than that of funeral businessman."[73]

IN SEARCH OF "TRUE" BUDDHISM

Popular, scholarly, and sectarian views of the priesthood, especially those linked to maintaining precepts, represent one barrier between the ideal of a priesthood elevated above secular society and the achievement of that ideal. Various opinions regarding what constitutes true Buddhism are a second barrier. Debates over the veracity of one Buddhist doctrine or another have taken place from the time of the Buddha. Japan is no exception. From the earliest times, different schools of Buddhist thought debated the depth and quality of other schools' understanding of Buddhist doctrine. For example, in the ninth century Saichō argued that the Buddhist schools of Nara relied not on the direct word of the Buddha, but on commentaries as their core and, therefore, were inferior to Tendai. Moreover, as discussed above, Saichō argued that they relied on inferior precepts no longer wholly appropriate to the times.[74]

Later, in the early Edo period, laws limited the number of new temples that could be built, as well as the ability of registered *danka* to switch affiliations. Buddhist schools, which up to then had maintained a certain amount of fluidity, drew stronger and stronger sectarian lines, and sectarian scholarship (*shūjō, shūgi, shūgaku*) blossomed. Sectarian scholars strengthened sect identity through positing the "truth" of their particular founders' teachings.[75]

During the Meiji period, to meet the needs of a modernizing Japan and to keep from being rendered irrelevant, Buddhists sought to interpret Buddhist history and teachings, in order. Buddhist scholars and leaders sought to create a "transsectarian" and "transnational" Buddhism that was immediately relevant to modern needs and that would deflect criticism, such as that lodged against the "premodern" ritual practices of Temple Buddhism.[76] The efforts of such scholars led to the modern construction of true Buddhism as a philosophy and not a religion marked by ritual practices.

The sectarian lines drawn in the Edo period and the reconstruction of Buddhism in the Meiji and Taishō periods created the criteria by which later Buddhist scholars and priests came to define true Buddhism. During the Taishō period the study of Buddhism by nonsectarian scholars began to flourish, leading to the import of Indic Studies (Indogaku) from the West. In Japan, these studies were used to place Buddhism and Japan on the world stage. Following their Western contemporaries, Japanese scholars of Indic Studies focused their attention on early Indian Buddhism, seen as closer to the true Buddhism of Shakyamuni than the Buddhism of Japan.[77]

The creation of Japanese Buddhism as philosophy—transsectarian, transnational, and modern—may have convinced some people of Buddhism's relevancy to Japan's modernization, but it also created an identity problem for priests. According to Yamaori Tetsuo, "Buddhism lost the source of its religious energy" in the Meiji and Taishō creation of a philosophical, universal, true Buddhism.[78]

Yamaori claims that the lifeblood of Temple Buddhism, namely commitment to local community involvement, ritual performance, and serving the needs of *danka* and adherents, stands in conflict with the modern construction of true Buddhism. Priests are forced to reconcile the modern vision of Buddhism with the Buddhism they practice in daily life, which is ritual-filled, sectarian, local, and traditional. This identity gap leads to the loss of religious energy, or sense of purpose. In the postwar period, as priests of Temple Buddhist sects have become viewed more and more as secularized ritual laborers, the contrast with the image of true Buddhism generated in the prewar period and advanced in the postwar period has become all the more striking.

A NUMBERS PROBLEM: LOOKING FOR A FEW GOOD PRIESTS

The crisis of identity centered on idealistic conceptions of real priests and true Buddhism is a defining issue for contemporary Temple Buddhism. However, the sects of Temple Buddhism face a more immediate practical threat as well: the number of willing applicants for the priesthood is dropping, and the number of empty temples is increasing. The second problem would appear to be directly related to the first, but the connection is not as obvious as it seems. At first glance, raw data would seem to show an opposite problem for the sects, namely, too many priests and too few temples. Sects of the Tendai lineage actually experienced a decrease in the number of temples still registered with them and an increase in the number of priests between 1974 and 1998; between 1987 and 1998 they did report a decrease in the number of priests, but the numbers show that there are now nearly three times as many priests as temples. Some of the surplus may consist of young priests (the sons of temple priests often ordain in their early teens) and second sons of temples who, while ordained, chose not to serve as priests. Even given this, there are more than enough capable priests to staff all temples. Yet according to a 1990 survey, 30 percent of temples report a lack of successors.[79]

There are several reasons for the decrease in the number of those opting for the priesthood and also for why so many temples go without successors, despite enough priests to fill the positions. First, the relaxation of restrictions against clerical marriage has led to a de facto system of temple inheritance, effectively choking off entrance into the priesthood from the laity. Second, the financial and managerial hardships that rural temples face make them unattractive postings. Third, there are numerous alternatives to the priesthood for people who desire to dedicate their lives to Buddhism.

INHERITED TEMPLES

Clerical marriage led to an unofficial system of temple inheritance. Approximately 74 percent of male priests are from temple households; virtually all economically viable temples are passed on from father to son and are not open to competition.[80] One Tendai priest comments,

> Temples where you can make a decent living have become secularized
> because of [efforts] to protect temple families; even individuals one
> wouldn't think appropriate become head priest. As for sons of rank
> eleven or twelve temples [low-ranked temples] who hope to switch to
> become the head priest of a large temple, they are forced to care for
> temples that have no future. How can you say, "Love the sect and
> protect the dharma" when you force on someone a temple to which,
> even at forty, one can't get a bride to come?[81]

Those entering the priesthood from the laity must work as assistants, take over an abandoned temple, or build a new temple. The first choice is not appealing to most, and the second and third are unattractive for reasons discussed below. The priesthood may lack appeal for women for the same reason. There are far fewer vacancies for nuns, and very few *danka* prefer the temple to pass on to a temple daughter, even if she becomes ordained.[82] In most cases, where there is no son to take over, a daughter is married to a priest from another temple family, and the son-in-law is adopted into the family, much in the way family businesses traditionally maintain family lines in Japan.[83] Thus, while as many as 90 percent of women who enter the priesthood come from lay backgrounds, their overall number remains comparatively small.[84]

In rare cases, someone entering the priesthood from the laity may "purchase" a temple. Though I have found no evidence of this occurring in the Tendai sect, evidence suggests that it does occur elsewhere. A temple is not actually purchased. What is purchased is the right to take over the position of head priest. In some ways, the practice is reminiscent of the buying and selling of member lists among pilgrimage group leaders during the Edo period. The contemporary price is calculated by multiplying the average price charged for a posthumous name by the number of households in the *danka*. This money is distributed among the previous head priest, *danka* leaders, and the head priests of temples that have long-term relations with the temple in question.[85]

The passing on of temples within temple families not only serves to block the temple gate to those from lay backgrounds; it also serves to fuel the negative image of priests as insincere. One survey found that 40 percent of temple-born priests entered the priesthood because it "seemed the natural thing to do." Another 8 percent entered after being convinced by others to do so. Only 20 percent answered that they entered of their own desire to do so.[86] Even among those who become priests of their own volition, there are many for whom the choice is made out of deference to the temple family and to the coinciding interests of the head priest and the *danka* in "defending" the temple (*tera wo mamoru*). One priest writes, "I have heard the term 'defend the temple' on many occasions and believed that to do so was the greatest duty of a priest. But, put another way, it is precisely this temple centrism (*jiin chūshin shugi*) that is the source of the critique of Buddhist corruption (*bukkyō daraku*) that is currently heard in society."[87]

These factors suggest a certain lack of sincerity or sense of calling. However, this survey fails to ascertain priests' current attitudes toward their work. I suggest that most priests do, in fact, see themselves as sincere practitioners. Discussions with priests on this subject revealed that many do admit to uncertainty at first. They entered the priesthood out of duty to their parents. However, after serving as priest for a time, and much reflection, they found faith (*shinkō*).

Growing up in a temple is often very difficult for children. They are teased at school, and, as one priest remarks, the atmosphere of a temple where memorial services are constantly being conducted is very dark (*engi ga warui fun'iki*). Many seek to get away from the temple, if only for a short period. "I went to the sect headquarters' school, Hieizan High. It wasn't that I was doing it to prepare to succeed at my temple; it was just that it had a dorm, and I could get out of the house and live a different lifestyle."[88]

Compounding such problems, training often starts young. Many begin to assist their fathers in the simpler services from late elementary school. One priest comments that when he appeared at the home of a friend wearing his robes, the friend was forced to treat him differently, forever changing their relationship.[89] Another priest comments that the temple household lifestyle is completely different from that of lay households: different family structure, different vacations, different rhythm of work for their father.[90] This is borne out by my own experience acting as caretaker of a small rural temple. Local farmers would drop by my living quarters at 5:30 in the morning with fresh vegetables, often walking in on my wife and me as we tried to sleep in. "What? You're still sleeping? A priest should be up before dawn!" Likewise, when I invited friends who were priests to visit the United States on my return, most complained that until their sons took over they could only rarely take trips abroad because they were never sure when they would be required to perform a funeral.

Furthermore, the line between secular and nonsecular life is thoroughly blurred for temple children. Regarding the concept of renunciation (shukke), one priest remarked, "For a child born and raised in the temple the lifestyle doesn't ever change. From where did a son leave, and to where did a priest go? I think each person has his own understanding [of where to draw that line]."[91] The difficult and unique life a child faces growing up in a temple often creates a sense of hostility toward the priesthood in youth, especially among first sons, on whom the pressure is the greatest. Many first sons with whom I have spoken go through long and trying emotional periods before they are comfortable in taking over their father's position. In the end, most become priests and take their role very seriously.

EMPTY TEMPLES

Despite a pool of temple-born sons to draw on, many temples, the majority of which are in rural areas, remain without resident priests. Recognizing the need to fill vacant temples, the Tendai sect commissioned the Vacant or Acting-head-priest-only Temple Countermeasure Committee (Mujūshoku Jiinkyōkai oyobi Kenmujūshoku Jiinkyōkai Taisaku Iinkai).[92] One measure developed was to encourage young priests to take over vacant temples.[93] However, there is no concrete plan yet for accomplishing this goal. Those who move into vacant temples receive no funding and no special training or benefits. Moreover, the priests of other temples administer such temples. It is often only by administering several such temples that some priests can earn enough to support a family and maintain the temples. Therefore, although many temples are vacant, the priests in charge of caring for them are not always willing to relinquish them to a new priest in search of a temple.

Another difficulty facing those who might wish to take over a vacant temple is that the danka have likely taken over the financial reins of the temple in the absence of a full-time priest. In such situations, an applicant is often called upon to expend vast amounts of energy slowly to wrest power away from the danka or forced to work as the danka's hired hand. The thought of having to go through such an ordeal, something most from lay backgrounds must consider, may play a role in keeping some from joining the priesthood. The following example of such difficulties appeared in a law advice column.

A young priest took over a temple that had long been without a priest.[94] His father, the designated head priest, had left the temple many years before. His grandmother had become a nun in order to care for the temple. When he graduated from college, he married, had a child, and took over as head priest. However, a "bosslike" responsible officer, along with several *sōdai*, had taken control of the temple during his father's absence.

The young head priest claimed that the responsible officer and *sōdai* set donation amounts and informed him each month by postcard of that month's services. They also claimed the right to appoint someone else in his place if he missed a certain number of services. The responsible officers, of whom there were six in this case, only elected people favorable to their position to the board of directors and excluded the priest from the meetings to calculate annual temple revenues and expenditures. Moreover, they circulated a letter to *danka* slandering the priest. Finally, whenever possible, they asked his grandmother to perform services in his place because, wrote the priest, she was more easily influenced.

The lawyer advised the priest to restore the temple as a religious center. He stated further that religious acts, and actions associated with such acts, are the head priest's responsibility. The duties of a responsible officer are the administering, disposal, and maintenance of temple properties. Decisions regarding donations and services are temple matters and, thus, the responsibility of the head priest. Furthermore, the lawyer wrote, the chief responsible officer and head priest, respectively, usually nominate the responsible officers and temple representatives for election. Thus, the head priest should be able to select people favorable to him. Also, in most cases the head priest retains the right to dismiss anyone acting with impropriety. Finally, the lawyer stated that determining budgets is the most important job of the responsible officers and, therefore, the head priest as chief responsible officer has the right to participate. Any decisions made without the knowledge of the head priest/chief responsible officer could be considered illegal. Although the lawyer's advice demonstrates that the young head priest should be able to control the *danka* who had taken over in the absence of a priest, it is clear the young priest must expend his energy taking back the reins of control over the temple.

ALTERNATIVE PATHS

In addition to the barriers represented by temple inheritance and the difficulties of occupying a long-vacant temple, there are now alternatives for those who wish to practice Buddhism, even to the extent of becoming ordained, but who do not find the traditional route to priesthood appealing or available. Lay-born individuals may still seek to enter the Buddhist priesthood via the traditional route of apprenticing themselves to a local priest, practicing and serving at the local temple part time or full time for a number of years, becoming ordained, continuing practice, and, when the priest feels it appropriate, going to a sect-approved training center to become licensed within the sect.[95] However, many who might otherwise wish to become temple priests do not wish to wait that long or do not like the opportunities awaiting them at the end of their training.

During the postwar period, numerous new religions, many with prewar roots, grew dramatically in size.[96] Beginning in the 1970s, new religious groups appeared and were dubbed new new religions by academics and the press. The new religions and new new religions were extremely successful in attracting members. One reason for their success is that they encouraged active participation within the organization—religious and administrative ranks were often open to all members. However, there are no statistics to show whether those who entered the new religions because of the possibility for advancement would have considered the priesthood in Temple Buddhism.

The type of commitment required of leaders or teachers in the new religions is generally understood to be different from that required in the sects of Temple Buddhism. Despite criticism that priests of Temple Buddhism are half secularized, theirs is still normally understood as a full-time commitment. The new religions and many new new religions do not envision leadership roles in the same light. Except in some instances, members are not expected to become full-time religious professionals. Therefore, it is unlikely that many of those who entered the new religions would have considered choosing the life of a temple priest.

However, the desire to become a priest/world-renouncer may not be the case with all of the new new religions. Many tend to attract a younger audience than the new religions, one that is often inclined toward religious austerities and in some cases world renunciation.[97] Before they turned to mass murder, Aum Shinrikyō members were often looked upon as radical but sincere practitioners of real Buddhist austerities. One contributor to an Internet discussion board wrote, "I can't say that I don't completely understand why the young are attracted to AUM, which takes world-renunciation to heart rather than corrupt Buddhism (*daraku bukkyō*)."[98]

The success of religions that stress the life of renunciation for certain members, such as Aum Shinrikyō, is evidence that there is interest among the youth in deepening their understanding of Buddhist principles through austerities.

Some in the new new religions may have turned to Temple Buddhism had it been better able to meet their needs. Yasui Yūji, a member of the Kyoto Buddhist Federation board of directors and a Tendai sect priest comments,

> Looking at it another way, those who run to cults are quite probably the very people who should be entering traditional sects. *Danka* members have little faith anymore, but these people act on strong faith . . . those who feel ill at ease and want to seek the source of their troubles, these are people with religion. Priests have been too spoiled by society. Unless they recognize this drive to seek the truth, such people will continue to leave their net.[99]

Few temple priests, however, are likely to allow such spiritual wanderers the chance to enter the priesthood. Many see youth who are aggressively interested in meditation or austerities as odd *(hen)*. Unfortunately, such views are often based on occasional personal experiences, and word spreads fast within the temple community. For example, I was witness to one such incident during fieldwork. A temple priest, who was in a hurry to find an assistant and open to training someone from the laity, took on a young man recommended to him by another priest. After purchasing robes and other material for him, the priest encouraged him to begin practicing sutra chanting and to come to the temple regularly to undergo basic training in preparation for training at the sect headquarters. The youth excitedly did as he was told, saying that he was suffering from stress because an ancestor had been improperly memorialized. The priest accepted this, although he told me he found it a little odd. As time passed, the priest decided to give the young man a Buddhist name. However, the young man refused the name. The name he had was just right, he said. He had had it looked over by various divination methods, and it was a powerful name. The priest was upset, but he offered to take one of the characters from the youth's name into the new name. The youth refused and begged for time to look for a name that would pass the diviner's test. Still, the priest, desperate for help, continued. However, in the end the youth was let go. One day, while helping with a memorial service, he had a little bit too much to drink and began lecturing the *danka* members at the table about ancestors, retribution, and proper memorialization. That was his last day as a priest in training.[100]

Moreover, competition for potential priests does not come only from the new and new new religions. Recently, additional alternatives have appeared, as in the following advertisement: "While continuing your current work and position, and without changing your current lifestyle, you, too, can become a priest from the comfort of your home. You, too, could soon be wearing these robes if you become a priest!"[101] This ad ran in several different weekly magazines and major newspapers. A study-at-home company that offers courses and licenses in numerous fields designed the lay-priest (*zaike sōryo*) program in conjunction with a priest who was hired to grade exams and answer questions. The priest's name and his temple's name were used in the advertisements. According to the priest, he also edited the texts used in the course. The following is a sample from one of the texts.

> In Japan today, the sects of established Buddhism have become ossified. They have lost their ability to lead the masses. Moreover, the Buddhist priesthood has become a form of labor or a business, and little teaching of Buddhism is taking place. It is no exaggeration to say that the only things that separate priest from laity are the robes worn and the ceremonies performed at funerals. I don't think I am alone in believing that lay people who sincerely seek the truth of Buddhist teachings and practice are far more deserving of the right to be priests than those who are priests in form only.[102]

Courses such as this appeal to those who are interested in traditional Buddhist teachings and practices but who do not have the desire to go through the regular route of apprenticeship. According to the priest involved, the majority of those who take the course are between the ages of thirty and fifty and work in the public sector. Established sects do not recognize the priestly name and rank granted. In an interesting turn of events, the sect (the Myōshinji branch of the Rinzai sect) defrocked the priest in February 2004 for ignoring repeated warnings about giving out unauthorized priestly ranks. Not realizing the irony of his own words in light of the predominance of married clergy today, a sect official commented, "Isn't the term 'lay-priest' itself a contradiction?"[103]

Another organization exists, however, that does offer the opportunity to prepare for entering the priesthood in several sects of Temple Buddhism. The Tokyo International Buddhist School (Tokyo Kokusai Bukkyō Juku) was founded in 1988 with the purpose of preparing retirees for a life in the priesthood. Most of its students (352 out of 529) are between the ages of fifty and sixty.[104] The school offers courses in the doctrines of most major sects taught by priests of those sects and lectures by prominent scholars; it also requires participation in retreats and ceremonial protocol classes. Once students have completed the courses, they may opt to undergo ordination at a temple of the sect of their choosing.[105]

This particular school aims at a growing interest in retiring into the priesthood. Several books have appeared in the past few years introducing the priesthood as a way to spend a fulfilling retirement.[106] Temple Buddhism sects do not discourage this trend because retirees are often able to support themselves and thus to work in rural temples and other areas where younger priests and their families cannot afford to go. However, the Tendai sect and others with difficult mandatory training requirements do not provide any special programs for elderly applicants. This effectively makes entry into the priesthood after retirement impossible for most. Furthermore, some priests claim that retirees can never become fully capable priests because they do not have the time to master the skills they need.[107]

The variety of alternative paths open to those who might wish to dedicate themselves to Buddhism make clear that there remains an interest in pursuing the priestly path. The alternatives also demonstrate the open religious marketplace in Japan today, in which Temple Buddhism represents just one opportunity among others.

IMAGES AND REALITIES

The image of the Temple Buddhism priesthood in contemporary Japan is in flux. The priesthood remains haunted by its long association with the state and especially with the war. The failure of the sects of Temple Buddhism to redress this problem allows it to fester. Related to this are modern interpretations of true Buddhism and its real priests that portray Buddhism as a philosophy and priests as proper practitioners of meditation and upholders of the precepts. Over and against this is an image of a funeral Buddhism whose priests are seen as funeral ritual specialists. The ritual specialist image is not easily overcome, for even as the mass media and scholars portrayed it negatively, it is in demand by those who support the temple—the *danka*. Finally, related to the demands of the *danka*, but also to the needs of the sects, there is the image of the temple as the property of the priest, his family, and the *danka* in which the priest is regarded as a defender of the local temple and its traditions. The manner in which the sects of Temple Buddhism seek to reinforce or to change these images will play a major role in shaping the future of the priesthood in Temple Buddhism.

5 New Priests for New Times?

The suicide rate in Japan is unusually high and the reason for this is that families are falling apart. Priests should take the sorrow of families into their hearts. That is the type of counseling [Buddhist] organizations have traditionally engaged in.[1]

Every temple has its own specialty. Maybe we should look to have each temple bear responsibility for Buddhist rituals or counseling [or whatever that temple's specialty is].[2]

It would be better to seek out a way to return to lay life than to [emphasize] world-renunciation.[3]

Counselor, ritual master, world-renouncer, or world-embracer, the roles of priests are under much debate today. Officials of Tendai and other sects are aware of the need to breathe new life into the priesthood and to overcome negative images associated with the temple as a family business or as a funerary services provider. This chapter will explore the contemporary efforts of the sects of Temple Buddhism to widen the net cast for new priests and to broaden the roles priests are actively engaged in.

Although they still rely on temple-born recruits and emphasize in their literature to priests and temple wives the importance of conceiving sons and then convincing them to become priests, most sects are also now exploring ways to increase interest in the priesthood from among the laity. The Tendai sect made headlines in all national newspapers in 1994 when it instituted what was deemed the first ever open call for recruits. In the following pages, I examine the Tendai sect's efforts to recruit and train people from lay backgrounds directly at sect headquarters, bypassing the traditional apprenticeship route.[4]

On November 22, 1994, the Tendai sect posted its first ever open call for priests. The program to recruit directly from the laity began as part of the fourteen-hundredth memorial anniversary for Chih-i. The call was widely publicized and elicited a large response—nearly three hundred inquiries. Most callers asked about the training, some further inquired whether the training would give them special powers. In the end, a total of ninety-one applications arrived by mail, including one from the United States. Thirty-two men were invited to Mt. Hiei to take the written exam and to undergo an interview on June 25, 1995.[5] Four failed to appear, and three excused themselves during or just before the exam. The remaining twenty-five took a written essay exam on the theme "life's turning point" in the morning and sat for interviews in the afternoon. The interview was in two parts. The first part covered the applicant's reasons for applying and impressions of Mt. Hiei and the priesthood. The second part addressed the life of practice and the applicant's health. Decisions were made two days later, and five candidates were selected. On July 21, an overnight orientation was held. Finally, an entrance ceremony was held on September 1, and the applicants began their new lives. On the day before the ceremony, the acolytes shaved their heads and were given robes, work clothes, a liturgy manual, prayer beads, and other items necessary for their training.[6]

Tendai officials stated that the call was initiated to throw open the gate to priesthood, which had become virtually closed as a result of patrilineal succession. The ratio of temple-born to lay-born priests in the Tendai sect is four to one. Furthermore, "that path is all but closed to those who have no relations with temples but who have the faith and desire to become priests."[7] Therefore, Tendai put out a public call, "in the spirit of Saichō," to find and raise top people who might one day go on to be "pillars" of Tendai. Moreover, Tendai officials stated that "through bringing in young people with the strong desire to overcome the difficult training, a new breath of life will flow into the sect."[8]

The program was not entirely without opposition. The idea of an open call was criticized from the beginning because, opponents claimed, it bypassed the old master-disciple relationship. In opposition to this, proponents argued that the point of the open call was to return to the founder's spirit of searching for people from all over and raising human resources to better the world.

The master-disciple relationship today is much different from what it was before, even in the prewar period. Today, more than two-thirds of priests become priests under their fathers. This situation drastically alters both the disciple-master relationship and the father-son relationship. Training is altered as well; fathers are generally less strict with their children than masters traditionally are with their disciples. Furthermore, the father-son relationship alters the attitudes of temple-sons toward the priesthood.

> Children who have grown up in the unique environment of the temple, and who have carried the unseen expectations of their master (father) and the people around them (*danka* members), to which they cannot but

wake up one day, either give in easily to their fate as the successor to the temple, or fight hard against it only to realize there are few other choices awaiting them. There are more than a few who neglect their studies, knowing that they are going to go on to take over the temple.[9]

Because the master-disciple relationship is also a father-son relationship, training in doctrine and ritual now generally begins at college.[10] For this reason Buddhist universities such as Taishō University have developed courses for temple children to teach them the skills they will need to perform rituals and to engage society as priests.[11] Moreover, priestly ranks can be acquired through successful completion of courses on Buddhist history, doctrine, and ritual at Buddhist universities, and the length of time required for monastic training can be shortened significantly, too.[12]

The open call sought to address the problem of overreliance on temple-sons and thereby to combat the various problems related to the inheritance of temples. The sect offered training and all expenses for the period of the program (roughly 3,500,000 yen per recruit for the full program). Those selected for the first class were from all walks of life. One worked at a computer company where he said he was very comfortable but "felt unease with such a life." Another was an art school graduate who, after bouncing from job to job, claimed he could not find his place in society. He felt drawn to the "Buddhist artistic frame of mind" and sought to change his life through the practices on Mt. Hiei.[13] A third had worked as a civil servant. In general, they claimed to share dissatisfaction with life in the everyday world and a desire to enter a new and radically different world on Mt. Hiei. Noting the similarities in the recruits' reasons for entering the priesthood with those of youth entering new religions and new new religions, Kobayashi Ryūshō, the proctor of the dorm in which they lived, commented, "There may be similarities with Aum [Supreme Truth] in their reasons for joining, but Buddhist practice is about living within nature. It begins with understanding that you are just one part of nature. It is totally different from such cults that define things based on fanaticism (kyōshin)."[14] In short, while acknowledging similar motivations for renunciation, Kobayashi highlights the belief that those who join new religious movements are somehow unstable, whereas those who join Temple Buddhism are not.

The program the recruits must go through is rigorous. The first seven months of the two-year program are devoted to basic training, in which one priest lives with them as proctor. Following basic training, they undergo a twelve-month learning period in which they commute to Eizan Gakuin (a Tendai

TABLE 3
Daily Schedule at Gakuryō

TIME	ACTIVITY
5:30	wake/wash
6:00	meditation/cleaning/services
7:30	breakfast/cleaning
8:00	class
12:00	lunch
13:00	work
15:00	class/work
17:30	services/clean
18:30	dinner
19:00	class/bath
22:00	lights out

sect two-year technical school of one hundred students).[15] From the second open call, recruits began to be required to attend Gakuin from the beginning of their stay. They participate in courses on Buddhism and Tendai history. Other classes include classical Chinese, sutra reading, and calligraphy. These are the basic skills deemed necessary for life as a priest. Additionally, the course work assists them in advancing through priestly ranks. During this period, they are also assigned various duties at temples in the Enryakuji complex (table 3).

The Gakuryō program is considered a mountain-seclusion practice (rōzan). The students are not allowed off-mountain, and outside contact is strictly limited. At their dorm they cook their own food, collect wood for a wood-fired bath, and tend their own vegetable and herb garden. After completing basic training and course work at Gakuin, the Gakuryō students enter a period of intensive practice (kegyō). This is a five-month course and includes the two-month training course required of all Tendai priests at Gyōin, which is completed in autumn of their second year.

The fifth open call was held in August 2000. Unlike the first call, later calls have received little press coverage. Indeed, some Tokyo-area Tendai priests I asked informally about the program were not fully aware that it was still in operation. The number of applicants has dropped accordingly. Only sixteen people sat for the examination for the second call. From the second call forward the original plan of bringing in five new recruits every two years was changed to three recruits every year to allow early recruits to help train newcomers and to provide for collegiality among dorm members.

The program has had only one mishap—the death of a recruit from the second call shortly after his arrival.[16] This recruit left the dorm late at night and called his parents to pick him up. He died on his way back to the dorm while awaiting their arrival. His death was first thought to be a suicide, but later it was determined that he had slipped and fallen from a narrow bridge in the dark on his way back from the phone to the dorm. This incident led some to believe that stricter screening was necessary. Because of stricter evaluation criteria, no new recruits were selected from among applicants in 1998.

The program has been in place since 1994, and the original recruits have completed the program and moved on. How successful has the program been in breathing fresh life into the sect? There is little evidence that it has managed, thus far, to bring about change. The dozen recruits who have been through the program represent only a tiny fraction of the total number (approximately four thousand) of priests in the Tendai sect. Aside from the numbers problem, the main stumbling block remains the division between temple-born and lay-born priests. Once recruits have finished the program, they are still faced with the same barriers faced by lay-recruits who follow the traditional apprenticeship route, namely, the barriers involved in finding a satisfactory post. For example, one of the early recruits found work as an assistant priest at a temple in Tokyo. The head priest of the temple expects his own son to succeed him. The recruit must choose either to remain as an assistant or hope for an opening somewhere else in the future. This problem may be particularly acute in a smaller sect such as Tendai.

Inherited temples are one problem. Professional networks, in which temple-born priests have an inherited advantage in participation, are a second. The term "Tendai as one family" (Tendai ikka) tends to confirm this. In the smallish Tendai sect few secrets escape the "family." This can be beneficial at times. For example, if one temple is in need, there is a tightly woven pattern of temple-to-temple relations upon which it can draw. However, the family-like nature of the Tendai sect also makes it difficult for outsiders to find acceptance. This tendency more broadly reflects Japanese society in which connections and group orientation are legendary. As one priest remarked, "Japan is a nattō (sticky fermented beans) society. If you pull up one bean, you will find many more pulled up with it."

The most critical relationship within Temple Buddhism is the master-disciple relationship, which is of lasting importance. It places a person within a specific lineage of priests, and it can determine the type of training one can apply for, the type of temple one can become head priest of, and even one's marital prospects. Open-call recruits, however, are neither born into such a relationship nor handpicked by a specific master. Their entree to the priesthood is through an open advertisement and testing by committee. This situation has led to a unique master-disciple problem. A priest who chooses to take on a disciple is usually cautious when doing so because, traditionally, the master is responsible for the lifelong welfare of the disciple and, equally important, the actions of the disciple reflect upon the master. The open-call recruits, however, are vetted by committee over a brief period and therefore are of an unknown quality. Thus, senior priests are often reluctant to take them on as disciples. Finally, priests on Mt. Hiei are loosely divided into different camps of supporters of one leader or another. The open-call recruits must begin their priestly life in the heart of Hiei politics. Those who make connections during their stay on Mt. Hiei expand their realm of possibilities for their postprogram career. Those who fail to do so face an uncertain future.

The open call has survived ten years, but the experiment has been far from successful. The inheritance of temples, professional networks, traditional views of the master-disciple relationship, and sect politics all combine to work against its success. Finally, as the previous chapter showed, the ongoing negative view of Temple Buddhism tied to the *danka* system and its ritual demands continues to limit interest in joining the priesthood and the prospects for those who wish to join it.

BEYOND FUNERAL BUDDHISM—LOOKING FOR NEW ROLES

In addition to the open call, which was designed to bring in fresh blood to the priestly ranks, the Tendai sect is also engaged in efforts to create or re-create roles for priests that go beyond the funeral Buddhism image. The sect is making efforts to construct a socially engaged priesthood and, thereby, a new image of priests as engaged, compassionate, "real" Buddhist practitioners.

Alongside the open call, involvement in social welfare activities is the core of the Tendai sect's efforts to create new priests and roles and is part of the efforts of other sects as well. The call for social engagement is not new. Inoue Enryō wrote in prewar Japan that world-abnegating Buddhism had to become world-engaged if it was to survive in the modern era.[17] Today the call for reform through social engagement is widespread. For example, Ishikawa Tōkaku, who

sees Japan and Temple Buddhism in a period of crisis, argues that Buddhist wel-
fare activities in the past occurred in times of crisis and calls for Temple Buddhism today to revitalize its "ossified" doctrines and to rethink its practices.
Shifting to meet the needs of today's welfare society, he argues, would guarantee
Buddhism's relevance and secure its future in the twenty-first century.[18] The creation of numerous public outreach and social welfare programs by the sects of
Temple Buddhism in the 1960s and 1970s, such as the Tendai sect's Light Up
Your Corner Movement, demonstrates their awareness of the value of such
activities. However, in a 1980 survey of Shingon sect priests, only 5.7 percent
responded that the purpose of the temple was to provide social welfare (com-
pared with 36.9 percent for funerals and 32.6 percent for this-worldly benefits).[19]
This finding implies that engagement in social welfare is not the norm for
Temple Buddhism priests.

Japanese Buddhist organizations have been involved on and off in welfare
activities for most of the twentieth century. The history of Buddhist involvement in welfare activities grounds many Buddhists today who call for the reform
of Temple Buddhism through social engagement.[20]

In the ancient and medieval periods, the basis of welfare activities was the
acts of individual Buddhist practitioners. The focus was welfare as a form of practice. Considering welfare as a social or political movement, addressing discrimination, and seeking to change oppressive social structures or other structural
issues developed much later. During the Nara period, welfare as an individual's
practice was understood as the manifestation of Buddhist teachings on compassion. During this period, welfare, practice, and the salvation of others were not
understood separately.[21] Activities included building bridges or digging wells.
Included here are Gyōki's (667–749) aid work among the masses and Dōshō's
(628–700) construction of roads, bridges, rest stops, and alms-houses. One notable
departure from this pattern is Shikoin (593), a temple system that is said to have
been founded by Prince Shōtoku (574–622).[22] The home of the Shikoin system,
which consisted of four facilities, was Shitennōji, a large temple complex that
still stands in current-day Osaka. In the Shikoin system, fields were planted to
feed the needy, herbal gardens were planted to provide medicines to the sick, a
hospital was built to provide the sick with treatment, and a shelter was set up for
those in need.[23]

The Tendai teachings on universal Buddha-nature, in which all sentient
beings are viewed as equal because of their possession of Buddha-nature, and
Tendai concepts of compassion based on the Lotus Sutra came to play a powerful role in Buddhist welfare activities from the ninth century onward. Saichō's

desire to train "national treasures," priests who could benefit the people and the nation through their knowledge and their actions, played (and still plays) an important role in how Buddhist practitioners envisioned welfare activities. Here we see the beginnings of a shift in emphasis toward welfare practice as an act for the betterment of society as a whole. The temples Kōsai'in and Kōjōin are the practical result of Saichō's welfare thought.[24]

In the Kamakura period the Pure Land teachings espoused by Hōnen (1133–1212) and Shinran (1173–1262) encouraged viewing salvation as equally possible for the rich and the poor, priests and laity. Moreover, the practice of calling on Amida (nenbutsu) marked a turn toward accessibility of practice for all. These teachings encouraged Pure Land practitioners, priest and laity alike, to seek salvation for members of all classes and walks of life and provided the spiritual foundation for welfare activities.[25] Another prominent Kamakura figure, Nichiren (1222–1282), fixed his attention on political reform. Nichiren linked the natural and man-made disasters that plagued Japan during his lifetime to the actions of the state. Nichiren viewed the state as having abandoned the teaching of the Lotus Sutra—an act that could only lead to dire consequences for all, according to Nichiren. Only through reform of the crumbling ritsuryō system of law and order through a return to the teachings of the Lotus Sutra, could Japan be saved and the populace granted reprieve from constant strife.[26] Here we see the beginnings of a shift from welfare as a personal practice to welfare as seeking structural changes in society.

Eison (1201–1290) and his disciple Ninjō (1217–1303) are also well-known for their welfare activities during the Kamakura period. Central to Eison's welfare activities were his views on the precepts and the bodhisattva Manjushrī (Monjushiri bosatsu). On the one hand, Eison taught strict adherence to the precepts through which one would naturally engage in right behavior including aiding others through compassionate acts. On the other hand, he viewed others as manifestations of Manjushrī. In particular, he saw members of the outcaste community in such a light. This led him to become involved in activities to seek their salvation, including conferring the precepts on outcastes.[27] Eison's disciple Ninjō became a tireless advocate for Buddhist welfare. He engaged in a variety of activities, everything from aiding individuals to administering medical aid to protecting animals. At one point he sought to revitalize Shotoku's Shikoin. To carry out his welfare activities, he actively sought out the aid of those in power.[28]

By the late premodern period, Buddhist welfare activities were centered on the temple's position as the focal point of local communities. The temple served as community center, school, and hospice, offering care for orphans and the sick.[29] One positive outcome of the temple registration system during the Edo period was that priests and the laity were brought into close and frequent contact throughout the country. This contact led to the spread of Buddhist thought on welfare to all levels of society. While the majority of welfare activities continued along previous lines, some Buddhist schools began to question the status system and other state apparati of social control. For example, the Shase branch of the Jōdo sect positioned itself against the recognized system of Buddhist education (the *danrin*) and the *danka* system.[30] Members of this branch of Buddhism based their actions on the view that those being helped and those helping are equal. Finally, as Yoshida Kyūichi and Hasegawa Masatoshi note, during the Edo period Buddhists became involved in every aspect of the dying process. From care for the dying to funerals and later memorial services, Buddhist priests became indispensable actors in death care. This extensive and active role of priests in the past is drawn upon today in discussions of how to move away from the limited role of funeral ritual professional and to better serve the needs of *danka* members through provision of care for the elderly, the dying, and the bereaved.

For the most part, Buddhist welfare activities, as they developed during the ancient, medieval, premodern, early modern, and the beginnings of the modern period, were still understood as private (for the salvation of the practitioner) rather than as public (for the salvation of society) acts and were based on efforts to aid the lower classes. In the Meiji period they developed in response to the advent of industrialization and capitalism in Japan. For example, in the mid-1800s, the government called upon Buddhist priests to preach against abortion and the killing of unwanted children in poor areas. Based on this experience, Buddhists began to open shelters and schools for unwanted children.[31] By the late 1800s, Buddhists were involved in a variety of efforts, from prison chaplaincies to schools for young children.[32] As industrialization advanced, the problems facing Japanese society changed, inducing a corresponding change in Buddhist efforts. Temples, for example, began offering day care for children whose mothers worked in factories. As imperial Japan grew in strength and went to war with China, temples played important roles in caring for Japanese war orphans. The teachings drawn upon in support of welfare activities changed as well, from the notion of equality found in the teaching that all possess Buddha-nature to a stronger stress on the teachings of compassion that highlight helping others.

Buddhists faced criticisms that they were of little use to modern society. Describing Buddhist efforts to redefine themselves against Meiji period criticisms, Ketelaar notes,

Each of the sects became involved in long-term projects for the aid of the destitute as well as in short-term relief in times of famine, disaster, or economic hardship. Numerous hospitals and clinics were constructed... [and Buddhists were] so entrenched in every aspect of Japanese "civilization" by the end of the nineteenth century that the earlier critique of an "other-worldly" Buddhism was no longer applicable.[33]

This massive effort to redefine Buddhism for the modern period laid the ground-work for Buddhist social welfare activities today.

Buddhists in the Meiji period learned a great deal about social welfare methods from Christian groups. Modern Buddhist welfare thought has been in constant dialogue with Christian welfare thought. While it would not be correct to say that Buddhist welfare activity did not exist before the influx of Christian welfare movements in the modern period, it is clear that Buddhist activities and thought on the subject developed over time through interaction with Christianity. Critics of Buddhism used Christian activities to portray Buddhism as ritual-centered and backward. The Buddhist response was impressive. By 1916, Buddhist welfare facilities outnumbered Christian ones 140 to 90. By the early Shōwa period (1930), they outnumbered Christian facilities 4,848 to 1,493.[34] During this period, Buddhist groups were involved in aid to the poor, disaster relief, orphanages, local development, education, prison chaplaincy, and social welfare movements such as the prohibition movement.[35]

By the Taishō period, welfare came to be viewed in social rather than individual terms. According to Ishikawa, Buddhist volunteerism began at this time. During the Taishō period, the number of sectarian Buddhist facilities and active welfare groups greatly expanded. The lifework of Hasegawa Ryōshin, one of the founders of Taishō University's social welfare education program in the prewar period, is illustrative. He began his life in social welfare education through street-level engagement. While a student at Taishō in his early twenties, he joined protests to allow imported rice to be sold inexpensively and worked at a home for foster children.[36] By 1919, he was lecturing on social welfare at Taishō University. In 1926, social welfare education became part of the official curriculum at Taishō University. Also about this time, Buddhist priests engaged in efforts to care for children began to develop national transsectarian networks. In 1928, the transsectarian Buddhist Child-care Association (Bukkyō Hoiku Kyōkai) was founded. It was also during the Taishō period that government policy began to incorporate such welfare work into governmental social policy.[37]

During the period of the Pacific War, welfare activities were part of a national, public effort to support the country. In 1944, the Imperial Japan Wartime Religious National Devotion Association (Dainippon Senji Shūkyō Hōkokukai) was established.[38] Buddhists were called on to develop programs to care for families of the war-bereaved and to care for orphans. However, as the war in the Pacific dragged on, funding, supply, and staff shortages led to temporary shutdowns of many facilities.

In the aftermath of World War II, Buddhist activities revolved around helping those in immediate need and were characterized by the social activism of the immediate postwar era. Later, projects such as kindergartens and schools developed. Unlike the prewar programs, which had been directed primarily at needy children, postwar programs sought to attract children from the local community. In the postwar period, Buddhist facilities outnumbered Christian ones 2,476 to 441 (1969).[39] However, the prevalence among Buddhist facilities of kindergartens, which generate income as well as educate, leads some to question whether many of these facilities were begun out of a need to generate income during the economic hardships of postwar Japan.

During Japan's period of sustained high economic growth (1950s–1960s), Buddhist sects developed social welfare programs, such as the Sōtō sect's Sōtō Volunteer Association (SVA), which has taken the lead in Japanese welfare efforts at home and abroad,[40] and the Tendai sect's Light Up Your Corner Movement. Some groups—such as the Tendai Sect Welfare and Youth Commission (Tendaishū Minsei-Jidō Iinkai), one of many groups officially affiliated with the Tendai sect (yet not defined within sect bylaws)—have more narrowly defined objectives. The stated purpose of this organization is to aid cooperative welfare and youth care programs based on the Tendai teachings. Other local Buddhist efforts focus on use of properties, by either building facilities on them or renting them out. Local priests are also engaged in a variety of efforts as public servants. Many serve on local welfare commissions (minsei iin kyōgikai) that advise and help develop programs for senior care, child care, or care for the handicapped.

By the 1980s, a new phenomenon had begun to emerge; facilities developed by individual temples began to break off and to establish themselves independently as private welfare or educational organizations. Sect officials have greeted this trend with a measure of alarm. The breakaway organizations provide needed services to their community, but there is some question whether a specifically Buddhist element will continue. In a later development, some priests have begun to develop welfare activities organizationally separate from (though often spatially contiguous with) the temple. The 1998 Nonprofit Organization Law (tokutei hierikatsudō hōjinhō) opened the door to increased involvement in welfare activities outside the bounds of the temple by making donations to non-profit organizations (NPOs) tax deductible. Reflecting the growing interest in developing nonprofit welfare activities through the temple, a conference titled "The Potential of the Temple as an NPO" (NPO toshite no Tera no Kanōsei) was held in 2000. Priests who had successfully developed nonprofit projects based out of their temples as well as priests who sought to do so attended the conference. Topics discussed included many of those already central to Buddhist welfare activities, such as creating educational or social-welfare NPOs, and new ideas such as beginning culture NPOs (sponsoring art shows and the like).[41]

BUDDHIST WELFARE ACTIVITIES TODAY

As we have seen, the *danka* system gives shape to contemporary Temple Buddhism. In particular, under the *danka* system, local needs—both those of the local community and the *danka* members and those of the temple family to protect and preserve the temple—have come to be paramount. Most contemporary Buddhist social welfare activities are the result of individual efforts by local priests. Temple priests who take an interest in the needs of their communities address those needs through their own efforts. Kindergartens and day-care centers make up the majority of local efforts.[42] These present temples with opportunities to provide much-needed services to the community (the waiting list at public day-care centers is always long; my daughter was number 348 for the April 2001 class in a Tokyo-area day-care facility). Kindergartens also provide temples with income and the opportunity to introduce the next generation to Buddhism. Other local efforts also generally focus on children. For example, some temples host scout troops.[43]

In keeping with the times, many temples have also begun to address the problems of Japan's aging society. Individual priests make visits to retirement homes to give lectures or sing songs. Local temples either open their facilities for use by the elderly or build new facilities on temple property. For example, one priest, who serves as acting priest at another temple in addition to his own, worked together with town and prefectural authorities to turn his second temple into a day-care facility for the elderly. Services are still held at the temple for *danka* members, but the temple is also opened daily to small groups of senior citizens as a place of relaxation. The town and the city provided funding for remodeling at the temple, including adding wheelchair ramps and a special bath.[44]

Some temple priests now participate in a Buddhist hospicelike movement called the Bihara Undō (Vihara Movement). This movement seeks to provide care to the dying and the bereaved based on Buddhist principles, much as the hospice movement in the West is based on Christian principles. Many young priests believe this movement offers the best way to combine traditional Buddhist death ritual roles with contemporary needs and to overcome the stale funeral Buddhism image.[45]

In addition to such measures, some temples have begun providing innovative rituals for the elderly. These include *pokkuri-dera,* temples where the elderly can pray for a quick death and thereby find peace of mind as they live out their final years knowing they will not burden family members if their prayers are answered.[46] In a similar vein there are temples dedicated to Yomeirazu Kannon, or the "no-need-[to-rely-on]-a daughter-in-law Avalokitasvara" (the bodhisattva of compassion), and others to the Boke yoke Jizō, or "senility-preventing Kshitigarbha."[47]

Ian Reader notes that social action by Buddhists is generally based on the efforts of individual priests because of sect structure; sect headquarters rarely have the power to set agendas within their own sects.[48] The examination of the Tendai sect's Light Up Your Corner Movement in chapter 3 supports this conclusion. Despite efforts to operate this organization in a centralized fashion, the sect has failed to energize its priests on behalf of this program in a uniform way.

Variation in local *danka* member needs also inhibits sect efforts to implement centralized social welfare programs. There is a general lack of interest in social welfare activities on the part of *danka* members, and temples must see to their primary constituents' needs first. Evidence suggests that most *danka* members prefer to avoid change and to leave the temple a secure place for the care of their ancestors. Efforts by priests require the participation or, at the least, the permission of the *danka* members. Without their support, little can be accomplished.

Many priests are risk averse. Their livelihood is based upon an intricate web of relations with *danka* members and the local community; should they throw that relationship off balance, the fate of their temple could change radically. Recognizing local variation and the needs of priests to service their own constituencies first, the Tendai sect makes grants to support local welfare programs available each year.

Fear of offending *danka* members, or simple lack of desire to stretch beyond stable roles, certainly plays a part in priestly inhibitions about beginning welfare activities. But so does a sincere belief on the part of many priests in the importance of their role as defenders of local and national traditions. For example, one large temple in Tokyo, which has the resources to begin welfare projects should it decide to do so, opts against engagement. The head priest sees his first duty to be looking after the needs of *danka* members and the faithful that gather there for various special ceremonies and festivals that take place throughout the year. These duties, so he and some members of his staff of priests argue, must come first. Too strong a move away from such duties, and the original meaning and importance of the temple as a place of practice and local tradition could be threatened. In short, what is involved here is less a fear of loss of a comfortable lifestyle than a fear that the true purpose of the temple would be lost. This opinion is echoed by another priest: "Priests defend traditions that would die without them there, traditions that would be a great loss to society if they died out. Priests are responsible for carrying on age-old traditions, preserving them and acting them out."[49] Hosokawa Keiichi, the director-general of the Myōshinji branch of the Rinzai sect, argues, "We cannot just ride the wave of modernity. We must maintain traditions while encouraging the social engagement of young priests. . . . If we only try to keep up with the times we will lose our original meaning . . . as a religious organization, the most important task before us is to train the next generation of priests."[50]

Defense of tradition is also heard from scholars. Yamaori Tetsuo, a scholar of Buddhism whose works sell widely among the general populace, states,

> Modern Buddhism has put too much emphasis on [the question] "What is our social role?" . . . But the social role that a religious should fulfill is a secondary role when viewed from the perspective of the original purpose of a religious. When that which is supposed to be a secondary role becomes the primary role, then big problems occur. . . . Putting it another way—and this may be shocking to hear—the original role of a religious is to live a nonproductive lifestyle. . . . They should be a model for life's last 20–30 years.[51]

Priests are trapped between two religious ideals. On the one hand, modern notions of the religious life assume that religious professionals should be engaged in aiding society in some way. (This is why the Religious Juridical Persons Law treats religious juridical persons as a form of public welfare juridical person.) On the other hand, *danka* and many priests demand the continuation of traditional roles such as providing care for ancestors. The challenge for priests who wish to engage in social welfare activities is to find ways to do so within their traditional roles.

Priests are also trapped between images of the temple as a local phenomenon and as part of something larger, namely, Buddhism. As we have seen, most *danka* temples are integrated locally and are seen by *danka* more as local religious organizations than as parts of larger, nationwide Buddhist sects. For this reason, welfare efforts conducted at the local, individual level by priests may not help to counter widespread images of corrupt priests engaged in funeral Buddhism. A national sectwide or transsectarian effort is required to replace pervasive negative images of priests and Temple Buddhism with positive images of socially engaged, compassionate priests. To this end, the Tendai sect has encouraged sect-centered welfare programs through the Light Up Your Corner Movement and through the Young Buddhist Association of the Tendai sect.

As we have seen, the Light Up Your Corner Movement is a broadly defined campaign with various aims, principally to redefine sect-*danka* bonds. In accomplishing its primary aim, the movement also works to involve priests in a variety of programs that have the potential to result in a positive image for the priesthood overall. As local leaders of the movement, priests are expected to become involved in local efforts to better society. It is hoped that, through such involvement, the image of the priest as solely interested in funerals will melt away under the warmth of compassionate social engagement. Moreover, the efforts accrue to the sect, because they are advertised as part of the sect's movement to better society. The most creative local efforts are co-opted by the center. Ideally, in this way, efforts that might serve only local needs can be applied to a wider audience. This co-optation of local efforts by the center serves to help more people and to draft local efforts into improving not only the position of the local temple, but also the image of Temple Buddhism as a whole.

YOUTH ASSOCIATIONS

Within the Tendai sect, as within in other sects as well, translocal involvement in welfare efforts generally occurs under the auspices of Buddhist youth associations (*busseinenkai*). Tendai sect youth associations are comprised of priests under the age of forty. Individual teaching district youth associations are organized under the sect-level Tendai Young Buddhist Association (Tendaishū Bukkyō Seinen Renmei), which was founded in 1970.[52] The association was formed from a handful of local associations in the midst of a tumultuous period. On the one hand, Japan had just pulled itself out of the confusion of the immediate postwar period, built a booming economy, and hosted the Olympics. On the other hand, traditional values were in question, riots were occurring over the U.S.–Japan Security Treaty (ANPO), and student protests were grinding college education to a halt. Out of this situation, an early leader remarks, young priests stepped forward to ask what they and the sect could do to address the problems of contemporary society. In 1966, the Tokyo Tendai Young Buddhist Association was founded, building on the emergence the year before of the Kinki Tendai Young Buddhist Association.[53] This was followed by the development of associations in all but two of the Tendai teaching districts within two years and the founding of the Tendai Young Buddhist Association in 1970. The final two districts developed associations by 1973.

The theme of the second league gathering in 1973, "Building a Tendai for Tomorrow," reflects the concerns of the young Tendai priests of the time. Sugitani Gijun, the first leader of the association notes, "The meaning of the Young Buddhist Association lies in enabling those of the new age to go beyond their elders through the use of new methods and to push forward fervently toward the realization of their goals without being afraid of making mistakes."[54] Statements such as this reflect the energy of the founding period. Founding members drew this energy from the anti–Vietnam War movement. Sugitani, for example, joined a Buddhist summit meeting in South Vietnam in 1965. The second leader of the association, Fuji Kōgen (who, like Sugitani, later served as director-general of the Tendai sect), devoted his energies to developing a summer retreat in which youth association members led young children on a retreat to Mt. Hiei. He also encouraged the development of similar local efforts to bring Japan's youth into contact with traditional Buddhism. The third federation leader, Nishioka Ryōkō (later president of the Tendai sect's Diet and currently the sect's director-general) was, and remains, focused on international aid efforts, especially in Southeast Asia. This interest began with the flood of refugees from Cambodia following the Vietnam War. The league later provided the support needed for the successful completion of the World Religion Summit on Mt. Hiei in 1987 in which religious leaders from around the world were invited to Mt. Hiei.[55] The league was also instrumental in arranging for special memorial services for the founders of Tendai.

The purpose of the Tendai Young Buddhist Association is stated today as "to bind together in friendship youth associations which conduct activities based on the teachings of the Tendai sect and Buddhist youth movements, to make Buddhism flourish, and to advance the cause of world peace."[56] The association seeks to meet these goals through holding an annual convention for all Tendai youth associations, an annual training retreat, and an annual young members summer retreat; through involvement in the transsectarian All-Japan Buddhist Youth Organization (Zen Nippon Bukkyō Seinen Renmei); and through acting as a center for organizing young Tendai priests throughout Japan so that they may be called upon when help is needed in welfare or disaster-relief efforts. The various teaching-district youth associations act to gather young priests to serve at regular local events or ceremonies. For example, local youth associations staff the Light Up Your Corner Movement conventions. Depending on their position within the group, members might do anything from holding signs on street corners directing guests to the event (usually a job reserved for the youngest members) to arranging and managing the event itself. Their presence is absolutely critical for the successful operation of conventions and other large events such as special exhibits of national treasures from Mt. Hiei or scholarly Buddhist conferences.

In combination with the Light Up Your Corner Movement, the association has proven an invaluable asset for the Tendai sect. It has provided young priests with a way to become socially engaged and to expand their sights beyond the temple grounds. Few priests have their own temple before the age of forty, so their time with their local youth association represents a period in which they are free to explore the possibilities of engaged practice. Moreover, when the priests connect their activities to and through the sect, the sect benefits as well.

The aid efforts of the various associations are their most public activities. Members participate in all Light Up Your Corner efforts abroad, including annual trips to Laos to build schools or to Thailand to aid in slum relief efforts.[57] Within Japan, the network of Tendai youth associations provides the sect with an efficient method for sending relief to areas affected by disaster.

The January 17, 1995, Kobe earthquake put the system to the test. League efforts were channeled through the Hyōgo Teaching District Youth Association.[58] The temples of many of the priests at the center of the aid effort were themselves damaged. On the day of the quake, a group of sect officials representing both the sect as juridical person (the Sect Administrative Office), and the religious body (the main temple [honzan]) visited the quake-damaged area, inspecting damaged temples and their environs. A Disaster Countermeasures Division (Saigaitaisaku Honbu) was set up within the sect administration, and an emergency headquarters opened in the Hyōgo Teaching District. The Hyōgo emergency headquarters became the conduit for aid and volunteers from Tendai temples and teaching districts around the country. During the first month, Tendai activities focused on providing food and water to temples, schools, and other evacuation centers. During the second month, Tendai efforts were still focused on providing food, but expanded to include providing daily-life goods. At this time, Tendai also offered a bath service, taking individuals living in evacuation centers to bathing facilities. They also began forty-ninth-day memorial services, and services to appease the souls of the dead were conducted at various sites within Kobe. In the third month following the quake, supplying food was no longer necessary, and efforts shifted to preparing meals for elderly victims and organizing an overnight rest retreat to Mt. Hiei. In the fourth month after the quake, the Tendai sect donated a hundred wheelchairs and organized a concert and a nature tour for victims.[59]

LOOKING TO THE FUTURE

Through the open call for new recruits, social welfare activities conducted under the Light Up Your Corner Movement, and Buddhist youth association networks, Tendai seeks to re-create itself for the needs and expectations of contemporary Japanese. Recognizing the need for a sect-level effort to focus the energies of priests on the contemporary problems facing Tendai and Temple Buddhism, Tendai founded the Tendai Sect Comprehensive Research Center (Tendaishū Sōgō Kenkyū Sentā) in early 2000.[60] The center will act as an information hub to aid priests in responding to contemporary needs. It is to cover topics ranging from education to proselytizing, from missionary and aid work to the training of priests.

The center was developed over a five-year period in which the needs of the sect were studied. The founding ideal of the center is the creation of "a Tendai sect that makes its presence felt" (sonzaikan no aru Tendaishū).[61] According to its bylaws, the purpose of the center is to seek out and devise plans to revitalize the Tendai sect, to conduct research into how to better respond to the changing needs of society, and to advance the Light Up Your Corner Movement.

Dissension within the sect regarding the creation of the center demonstrates difficulties the sect faces today. First, "there are many [priests] who did not feel such a center was necessary. . . . They are satisfied with a life of conducting funerals and memorial services."[62] Second, some priests felt that the whole project was a one-sided effort on the part of the sect administration and that it failed to take into account the voices of local temples. And, third, signaling the fight over how best to address the modern needs and goals of the sect, others protested the name of the center. Originally planned as the Tendai Sect Comprehensive Teaching Center (Tendaishū Sōgō Kyōka Sentā), the name was changed at the last minute. One leading member of Tendai's Diet argued, "I am not happy with the change from 'teaching' to 'research.' Teaching and proselytizing are the lifeblood of the Tendai sect. If we do not push teaching and proselytizing Tendai, we will not be able to keep up with modern society!"[63]

An examination of the Tendai Sect Comprehensive Research Center brings to light (1) problems that focus on the proper role of the priest (e.g., Should they be ritual specialists, preachers, or social welfare workers?), (2) the differing needs and goals of the sect and local temples, and (3) differing opinions on the proper goals of the sect (e.g., Should it focus on doctrinal research and debate or on proselytizing?). The examination of the priesthood in this chapter has shed light on these problems faced by the priesthood as well as on the countermeasures taken by the Tendai sect.

The priesthood of Temple Buddhism faces numerous problems in contemporary Japan. Negative images of priests abound, based on views of contemporary Buddhism as corrupt or on certain ideas (often related to precept maintenance) about what constitutes a real priest. Priests, scholars, and laity all hold these images. Furthermore, the secularization of temple ownership through inheritance has created a lack of opportunities for priests of lay family backgrounds. Alternative avenues for the pursuit of religious practice (new new religions, Buddhist academies) exist in perhaps wider variety than ever before. The influence of the *danka* member system has curtailed efforts to extend the benefits of social engagement and to recruit new personnel to counter the overall image of Temple Buddhism as corrupt or moribund. Today the priesthood of Temple Buddhism remains trapped between image and reality, between lofty goals and shifting realities of practice, and between the needs of the sect, the priest, and the laity.

6 Coming to Terms
Temple Wives and World-Renouncers

[Temple-wives] are the head priest's partner. They raise and educate
the priest's successor. They act as the temple's warmhearted and kind
reception[ist], greeting *danka* members, the faithful, and society at large.
They are vitally involved in activities; sometimes they share the head
priest's temple duties; and there are many examples of them handling the
temple's finances.[1]
—Tendai sect priest, 2000

I suppose that, in the end, if we are to try totally to protect the livelihood
and status of the temple family of a head priest who has passed away, that
is, the bereaved family, there is nothing else to do but adopt an officially
recognized system of family inheritance [of the temple] like in Jōdo Shin.
Make the successor someone who is related by blood. This would be a
reasonable way to protect bereaved family members as well as pass on the
Dharma. For better or worse, this is the only route open to maintaining
today's temple system. In principle, it's not actually an end-of-the-world
thing, but . . . you reap what you sow and world-renouncers have come to
have families, and this is the bitter repercussion. We can no longer think
this is someone else's problem.[2]
—Shingon sect priest, 1979

REPORTER: What kind of place do you believe the temple is? After the
head priest has passed away, on what would you base the family's right
to go on residing in the [temple] living quarters?
ELDEST DAUGHTER: We women don't understand such difficult discussions.
We haven't had the free time to think about such things because
we've been working. We did as the priest said, we did as the priest did,
we just worked and worked. But we were not dissatisfied. We have no
regrets. We saw it as only natural since we were receiving the Buddha's
rice. We didn't seek anything in return. Far from it, mother even
invested her own money in the temple. If you ask us temple family

what the temple is, it is life itself. [Our] lives and the temple were one
and the same.[3]
—Shingon sect temple family member, 1979

You always tell us "work, work, work." Then what have we got when our
husband dies? Nothing is guaranteed for us, the *jizoku* [temple family].
We are just like ordinary women with no special skills or training. There
should be proper guidelines to assist us as *jizoku* women.[4]
—Sōtō sect temple wife, 1982

Up to now I have contributed to the development of the temple from the
sidelines as the abbot's wife, but now that I have taken the precepts
myself and become a disciple of the Buddha, I have really come to feel a
burden of responsibility.[5]
—Tendai Sect temple wife on taking the new temple wife ordination,
1998

In previous chapters, I have shown how the sects of Temple Buddhism
struggle to redefine the relationship between *danka* members and the temple and
to re-create priestly roles. I have also shown that despite their best efforts the
sects have yet to achieve real success because of failure adequately to remedy
underlying problems. Most important, they remain trapped between their sincere desire to meet the needs of modern society and their equally sincere desire
to continue as world-renouncing defenders of tradition. There is perhaps no
point at which this conflict is more pronounced than in the debate over the
place of temple families and temple wives.

As clerical marriage became the norm within the sects of Temple
Buddhism following legal changes in the Meiji period,[6] women came to play ever
greater roles at temples. Today, a typical day for a temple wife might run as follows: wake up early (5:00 A.M.), open the temple gates, prepare breakfast, send
the children to school, clean the living quarters, clean the temple, and sweep
the grounds. As the day wears on, people might start to appear to visit their family graves. The temple wife greets them. Some stay for tea. Meanwhile, she must
answer the temple phone, set the priest's schedule, and arrange for grounds or
building maintenance. If there is a memorial service that day, she must prepare
tea and snacks, or even whole meals, for those in attendance, and serve them.
Like other mothers, she is charged with managing the children's education.

More than likely, she is active in the local parent-teacher association and community groups. Many temple wives also teach *goeika* (Buddhist hymns) or a traditional Japanese art, such as the tea ceremony.

Despite the critical nature of their wives' work to the functioning of the temple, many priests prefer that the lives of temple wives and families be kept hidden. For this reason, temple wives have earned the sobriquet "the hidden strength of the temple" (*tera no en no shita no chikaramochi*). Another commonly cited description runs, "The priest and his wife are like kimono. The priest is the outside (what everyone sees), the wife is the lining (there, but not to be seen)."[7] This chapter examines the lives of temple wives and temple families and the contemporary controversies surrounding their presence at the temple. Special attention is paid to the efforts in the postwar period within the Tendai sect to come to terms with the status of wives within Temple Buddhism.

Clerical marriage is not new to contemporary Japan. There is evidence of clerical marriage from more than a thousand years ago. Jaffe notes, "The practice was common enough that as early as the Heian period the rights of a blood-child to a deceased cleric's property were legally recognized."[8] The retired emperor Goshirakawa (1127–1192) is said to have stated the following regarding monks who kept women on the side. "Those who hide it are saints, those who don't do it are Buddhas."[9] Later, Edo period legal codes strictly forbade clerical marriage, but infractions abounded. The following passage is from a story by Ihara Saikaku, a famous seventeenth-century writer.

> In recent years, however, with the growing prosperity of temples, the priests have become even more licentious. In the daytime they wear vestments, but at night they sally forth dressed in short coats. Furthermore, they install women in their temples. For this purpose the priest will have a deep recess built in the corner of his private apartment.[10]

Although present from early on, clerical marriage was not considered the norm. However, with its legalization in the Meiji period, clerical marriage became so pervasive that it could no longer be understood as a heterodox practice or successfully secreted away. It had become the norm. However, for sects such as Tendai that consider themselves world-renouncing organizations, clerical marriage remained, and in some cases still remains, something to be hidden from view. For example, Rinzai sect bylaws had already made provisions to allow a priest's son as possible successor by the Taishō period; however, there was no mention of the priest's wife.[11] While other households might hang their laundry outside to dry, or hoist a streamer on Boys' Day to celebrate their son, until recently, temple wives were requested to work quietly, and temple children to not call unwanted attention their way.[12] As we have seen, the practice of marriage caused numerous image, practical, and ideological problems for the sects of Temple Buddhism. However, as male priests delay in taking decisive steps to solve these problems, it is temple families, and temple wives in particular, who suffer.

The second and third excerpts at the beginning of this chapter are taken from a case that began in 1978 when a temple priest passed away, leaving behind his wife and three daughters. After three years of negotiation, the family was forced to leave the temple they had rebuilt with their father. They took with them their personal belongings and a 40,000,000-yen cash settlement.[13] They were luckier than many temple families, which are often turned out of the temple with at most a few million yen. For example, in 2000, the courts forced the wife of a head priest in one case to sue the temple for compensation.[14]

When her husband passed away, Ms. Jifu was permitted to live at the temple with her mother-in-law.[15] To guarantee that the family of the deceased priest could continue to reside at the temple, her older brother, Mr. Tazaki, who was a teacher and already the head priest of his own temple, was selected as the acting head priest (*kenmujūshoku*). After Ms. Jifu's mother-in-law died and her brother retired from teaching duties, *danka* members asked Mr. Tazaki to become their full-time head priest. He refused, and they sought a new priest. However, Mr. Tazaki then demanded 50,000,000 yen to compensate him for his work up to then and to take care of his sister, Ms. Jifu.

Citing the inappropriateness of such a demand, *danka* members petitioned the sect to have Mr. Tazaki removed, which it did. In his place the sect appointed a new head priest. However, that priest requested that Ms. Jifu leave before his arrival. Citing sect rules that temple family members must be cared for in the event of the death of the priest, Ms. Jifu placed a claim with the temple for compensation. The temple refused. The case then progressed to the local sect office, which tried to intervene. However, because the temple did not have sufficient funds, the mediation went poorly. Finally, the incoming priest offered 5,000,000 yen. Ms. Jifu, however, refused. Although a large sum of money, it would never be enough to support a middle-aged woman with few marketable skills in Japan.[16] She sued for 20,000,000 yen.

The sect did not intervene in the matter. Sect officials preferred that the matter be handled locally. Moreover, the sect bylaws governing such incidents were intentionally written vaguely to allow for great variation among individual temples, and to mask the presence of temple wives. The vaguely written bylaws allowed the sect the space to stand aside. The matter was eventually tried before the Nagasaki local court. Ms. Jifu lost and soon appealed. The Fukuoka High Court turned down her appeal. The court ruled that the sect bylaws were designed to cover such problems and that the matter, therefore, was an internal problem in which the court could not interfere. Thus, Ms. Jifu was forced to move out of the temple. She left with nothing.

The weak economic and legal position of temple wives results from the lack of clear recognition of their role in the sect bylaws.[17] Whereas such bylaws state that temple wives should be cared for in the event of the death of their husband, the head priest, they do not specify what form that care is to take, or how much financial aid will be made available. Actual interpretation and implementation of the sect bylaws are left to individual temples, which have wide leeway to do as they see fit regarding the temple family. Lack of recognition of temple wives, in turn, is due to their unique position as the wives of supposed world-renouncers and to gender role ideals in the larger society.

WOMEN IN JAPANESE SOCIETY

Despite legal changes, such as the passage of the Equal Employment Opportunity Law (danjo koyō kikai kintōhō) in 1985 (effective April 1986), women in Japan throughout the postwar period have been socialized for marriage and motherhood, not for careers outside the home.[18] A woman's social success in life is still primarily based on her domestic, rather than career, success. This has changed somewhat in the recent past, with career women slowly becoming accepted. However, such individuals generally are expected to give up a family life. Their success is accepted because they have in effect managed to switch gender roles. Those who attempt to be both mother and businesswoman are less likely to be socially accepted.[19]

Nevertheless, gender roles are slowly changing. One study of the popular literature consumed by young women in Japan shows that images of successful single mothers and divorcees are common and popular.[20] Furthermore, rather than staying permanently out of the workforce after the birth of their first child, as had once been the norm, by the 1980s, women began to reenter the workforce after several years off to raise children and today regularly seek fulfilling work.[21] Women today also have longer life expectancies than they did in prewar Japan and are thus more likely than their predecessors to have time to devote to work in their post-child-rearing years. Furthermore, they have attained higher levels of education than ever before and have concomitant expectations.[22]

Despite a trend toward change, however, the dominant female ideal type remains woman as mother and nurturer, self-sacrificing and persevering. Women are socialized in these traits from a young age, but true pressure is applied with motherhood. For example, kindergartens expect mothers to devote themselves full-time to their children's education.[23] This ideal is reinforced as schooling continues, leading to the creation of so-called education mothers (kyōiku mama), mothers whose life is utterly devoted to their children and whose social success is linked firmly to their children's educational success. Furthermore, Japanese companies rely on wives to manage home affairs so that their husbands are able to dedicate their lives to the company.[24] Companies therefore tend to discourage female employees from beginning full-time careers.

Such gender ideal types are also pronounced in the new religions. Hardacre notes, "Women should work to build up their husbands and not put themselves ahead of men, especially in public. Where work is concerned, the crux of the matter is the notion that a woman's income should not be greater than her husband's, because that would be a blow to his ego, which it is a woman's job to support."[25] In a study of members of Risshō Kōseikai and of the Episcopal Church of Japan, Nakamura Kiyoko finds that, although men agree to equality in principle, in practice the conservative view remains strong.[26] Nakamura's findings also show that such a view is supported by nearly one-third of female respondents.

WOMEN IN TEMPLES: TEMPLE WIVES AND DAUGHTERS

The ideal types found in the wider society, and practiced in new religions such as Risshō Kōseikai, are also entrenched in temples, which tend to reflect conservative, traditional values such as those observed in the prewar government campaign to create "good wives and wise mothers" (ryōsai kenbo).[27] For example, Fuji Kōgen, then director-general of the Tendai sect, opened his New Year's greetings to Tendai sect temple wives as follows: "I always respect and admire all of you for giving everything day and night tirelessly assisting the head priest, interacting with danka members, raising the disciple [their son], and working to make the temple flourish."[28] Kobori Setsuko, then the president of the Tendai Sect Temple Wives Federation (Tendaishū Jiteifujin Rengōkai), opened her 1997 New Year's greetings to Tendai sect temple wives with this salutation, "Temple wives from across the country, how are you? Thank you for your diligence in receiving danka members, raising the disciple, assisting the head priest, and working for the temple."[29] These statements reiterate the Tendai sect bylaws, which read,

Those who are family members of a priest whose residence in an authorized temple or teaching center is recognized and who live with the head priest or teaching center administrator and work to support, maintain and expand the temple or teaching center are called temple family members (*jizoku*). Temple wives (*jiteifujin*) must work to support the head priest, care for the temple grounds, teach/proselytize to the *danka* members and faithful, and educate and raise the children.[30]

The duties temple wives are expected to fulfill are clear: assist the priest, raise the children (the next generation of priests), greet the *danka* members, and otherwise work to benefit the temple. These duties are recognized and confirmed by most temple wives. A 2001 survey of more than fifteen hundred temple wives of the Ōbaku sect and the fourteen branches of the Rinzai sect found that they ranked temple administration and management as their primary role (30 percent), followed by interaction with *danka* members (17.1 percent).[31]

In many ways, however, the current bylaws represent significant advances for temple wives and families. Before World War II, temple wives were expected to remain hidden from view as best as possible, and their roles at temples were restricted to caring for the needs of the priest and raising their children. They also had no guarantee of legal or financial protection. It was not until 1916 that the Honganji branch of the Jōdo Shin sect became the first to recognize temple wives officially within sect bylaws. The Jōdo sect and the Ōtani branch of the Jōdo Shin sect followed the example of the Honganji branch in 1919 and 1925, respectively. It was not until the 1960s that the other sects of Temple Buddhism began to recognize temple wives within sect bylaws.[32]

During World War II, many temple priests were sent to the front to fight. In their absence, sects were forced to rely on temple wives to care for the temples. This brought temple wives out of their previous behind-the-scenes role and dramatically increased their responsibilities at the temple. In the case of the Jōdo Shin sect, for example, women were allowed to become priests, but not head priests, in 1941, and in 1944, they were permitted to become doctrinal instructors (*kyōshi*).[33]

The expanded duties of temple wives continued in the postwar period because land reformation threatened the economic viability of many temples, forcing priests to work outside the temple. The wife, therefore, had to care for the temple in his absence. Moreover, as one temple wife, now in her eighties, explained bluntly, "You don't have to pay a wife."[34] This meant that temple wives were left to care for the temple, managing an ever greater range of duties, from cleaning to greeting and advising *danka* members to managing temple finances.[35] In this way, their roles, and the sect's hopes for proper fulfillment of those roles, came to be similar to those of middle-class housewives and their husbands' companies, respectively. Temple wives were no longer hidden, and they were playing important supportive roles. However, their roles were generally far more extensive than those of lay housewives. They were closer in comparison to those of the wives of small shop owners.

In the space of less than fifty years, temple wives became indispensable assistants to the head priest. Wives generally now manage the temple household and often the temple's finances. They manage the priest's schedule and act as his receptionist. They are also frequently responsible for preparing the hall for rituals (setting and lighting incense and candles, cleaning, etc.).

Tendai sect literature addressed to temple wives constantly affirms this role of assistant to the head priest and seeks to encourage temple wives to fulfill their duty to support the head priest so the temple will thrive. Work at the temple, for example, is related to religious practice. A temple wife writes to the Tendai sect temple wife newsletter, "I hear that there is a practice called the Cleaning Hell that has long been one of the important practices on Mt. Hiei. This must be about none other than purifying your own heart and drawing closer to the spirit of Dengyō Daishi through the work of cleaning. Cleaning and caring for the temple when the priest is away are among my most important jobs."[36] In addition to cleaning, the work of temple wives includes greeting, advising, and putting at ease *danka* members. "It is said that the key to the twenty-first century is within [the teaching of] 'living together.' . . . We religious must support that kind of age. The temple, as a place where faith is put into practice, is a place of rest where people can seek salvation. The warmth of the temple wives is the shining light [of that place]."[37] Here basic contemporary Tendai teachings, such as the teaching that people are given life by those around them (*tomo ni ikiru*, literally, "living together"), are linked to the role of temple wives.

Temple wives are no longer hidden behind the scenes. They are expected to be role models for *danka* members. Wives, however, generally do not perform administrative roles as officials of the sect or perform ritual roles (on-stage roles), but support and advisory roles (off-stage roles) are standard. This is very similar to conclusions Helen Hardacre came to regarding the roles of women in the new religions. Hardacre writes, "Whether the family or the religious group, men should represent the collective to the 'outside' (*omote*) while women are active on the 'inside' (*ura*). As long as the 'inside-outside' distinction is honored and the hierarchical principle affirmed, there is no objection to women taking active roles. This is why women are so active as counselors and healers, but less often fill positions in the administrative hierarchy."[38]

This similarity between the new religions and Temple Buddhism reflects their conservative understanding of gender relationships. However, temple wives also represent the incursion of the worldly household into the world-renouncing realm of Temple Buddhism. Their position as role model for *danka* members, moreover, is at odds with the desire of the sects of Temple Buddhism to portray themselves as world-renouncing organizations.[39] Therefore, the relegation of temple wives to supporting roles is not due solely to conservative gender values, but also to the emphasis on world-renunciation by the sects of Temple Buddhism. This inconsistency—a sect policy of supporting wives as role models for *danka* members while failing openly to recognize wives within the sect because their presence undermines basic assumptions held by the priesthood regarding its world-renouncing status—demonstrates the peculiar space temple wives occupy. Kawahashi Noriko argues that because of this fact the experience of temple wives cannot be likened to that of everyday wives.[40]

One might assume that the peculiar space temple wives occupy as the wives of world-renouncers could lead to discontent among *danka* members. After all, their presence would appear to undermine the sincerity of the priest's practice. However, *danka* members are not troubled by the presence of the priest's wife; they are more likely to be troubled by the lack of a temple wife. For example, one temple wife related in an interview that her presence was not a problem at all; her temple's *danka* members were far more disturbed by the fact that she and her husband had yet to persuade their daughter to marry a successor.[41] This and similar stories are common enough to suggest that *danka* members do not see local temple priests as world-renouncers. *Danka* members are more concerned about the care their ancestors receive and about the temple caretaker's (head priest's) family's smoothly continuing in their role.[42]

When read against the images of real priests and true Buddhism discussed in the previous chapter, the general lack of concern regarding clerical marriage on the part of *danka* members suggests that there are two divergent images of priests: one of local temple priests whose primary responsibility is to carry out religious duties related to care for the ancestors and one of real priests who are practicing world-renouncers.[43] The Sōtō sect confirms this possibility. According to a Sōtō sect survey, approximately 50 percent of the two hundred respondents said that they would like their local priest to look like an ordinary person and dedicate himself to propagation of the temple, whereas 35 percent wanted their priest to shave his head and wear robes.[44]

Continued emphasis by sects on the world-renouncer ideal leaves little room to explain clerical marriage, thereby reinforcing the image of temple priests as something other than real priests. Kawahashi uses the biting term "fake world-renouncerism" (gisō shukkeshugi) to describe the gap between sect insistence on world-renouncer status and the reality of everyday practice.[45]

In addition to being assistants to the head priest (or the temple's Ministry of Finance and Ministry of Communications, as one priest said), temple wives are expected to be selfless mothers. This is symbolized by the 1997 enshrinement of a statue of the mother of the Tendai sect's founder as a child-rearing bodhisattva of compassion (ko sodate kannon) at Daikōdō, a temple in the Enryakuji complex on Mt. Hiei, the headquarters of the Tendai sect. The caption under a picture of the statue in the Tendai newsletter for temple wives reads, "Her figure of loving compassion resembles that of temple wives."[46]

Of all the roles a temple wife plays, that of selfless mother is perhaps the one most counted upon by the sect. The sect relies on her to raise the next generation of priests and thereby to secure its future. This message is found in the sect bylaws, created by the male priesthood, but it is also reiterated within the writings of temple wives, such as those found in the official sect newsletter for temple wives. "I believe that the duties and responsibilities of temple wives, to be a temple wife whom the danka members and faithful trust and to raise the future successors of the temple, and so on, are extremely important."[47] The newsletter is made up primarily of short essays by temple wives who describe their participation in study sessions or tours sponsored by the sect or the Temple Wives Federation.

Some letters relate stories of how fulfilling it is to raise an heir to the temple and to see him successfully complete the required training on Mt. Hiei. Occasionally, a letter reinforces the message of motherhood from the side of failure: "The raising of a successor to the temple is an important duty of the temple wife. I feel terrible that, although I had two sons, I was not able to raise a successor."[48] The successful raising of an heir is important to temple wives not only so that they may find social acceptance within the temple world (and, indeed, from danka members as well); it is also the only sure means of guaranteeing their own security in old age. As the court case cited early in this chapter demonstrates, those wives who fail to raise a successor to the temple face expulsion, penniless, from the home in which they have spent their whole adult lives. In part because of this pressure, and in part out of a sense of responsibility to their temple and the sect, temple wives therefore maintain informal networks through which eligible sons and daughters can be matched. The annual and semiannual meetings of temple wife associations serve as informal matchmaking sessions, according to two temple wives interviewed.[49] Nevertheless, despite the intense pressure to sacrifice all in raising their children in the hopes that a son will take over the temple or that a daughter will marry in a successor, I have not encountered temple families, at least within Tokyo- and Chiba-area Tendai, that openly pressure or require their sons to take over. Still, the unspoken pressure is palpable.[50]

To be the mother of an heir to the position of head priest is understood to require special training. The goal of heir-production is, therefore, systematized. Sect leaders realized that if temple wives were to produce and educate heirs, they had to be made faithful Buddhists. Unlike priests, temple wives do not enter the temple as religious professionals. In fact, 69 percent report entering from lay households and thus from outside the temple world.[51] However, once there, they are called upon to be models of faith for *danka* members and educators of the head priest's disciple (their son). "The first thing sought from temple wives is confirmation of their faith."[52] This requirement, too, separates temple wives from average Japanese wives: their home is a site of religious practice, and their role there today is as manager of that site. *The Temple Wife Handbook (Jiteifujin techō)*, published by the Tendai sect in 1997, provides temple wives with basic information on the history and teachings of the Tendai sect (though not nearly as detailed as the information found in the priest's handbook). For example, there is a short introductory essay titled "The Teachings of the Tendai Sect" with subheadings such as "Buddhism is...," in which the four noble truths and eightfold path are introduced, and "The Life of Dengyō Daishi," in which the life and goals of the founder of Japanese Tendai are introduced.[53] This information, along with information passed on at study meetings, is designed to ground the temple wife's faith in Buddhism and to create a sense of shared belonging in an authoritative tradition so that she can educate the Dharma-heir and interact with *danka* members with confidence.

The need for training of temple wives as religious in order that they might better fulfill their roles at the temple was also recognized by early leaders of the Tendai Sect Temple Wives Federation. Realizing that temple wives could not read sutras, federation leaders embarked on a program to teach them how to do so.[54] If they could not read sutras, it was reasoned, it would be difficult for them to raise the heir to the position of head priest. To this end, a sutra-copying campaign was organized. Through repeated sutra copying (a classical form of both sutra memorization and meditation), temple wives were taught the sutra.[55]

HOMELESS AT HOME: THE PLACE OF TEMPLE
WIVES AND FAMILIES

> We are called upon to bear and raise children, educate the successor,
> support the head priest from the shadows, and act as a model woman,
> wife, mother, and Buddhist layperson. We are categorized as having to
> spend our whole lives within a home called "temple," and the only right
> of a temple wife is to be issued condolence money [when the head priest
> dies] or a special posthumous name [when the temple wife herself dies].[56]

Despite their role as managers of a religious site, temple wives are often
looked upon by sect officials as outsiders—outside doctrinal categories and outside
the male-gendered temple world. Women, some priests argue, "have no head for
discussing religion,"[57] and, regarding the prospect of women instructing the
danka members, "It's impossible for women to discourse on peace of mind" (i.e.,
about having a heart of faith).[58] Study retreats, at which it is the norm for male
priests to lecture temple wives, also illustrate this view. In fact, 2001 was the first
year that someone other than a male Tendai priest was invited as special guest
speaker at the annual meeting of the Tendai Sect Temple Wives Federation.

This view of temple wives as outsiders and as incapable of fathoming the
depths of doctrine (which priests are assumed to be able to master) leads to a
common view of temple wives as the "property" of the priest.[59] They arrive with
the priest. They don't belong in a world-renouncer's realm. There is no recognized ideological space for them within the temple. What space they have is borrowed through their husband, the priest. The borrowed nature of their space is
made clear in death. For example, in some regions it is customary at Sōtō sect
temples to not permit temple wives to be buried with their husbands.[60] In a
representation of the continuation of the dharma-lineage over time, head priests
are buried in a special grave for priests. The temple wife is not part of the
dharma-lineage.[61] Therefore, when the priest is gone, temple wives are expected
to disappear quietly, as the court case cited earlier demonstrates.[62]

The creation of a recognized space for temple wives within the sects of
Temple Buddhism is now the primary objective of some temple wife activists.
They argue that doctrine must be rethought to include a space for temple
wives.[63] Against such arguments, some priests counter that there are only four
categories recognized within Buddhism: monks, nuns, laymen, and laywomen.
Temple wives should be content within one of the two female categories. However, given their role as assistant to the head priest and trainer of the disciple

(head priest's son), temple wives cannot be easily classified as strictly lay. And because most have no formal training as priests, they cannot be classified as nuns, either. Some temple wives consider themselves laity; others are ordained as priests. Some seek recognition as religious practitioners (though not as priests), others as assistants. For example, 23 perceent responded in a survey that they should be able to perform religious duties alongside their husbands, while 25.3 percent were against the idea (with some arguing that to do so would eliminate the meaning of monastic training). As Kawahashi notes, "temple wife" is left an "ambiguous category."[64]

Temple wives are left in their ambiguous category in part because male priests are themselves trapped in an ambiguous category. As married clergy, priests cannot claim to be monks as understood in the traditional four categories (i.e., as world-renouncers), yet as trained priests, they cannot be seen as simply laymen, either. Before an unambiguous category can be created for temple wives, leaders of the sects of Temple Buddhism face the challenge of creating a new understanding of the categories of world-renouncer and householder.

The debate continues over how to structure a space for temple wives through the category of temple wife (*jiteifujin* or *jizoku*). In 1999, a series of essays was sparked when Minami Jikisai, a senior priest in the Sōtō sect, declared in an essay in the newspaper *Chūgai nippō* that the category of temple wife or temple family should be eliminated: "I am ready to recognize the existence of monks' dependents. But I question the category of temple wife. I am against the idea of systematically increasing their rank, and especially against placing temple wives within the system to the point of pulling their rank up to being on a level with monks."[65]

Countering Minami, members of the Tōkai/Kantō Network for Women and Buddhism (Josei to Bukkyō Tōkai/Kantō Netowāku)[66] first questioned his use of the term "rank": "I must admit I was honestly shocked at the idea that monk[hood] is a rank."[67] They then attacked his assumptions that temple wives did not need a specially recognized category to guarantee their security in the event of the death of the head priest.

In response to Minami's proposal to eliminate the category of temple wife, Taki Eishin, then director-general of the Tendai sect, stated in 1992 that the problem was not a lack of definition, but a lack of implementing bylaws concerning their recognition. "In Tendai, temple families (*jizoku*) are already thorough members of the sect. [They are defined] within the sect constitution. They are defined as important members along with head priests, disciples, and *danka* members and the faithful."[68] Taki went on to explain that problems over the standing of temple families occur when matters concerning their support in the event of the death of the head priest are not made clear within the bylaws of individual local temples ahead of time. However, as we have seen, local ambiguities are the result of the vaguely written sect bylaws. This is another clear indication of the center's lack of direct power over the periphery in the sects of Temple Buddhism.

Perhaps the most critical question affecting not just temple families but *danka* members and the sects in general is Who owns the temple? Legally, the answer is straightforward: temples that are registered as religious juridical persons are owned by the religious juridical person. However, we have seen that legal definitions do not adequately take into account traditional, local, or personal understandings regarding temple ownership. In particular, such extralegal understandings of the temple are not always based on physical assets. The temple is history, it is site (of religious rituals), it is home (to ancestors), it is house and home (for the temple family), it is cultural asset (public space or touristic site), and more.

As it concerns temple wives and families, the problem of temple ownership centers on four groups of actors: the sect, the priest, the temple families, and the *danka* members. For example, there is a perception on the part of some sect leaders, such as Tendai's Taki, that temple wives who believe they have the right to remain at the temple even after their husband's passing account for the difficulties in filling vacant posts (he states that 10 percent of vacant temples are at stake).[69] Sects also want to avoid public disputes between temple families and *danka* members, fearing that such disputes could damage *danka*-temple and *danka*-sect relationships. Therefore, sects of Temple Buddhism seek ways to incorporate temple wives and families into the sect and to prevent trouble before it begins. One method is to encourage temple wives to study about the sect and to participate in retreats. For example, each year leaders of the Tendai Sect Temple Wives Federation participate in a retreat on Mt. Hiei. The temple wife retreats are similar to retreats that *danka* members are encouraged to attend to strengthen their bonds to the sect by introducing the cultural and religious legacy of the temples on Mt. Hiei. At these retreats it is hoped that temple wives will learn more about temple management, touch the spirit of the founder, and deepen their self-awareness as the wives of temple priests.[70] The development of the temple wife precept ordination system is another method (see below for details). However, most sects fail to realize the full benefits of such methods because gender discrimination and lingering attempts to maintain the facade of world-renunciation keep them from incorporating temple wives and families into the religious and administrative structures. Moreover, such efforts to strengthen the awareness of temple wives as members of a larger religious organization do little to address the economic security of temple wives.

Sect efforts to encourage a sense of belonging and duty among temple wives and thereby to discourage perceptions of the temple as private property often fail because they are unable to penetrate the daily life of temple wives. Sect leadership is too divorced from local concerns. Local temple priests rely extensively on their wives. Together, many priests and their wives spend countless hours working to expand or rebuild the temple. Because of these joint efforts, a sense of ownership regarding the temple may develop. This is no different from a young family that struggles to build a small business or enterprise. The physical, financial, and emotional investment is considerable, and attachment to the project is almost inevitable.

Moreover, the temple is home to the priest as head of the family. His children will grow up there. More than likely the family members will spend long hours from childhood helping to manage the temple, whether through cleaning, greeting guests, or helping prepare for ceremonies and festivals. Therefore, they come to know the temple as home. In some instances, the family may also build a house on the temple grounds, further strengthening their emotional and physical bonds to the temple.[71]

The relationship of the wife to her husband, the priest, may also lead to a kind of privatization of the temple. The Tendai sect, for example, expressed concern that temple wives understand their place within the temple as being more than just that of wife.

> The secularization of temples today continues. The existence of a family living along with the head priest and his disciple is now the norm. This [family] is regularly called the temple family (*jizoku*) within the Tendai sect. But in order that they are able to fully develop their functions at the temple (*danka* member proselytizing/assistance at services), it is important that they become aware of the Buddha's grace by which they live in the temple and receive the Buddha's rice, and that through this awareness they work in service to the main deity (*honzon*) and for the development of the temple. If it wasn't for this they would simply be the head priest's family, they couldn't be called the temple family.[72]

In one survey, the majority of temple wives responded, "It just so happened that the person I chose to marry was a priest." In response, a nun commented, "Now the truth is coming out. It is clear they do not think of the temple as a religious or public welfare juridical person. Nor do they think of the head priest himself as a monk practitioner."[73] Not only this nun (and others[74]), but also many priests fear that temple wives will see priests not as priests, but as husbands, and, therefore, will see the temple as personal property rather than as a religious organization.

Moreover, some nuns see clerical marriage as a break from true Buddhist practice. This attitude is clearly demonstrated in Paula Arai's work on Sōtō sect nuns in Japan. Arai remarks, "According to the abbess Aoyama, to be a renunciant means not to pursue worldly things and not to behave in worldly ways. In keeping with Dōgen's teachings most nuns draw a clear distinction between the lifestyle of a renunciant and a householder."[75] Aoyama states elsewhere,

> Religion is, if in nothing else, epitomized in the point of "abandonment."
> . . . It is a realm that even someone as great as the Buddha Shakyamuni
> could attain only when he abandoned his concubine and his son Rahula
> and risked his life in practice. How is it that deluded people like us
> could perfect this path, with a wife and children and our property and
> reputation, and even our secular work, on our hands? . . . The temple,
> which ought to be a place for *danka* members to participate in *zazen*
> and hear the Dharma, a place of practice for priests, and a space for
> proselytization, has now changed into a residence for the head priest and
> his family. Someone who has a family, ensconced in a private castle of
> delusions, is no renunciant but rather a householder. . . . Priests take
> wives, temples are mistaken for the residences of families, and thus is
> born the misunderstanding that temples are private property.[76]

Setouchi Jakuchō, a famous novelist and Tendai sect nun, concurs, clearly indicating in an interview that clerical marriage is a major problem, and that temple wives have no place in a real Buddhist temple.[77] The fact that many nuns are from lay backgrounds, whereas most priests are from temple family backgrounds, shapes their respective views of clerical marriage. In a similar fashion, the views of male priests from lay backgrounds appear to be more conservative regarding proper priestly practice and conduct than those of male priests from temple family backgrounds.

Privatization of the temple occurs outside the temple family, too. *Danka* members often consider the temple their property. It is through their donations that it is built. It houses their family graves. In many cases it also serves as a local gathering center. Moreover, through the *danka* representative system (*sōdai seido*), *danka* members often participate in the management of the religious and

administrative affairs of the temple. In some instances participation as a representative is a hereditary position. These activities and connections serve to
encourage a sense not only of belonging, but also of ownership. In this fashion,
temple families often come to be seen as caretakers of the "*danka* members' temple," and a bond between the *danka* members and the temple family as such
develops.

These conflicting views of temple ownership are the basis for misunderstandings regarding temple wives and families. The 1979 case cited earlier, in
which a temple family was awarded 40,000,000 yen in compensation, demonstrates that such conflicting views lead to misunderstandings. The priest passed
away, leaving behind three daughters. Because of years of work for the temple,
lasting well into their adult lives (the eldest was thirty during the time of the
conflict, the others, twenty-eight and twenty-six), the daughters felt that they
had the right to remain on the temple grounds. Before his death, their father, the
head priest, attempted to arrange a marriage for his oldest daughter with a young
priest. This would have guaranteed his family's security, and the *danka* members
were supportive of the idea. However, his daughter refused because she was seeing someone else at the time (whom she later married). Her refusal to marry the
priest upset *danka* members, who had hoped that "their" temple family at "their"
temple would stay on. Significantly, there was no discussion of one of the daughters' becoming a nun.[78] The daughters noted that the temple representatives
were all elderly men and community leaders and, therefore, had little sympathy
for the difficulties the women would face outside the temple.[79]

Complicating the competing interests in temple ownership is the de facto
system of patrilineal succession of temples. The 2001 survey of Rinzai and Ōbaku
sect temple wives found that there was less interest in ordaining daughters than
sons and that one of the main reasons for ordaining sons was to ensure a successor.[80] This system of patrilineal succession encourages the privatization of the
temple and is a major source of problems related to temple families.
Nevertheless, this system is encouraged by sects to combat declining numbers of
priests. *Danka* members, who develop ties to particular temple families and prefer to see the same family observe rituals for their ancestors over time, also
encourage it. Priests encourage the system as well, because they can guarantee
their family's security, as do temple wives for the same reason (14.8 percent of
temple wives ranked succession as the number one problem they worried about,
second only to temple administration).[81] This leads to a vicious circle in which
temples become emotionally privatized through efforts to support the temple
family, which in turn is left in dire straits when the male lineage stops and the

family is forced to move out of the temple—which is in fact a juridical person, not personal property.

Securing the welfare of temple families is currently a major topic within sects of Temple Buddhism. The extent to which temple families are entitled to funding and other means of support is directly related to the degree to which clerical marriage is recognized and to which temple wives are integrated into the organizational and religious structures of the sect. Tendai sect leaders, for example, argue that the sect has already incorporated the protection of the temple families into its structures. Problems arise from lack of compliance with registration procedures. According to the head of the Tendai Sect Miscellaneous Affairs Section (Shomuka), in 1992, 74.6 percent of temples had temple families, but only 69.2 percent of these were properly registered with the sect and, therefore, eligible for benefits.[82]

At the same time, temple wives in Tendai and others sects argue that the provisions in sect bylaws are hollow. There is little detail concerning concrete measures to support temple families. The following is the Tendai sect bylaw concerning temple family support.

> Article 6: Support for Temple Families in the Absence of the Head Priest
>
> [Clause 1]: In the event of the head priest's death or absence, the dharma-relative [temples with a specially recognized relationship with the temple] and other temples with a relationship with the temple must provide appropriate support for the temple family.
>
> Clause 2: The head priest in conjunction with the dharma-relatives and/or temple representatives may arrange the above methods for support in advance. However, the permission of the board of directors [of the juridical person] must be obtained.
>
> Clause 3: In case of Clause 1, when there is a temple family member at the temple who has the promise to obtain licensure as the temple head priest, then, in accordance with Article 4 Clause 1 of the bylaws governing selection of head priests and teaching center administrators, an interim head priest will be appointed who will care for and educate that family member until licensure is obtained.
>
> Clause 4: When the temple family member, in accordance with the above clause, obtains licensure as head priest, that person may become the temple's appointed head priest.[83]

The bylaws clearly relegate specific details regarding actual support to the local temples. Yet they provide no concrete support for temple wives. They also make clear that the preferred method of support is to pass the position of head priest on to someone from within the temple family. This preference serves to pressure temple wives into the motherhood role. This pressure is confirmed by a 1980 survey of Chizan branch Shingon sect temple wives, in which it was found that the majority planned to rely on grooming a successor to guarantee their security in the event of the head priest's death.[84]

In most instances, where a successor is not present or ready from within the temple family, care for the bereaved temple family is left to the temple's dharma-relatives (*hōrui*). Dharma-relatives are temples that have a relationship to each other that is registered within the sect. They form a support group for each other. Priests from related temples assist with ceremonies and provide advice for each other; they also often sit on the board of directors of each other's juridical person. Unfortunately, if the head priest of a temple dies and there is no cooperation from the dharma-relatives regarding support for the temple family, "the temple family is left in an extremely unfortunate position," as one priest remarked.[85] As the case cited at the beginning of this chapter shows, sects first hope that the issue will be resolved within the temple. Barring that, sects hope that the dharma-relatives will solve the problem. Should these methods fail, the local sect office is expected to mediate. Only after all these avenues have been tried will the main sect office intervene—if it intervenes at all.

To avoid disputes and encourage the timely departure of temple families from the temple after the head priest's death, most sects have established life insurance and retirement programs. The Tendai sect, for example, developed a program through Chiyoda Life Insurance and engaged in a concerted effort to enroll temple families in the program, hoping that this action would encourage them to prepare for the eventuality of retiring out of the temple after the head priest passed away.[86] While sects also encourage local temples to develop retirement plans, most do not have the funds to support an adequate program.

Despite the inadequacy of most insurance and retirement programs, some individuals insist that temple wives should leave the temple, just as company wives must leave company housing. "What about when the head priest dies before the temple wife? It is only natural that she should leave the temple. It's the same as company wives and their children; there is no way they can stay on in company housing."[87] To this a temple wife responds,

> In the case of companies, [families] collect retirement funds when they leave company housing. One who manages to work through to retirement gets probably about 20,000,000 yen. Last year 180 Sōtō sect head priests

died. That means that there were 180 people who had to leave the temple (company housing). [Multiplying] 180 [by] 20,000,000 [gives] 3,600,000,000. The juridical person Sōtō sect had an operating budget last year of 4,750,000,000. Take 3,600,000,000 from that. If we do as Mr. Minami says and treat the support of those who leave the temple as in regular society, this is what will happen. If he says, "We can do it, no problem," well then that is just fine by the temple wives.[88]

The temple wife's point is clear. Regardless of problems concerning their religious status or the priest's world-renouncer status, temple wives cannot be treated as company wives. Temples and sects do not have the financial wherewithal to attempt such an endeavor.

A third option often presented is that of temple family members joining the priesthood themselves. In particular, critics often claim that temple wives ought to become nuns if they strongly desire to remain at the temple. Only 2 percent of temple wives in a 1980 survey responded that they would want to take over the temple if their husband passed away, and in a 2001 survey only 7.2 percent expressed interest in undergoing training as nuns.[89] For most this is an unrealistic option. Few of the sects of Temple Buddhism have the facilities to train a large number of female priests.[90] Moreover, training programs are two months to three years long, depending on the sect. The daily schedule of temple wives does not permit them to take such lengthy amounts of time off.

Many other barriers exist for those temple wives who might choose the priesthood. Foremost is the attitude of most male priests. Evidence strongly suggests that they prefer their wives to remain housewives. Priests frequently argue that women do not wish to become nuns because a nun must shave her head. However, one temple wife, who is also a priest, pointed out that the problem is generally not that temple wives are against shaving their heads; it is that priests are against having bald wives. Within traditional conservative gender ideal types, when a woman shaves her head to become a nun, she is becoming a professional. But as we have seen, professional women are generally accepted only if they also give up family life. Those who fail to choose one or the other path are open to scrutiny. In one case, a temple wife who became a priest and sought to succeed her father as head priest claims that *danka* members spread rumors questioning her sexual life.[91] This embarrassment helps to demonstrate the difficulties temple wives face should they choose to become ordained as priests and wish to be accepted both as priest and as mother. Moreover, a priest whose wife chooses to ordain often meets with varying degrees of ridicule from fellow priests, specifically because his wife has transgressed traditional role boundaries.[92] In this way, male priests are similar to their counterparts in the business world. They can accept a woman who is a professional at the expense of being a mother and homemaker, but they find it difficult to accept a woman who attempts to be both mother and professional. This is one reason why many priests (and many nuns as well) do not consider nuns who marry to be real nuns.

Despite the many barriers to becoming a nun, a growing number of temple wives are seeking ordination. Within the Tendai sect, those who undergo priestly ordination must undertake the same training as other Tendai priests. In the Tendai sect, there is no special program for female priests. All prospective priests (male and female) must undergo the two-month training course on Mt. Hiei at Gyōin. The experience of temple wives who have become priests varies from person to person. Some choose to work alongside their husbands as assistant priests; others choose to return to their previous position and confirm their faith through their work as temple wives. In addition to a growing number of temple wives seeking priestly ordination, there appears to be a growing number of temple daughters seeking priestly ordination. Nishioka Ryōkō, at the time the president of the Tendai sect Diet and a member of the Board of Directors of Taishō University, claims this trend is visible at Taishō University. He states that more and more temple daughters are seeking ordination early on and training for the priesthood in college. This is especially so for temples that lack a male heir. He argues that the sect must begin to take this trend seriously and consider the possibility of daughters as heirs to the temple.[93] His comments are echoed in those of a Sōtō sect priest and sect Diet member who, regarding one *danka* member's attempt to prohibit a temple wife who had been ordained as a priest to succeed as head priest, stated, "It's not like the head priest's children are going to be limited to boys. Since there is a daughter with the desire to do it, the *sōdai* should strive to help raise her. Basically, the *sōdai* have no right to tell her to get out of the temple."[94] Statistics would seem to support the potential to fill vacant head priest positions with female priests, including the wives and daughters of temples. Currently 11 percent of all priests are female but only 2.76 percent of all head priests are female (table 4).

Though still few in number, temple wives who seek priestly ordination represent what some believe is the ideal solution to clerical marriage—a family of clerics. However, married female priests represent a challenge to those nuns who define their legitimacy over the male priesthood by their adherence to

TABLE 4

Numbers of Female Head Priests and Priests in Ten Sects

SECT	HEAD PRIESTS (% OF TOTAL)/ PRIESTS (% OF TOTAL)	RECENT TRENDS CONCERNING FEMALE PRIESTS	TONSURE	TRAINING CENTERS
Tendai: 3,350 temples; 4,007 priests	99 (2.9%)/ 528 (13%)	Number is increasing: 7.8% in 1992, 11% in 1999.	Required only for Shidokegyō, Kanjō, and Tōdanjukai	Taishō University Eizan Gakuin, area training centers (gakuryō). Training at Gyōin on Mt. Hiei is required.
Kōyasan Shingon: 3,629 temples; 3,437 priests	Unknown/ 312 (4.9%)	Number is decreasing: 5.9% in 1992, 5.2% in 1999.	Required only for Kegyō	Kōyasan University, Kōyasan Nisōgakuin
Shingon-Chizan branch: 2,896 temples; 3,437 priests	Unknown/ 45 (1.3%)	Slight increase. In 1995, Chizan Nisō no kai was formed.	Required only for Shidokegyō, Kanjō, and Tōdanjukai	Chishaku Senshūgakuin, Naritasan Kangakuin, Chizan Kyōgaku Kenshūjo, Taishō University
Shingon-Buzan branch: 2,641 temples; 3,081 priests	75 (2.8%)/ 109 (3.5%)	Number is increasing. In 2003 a symposium on female head priests was held at Honzan.	Required only for Tokudo, Shidokegyō, and Kanjō. Close-cropped hair is permissible during training.	Jisō Senmon Dōjō, Senshūgakuin, Taishō University (for Shūgaku [sectarian studies] only
Jōdo: 7,077 temples; 10,553 priests	Unknown/ 841 (7.9%)	Number is increasing: 7.3% in 1993, 7.9% in 2003.	Only required when entering the Denshūdankai Dōjō	Jōdoshū Nisō Dōjō, Ritsushi Yōsei Kōza
Jōdo Shinshū-Honganji branch: 10,310 temples; 7,549 priests	259 (2.5%)/ 1,811 (23.9%)	Number of head priests is increasing.	Not required	Chūō Bukkyō Gakuin, Tokyo Bukkyō Gakuin, Ryōkoku University Distance education programs, etc.
Rinzai-Myōshinji branch: 3,389 temples; 3,461 priests	102 (3%)/ 135 (3.9%)	Approx. 80% serve as head priests.	Not required	Ten'eji Nishū Senmon Dōjō

Table 4 (continued)

SECT	HEAD PRIESTS (% OF TOTAL)/ PRIESTS (% OF TOTAL)	RECENT TRENDS CONCERNING FEMALE PRIESTS	TONSURE	TRAINING CENTERS
Sōtō: 14,723 temples; 16,621 priests	475 (4.3%)/ Unknown	Number is decreasing: 5.1% in 1985, 4.3% in 1995.	Not required	Aichi Senmon Nisō Dōjō, Niigata Senmon Nisō Dōjō, Fuji Senmon Nisō Dōjō
Nichiren: 5,188 temples; 8,211 priests	273 (55)/ 1013 (12%)	Number is increasing. In 2001 the training center that did not require tonsure was closed.	Must crop hair to 5mm or less for ceremony to become a head priest. Those who graduated from the training center with no tonsure requirement wear a hat.	Training center is opened once each year to new applicants.

Source: Jimon kōryū, March 2004: 87.
*The total number of priests and temples does not include those sects and branches for which total numbers of female priests and head priests were not available. The totals are based on responses from each sect with the exception of the Sōtō sect, which is based on a 1995 survey.

monastic vows of celibacy. Such nuns fear that widespread acceptance of the marriage of nuns could lead to the same secularization that they see among their male counterparts.

In any case, becoming a priest does not guarantee that the temple wife can take over her husband's temple. In most cases, especially if the decision to become a priest was not made early on, *danka* members prefer a male priest. They are often willing to work with the temple wife to secure a husband for her daughter, or to encourage her son to succeed his father, but they are rarely open to having the wife or daughter switch roles and become their priest.[95] For example, there was one case before the courts in 2002 in which *danka* members refused to allow the ordained daughter of a temple priest to succeed as head priest despite the backing of the sect. They expressed fears that she would turn the temple into a nunnery on the one hand and concerns about her private life on the other. Prejudice against female priests also stems from the view that they are second-best to male priests for performing funerals and memorial services. Gender expectations, as well as *danka* members' expectations regarding local priests (as opposed to the ideal of real priests), appear to trump attitudes regarding real priests that are shaped by images of precept maintenance, celibacy included.

Though many temple wives seek change, effecting change within the sect is difficult for them. For example, although the Tendai sect established a Temple Family Information Center (Jizoku Sōdanjo) within the Social [Services] Division (Shakaibu) of its administration, the center is under the leadership of male priests and allows little input from women. Temple wives in the Tendai sect also have no direct representation within other aspects of sect administration. The realm of sect administration is understood in Tendai and other sects as the domain of the world-renouncer. As is common in most sects, Tendai temple wives must have a priest speak for them before the governing Diet. One temple wife writes that "women obtained the right to vote in our country after the Second World War. Half a century later and temple wives have yet to obtain the right to vote in the sect Diet."[96] A recent survey of sect Diet members representing ten of the major sects of Temple Buddhism revealed that only 17.6 percent held any interest in the topic temple families or temple wives.[97] With such minimal support, it is little wonder that some temple wives seek direct representation within the sect.

Lack of representation reflects the conservative gender views male priests hold. Regarding male priests in the prewar period, the Jōdo Shin sect doctrinal instructor, Watanabe Noriko writes, "It must have been terribly difficult for male priests to understand the liberation thought of the 'new woman.'"[98] This attitude toward women remains strong. Lack of representation also stems from the division assumed within the sect between official, active members who comprise the sect (i.e., the priesthood or world-renouncers) and the secular world.

Lack of representation also stems from minimal participation by most temple wives in efforts to bring about change. This lack of participation is the result of several factors. Some temple wives have no interest in changing things. They are content with the life they lead. Others are against moves by members who seek status as religious within the sect and whom they consider to be radical. They either believe in the system as it is structured or believe that rank as a religious practitioner is not appropriate. Others are simply too busy. Their temple duties leave them little free time for participation.[99] Finally, many priests are against their wives' participation in such activities—because being onstage is not the "proper" place for a woman and because such activities distract a wife from performing her duties at the temple.[100]

TEMPLE WIFE PRECEPT ORDINATION: A FAILED EXPERIMENT?

One response to the various problems surrounding the existence of temple wives has been the founding of temple wife ordination ceremonies by Tendai and other sects of Temple Buddhism. It was hoped that the ordination system for temple wives would openly integrate them into sect administrative and religious structures. Integration was understood as critical to guaranteeing the financial security of temple wives and to making sure that they would perform their proper roles at the temple (in particular, to educate the heir and to support the priest). In the case of the Tendai sect, the ceremony was called the temple wife precept ordination ceremony (*jiteifujin tokudo*; hereafter, temple wife ordination).

> It goes without saying that temple wives play a number of important roles within the temple, from proselytizing *danka* members to educating the heir. . . . We would like to switch to a system whereby, because we want them to fulfill their important roles as temple wives, they are not referred to as the head priest's wife. Those temple wives who undergo the temple wife precept ordination ceremony are registered in the temple wife register and licensed.[101]

The Tendai sect's temple wife ordination was begun in 1996. As the Division of Doctrine (Kyōgakabu) wrote that year:

> Up until now "temple wife" (*jiteifujin*) was just a way to refer to the head priest's wife. Therefore, the "temple wife precept ordination ceremony" was instituted. As a form of license, along with reaffirming the self-awareness of being a temple wife through study retreats, it will give the unshakable faith of being supported by the Buddha's compassion and allow the courage needed to engage in each day's activities. Of course, it would be best if temple wives took the precepts of a world-renouncer and became priests. But, on the other hand, in order to make clear the role of the temple wife and her position vis-à-vis *danka* members and the faithful, the temple wife precept ordination ceremony was felt to be the most appropriate step.[102]

The temple wife ordination was based on the priestly precept ordination. In temple wife ordination, the Ten Good Precepts are administered along with the

Three Refuge Precepts (sankiekai), and bodhisattva vows (shiguseigan) are taken.[103] The main differences between priestly and temple wife ordination were that the temple wife did not have to shave her head and was not granted priestly robes during the ceremony.

Shortly after its official creation, temple wives began to take the temple wife ordination. Ordinations were conducted at special gatherings. The first were in the Kanagawa and Gunma teaching districts, followed by one on Mt. Hiei at the annual meeting of the Tendai Sect Temple Wives Federation. In the following months, ordination ceremonies were held in one teaching district after another. Participants numbered from as few as ten to more than seventy. By 2000, the majority of Tendai sect temple wives had taken the temple wife ordination.[104]

This new system was not the first such opportunity for temple wives to seek ordination or initiation. On several occasions in the past (postwar), some temple wives were given special permission to undergo priestly ordination without shaving their head. Such individuals were retroactively recognized as licensed temple wives under the new ordination system if they filed proper paperwork with the sect headquarters. More frequently, temple wives in the past were given the lay precepts. This situation led to some confusion when the new system was begun. One priest stated at the Tendai sect's annual Diet meeting in 2000 that many temple wives in his district were upset.[105] They had undergone a lay ordination that was given only once every fourteen years by the head priest of Tendai at a special ceremony in their district. Those who had undergone this special lay ordination believed they should be granted the same temple wife licensure as those who underwent the new ordination. The sect Division of Doctrine declined their request, because they had only been given the lay precepts and not the Ten Good Precepts. In addition to receiving lay precepts, many temple wives also had the opportunity to undergo a special initiation called kechien kanjo.[106] Although not an ordination, it had long been used as a way to encourage deepening of faith among temple wives and danka members. It did not, however, count toward recognition as a temple wife under the new temple wife ordination system.

The new temple wife precept ordination ceremony was instituted on a five-year trial basis. The tenure of the trial expired in 2000. In a move that surprised many and made headlines in all newspapers covering religion, the Tendai sect announced that the ordination system would be discontinued. I will make clear the reasons for this shortly.

What was the purpose of the temple wife ordination? Tendai officials quoted above make it appear that the goal of the ordination was to grant a special status to temple wives within the sect to encourage them in their work at the temple. A temple wife was no longer to be just the head priest's wife; the term "temple wife" was to be the title of an office that required the licensure of ordination. Moreover, the status of the temple wife was to be recognized as religious in nature.

> It is not overstating things to say that temple wives are [a kind of] religious. Even so, just because they married the head priest or were born and raised at a temple, there must be some doubt concerning the spiritual foundation supporting a temple wife. On the other hand, if some kind of spiritual support exists, they can take confidence in the daily affairs of the temple and be satisfied. That spiritual underpinning can be found through taking the temple wife precept ordination.[107]

Furthermore, temple wife ordination was instituted to ensure that the temple wife would receive support from the sect. But although the temple wife ordination clearly was designed to grant temple wives secure, recognized status within the sect, the quantity and quality of that support was not clearly defined.

Furthermore, the type of status granted through the temple wife ordination was ambiguous. It can be read as a status within the administrative organization that confirms certain rights to support, but it can also be read as status as a religious within the sect. The fact that the temple wife ordination was based on the priestly ordination and is understood differently from lay ordination points to this conclusion: "It is only natural that your outlook and that of the average *danka* member's should differ. In that sense the significance of taking the temple wife ordination, which is based on the priestly ordination and receiving the precept body from the Buddha, is without measure."[108] While it is clear that the temple wife ordination was understood to be different from lay ordination, it is also clear that it was not to be considered on the same level as that of priests. It granted neither the right to teach or to perform rituals nor the duty to proceed to higher levels of priestly initiation and training.[109] This difference was present even in the pricing structure for ordination: 30,000 yen for priestly ordination, 20,000 yen for temple wife ordination, and zero yen for lay ordination.[110]

Temple wives who made firm the foundation of their faith through taking the temple wife ordination were repeatedly encouraged to engage in proselytizing efforts. However, they were encouraged to do so not as priests might (e.g., through sermons expounding on Buddhist doctrine), but rather by example, through their lives as wives and mothers. At times, fellow wives encouraged them. One writes, "With [the temple wife ordination] as a base, we temple wives, too, should deepen our studies and, with confidence and pride, engage in a form of proselytizing that as [it is done by] wives, is a different, more homey type than the proselytizing done by the head priest."[111] Encouragement also came from the sect: "Temple wives have an ease of mind and approachableness that the head priest does not. It is important to be a good talking partner and advisor to those who come to visit the temple. It is also important to participate in many activities and, through methods such as providing use of the temple grounds, to become involved in the local community."[112]

Both of these statements show a clear gendering of roles. A temple wife is more "homey" and "approachable" than her male counterpart, the head priest. The sect clearly hopes that temple wives will play a role within the religious operations of the temple, but only as women in a specifically gendered fashion. This gender division of religious labor applies not only to temple wives, however; it can also be seen in the attitude of male priests toward nuns. A nun is often seen as the "office lady" of the temple world, there to serve men tea. This is most ironic, considering that many nuns pride themselves on maintaining an image of what a real priest should be (e.g., celibate). Thus, temple wives may have gained recognized space within the sect through the temple wife ordination, but it is still a gendered and subordinated space: the world-renouncer-wife to a world-renouncer-husband.

When the temple wife ordination was first implemented within Tendai, there was discussion about making it the first step toward the creation of a temple wife track within the religious ranks. Some suggested that temple wives should be able to undergo training to become doctrinal instructors after ordination.[113] Many temple wives seek equal status, but others do not desire equality as religious actors at the temple. The Tendai sect plan to advance temple wives from temple wife ordinands to doctrinal instructors disappeared with the end of the temple wife ordination system in 2000.

Related to the creation of a status space between religious professional (however gendered in its nature) and layperson, the temple wives ordination was also implemented to confirm temple wives in their role as assistants to the head priest: "The performance of morning, evening, and memorial services in the main hall by the head priest are all in the service of the Buddha. The work of the temple wife is to support the priest in this work and to create an atmosphere in which he can further the work of the temple."[114] The role of assistant also demonstrates the gendered role of temple wives. Like everyday wives, temple wives are expected to care for the household, thereby freeing their husbands to dedicate themselves full-time to their work. However, in the case of temple wives, the household is a religious site, and the children (at least the male children) are the disciples of the head of that site (who is both head priest and husband). The temple wife, therefore, was given special recognition and the imprimatur of authority through the temple wife ordination.

Finally, the temple wife ordination was begun to further systematize the role of the temple wife as mother to the successor to the position of head priest. The temple wife ordination itself was first considered within the Tendai sect by the Special Committee to Study the Temple Successors Problem (Jiin Kōkeisha Taisaku Tokubetsu Iinkai).[115] The goal of creating good (temple) mothers is clearly stated in the *Temple Wives Handbook*. "Temple wives should first see to the [religious] instruction of the temple family [i.e., their children] and give life to the teachings of the Buddha within their role as mother and their work as wife."[116] With the foundation in faith built through the temple wife ordination, temple wives were expected to see first to the instruction and indoctrination of their children.

Through their work as exemplary mothers, they were expected to be able to lead *danka* members by example. "If you cannot succeed at instructing your own family, you will not succeed with *danka* members. Implanting the seeds of faith within the family will, in turn, lead to instruction of *danka* members."[117] The effort to systematize the role of motherhood most clearly demonstrates the difficulties the sect and temple wives face in coming to terms with the institutionalization of householding world-renouncers. Through ordination, the temple wife was given special religious status to authenticate her presence at the temple and her role as the educator of the head priest's disciple, her son. The ordination also guaranteed her space within the administrative structure of the sect, allowing her protection (at least in word) in the event of the head priest's death. Whereas the sect openly declared the purpose of the temple wife ordination to be that of granting secure status to temple wives, thereby guaranteeing them protection within sect bylaws, the granting of religious status can be seen as an attempt to solve the clerical marriage problem by making the temple family a world-renouncing family (husband and wife both ordained). "Holding dear the history of Mt. Hiei, no matter how secularized [temples have become], as long as you are in a temple of the world-renouncer organization—the Tendai sect—you must hold to the spirit [of the precepts]. This is the [purpose of the] temple wife ordination that this sect is trying to implement now."[118] Temple wives were allowed recognition and, therewith, the basis for support, but only within prescribed gendered boundaries: they were expected to be good wives, wise mothers, and persevering assistants. These are the very qualities of the traditional Japanese housewife; though growing weaker, such qualities are still portrayed by the state and media as the ideal for women. It is as a living ideal type, thereby inspiring the laity, that temple wives are to perform their religious role within the sect.

Recognizing the various problems with the way temple wife ordination was implemented, the Tendai sect ceased this ordination system at the end of 2000. Despite the support of many temple wives, there were complaints regarding the way in which the system had been established and administered. Many elderly temple wives were led to question their previous status. Had they not acted out of deep faith before? Why must they be ordained now?

Moreover, the system was seen by some as a purely cosmetic move, an attempt to paper over the serious problem of lack of financial support for a temple wife in case of the death of her husband. Although the system clarified the place of temple wives within the sect, it did little in the way of providing concrete measures for assistance to them. Furthermore, the system was developed without consultation with leaders of the Temple Wife Federation. In short, there was no input by the very people it was going to affect the most. This exclusion from the decision-making process only served to highlight the outsider status of temple wives and helped to undermine the sect's attempts to include temple wives within the sect. Finally, ordination may have served to alienate those who had no interest in furthering their religious commitment to the sect. The temple wife ordination bylaws forced all temple wives who wished support and recognition to take the temple wife ordination, regardless of the extent of their desire to pursue deeper religious commitments.

The temple wife ordination system had been aimed at creating faithful temple wives. It was hoped that through its implementation, temple wives would be incorporated into the sect and its worldview. If this could be accomplished, problems centering on the place of temple wives in the sect, privatization of the temple, and support for temple wives would be solved. In some ways the temple wife ordination system was similar to the Light Up Your Corner Movement, which seeks to (re)integrate *danka* members into the sect. The Light Up Your Corner Movement has yet to realize its potential because it has not developed a system for bringing *danka* members into the decision-making processes of the sect. They remain in subordinate and outsider roles within the sect, which still sees itself as a world-renouncing organization. In a similar fashion, temple wife ordination was in danger of failing to meet its goals from the beginning because the male priests who created it failed to consult temple wives and because it failed to address the critical problem of the status of the clergy themselves. In effect, rather than seeking to come to terms with the secularization of the clergy (to come off the mountain, as it were), the Tendai sect attempted to create a sect of married world-renouncers. Moving away from the rhetoric of renunciation is difficult. For centuries, the sects of Temple Buddhism have relied on such rhetoric for their legitimation. Rather than abandoning the rhetoric, the Tendai sect, attempted through temple wife ordination, to breathe new life into it. Even if temple wife ordination had survived, there is little evidence that it would have succeeded in bridging the gap between the rhetoric of renunciation and the ideal image held by priests and the public alike of what a real priest is supposed to be and the reality of married priests engaged (however sincerely) in seeing to the ritual needs of their *danka* members and the financial needs of their temples.

Finally, as we have seen, Temple Buddhism rests atop the traditional family system. Temples, and through them sects, rely on the support of *danka* families. To secure this base, sects of Temple Buddhism engage in efforts to maintain the traditional family system, such as the Tendai sect's Light Up Your Corner Movement. In this attempt to place temple wives within the religious and administrative structures of the sect, and thereby to provide them with the authoritative base to be part of a role-model family, sect leaders not only sought to address the problem of the existence of temple wives, they also sought to create a strong base for teaching family values and thereby to strengthen *danka* families. *Danka* families provide one leg of the base upon which Temple Buddhism rests, while temple families provide another. In short, the world-renouncing sects stand atop lay families and temple families. In response, the world-renouncer, as role model for what householders are capable of becoming, is today put forward as a role model for household life itself—an inherent contradiction that it appears the sects of Temple Buddhism are not yet prepared to face.

7 Money and the Temple
Law, Taxes, and the Image of Buddhism

[The new religion] Aum is reproached for taking illegal offerings and selling supernatural powers, but there are temples that charge exorbitant prices for posthumous names and conduct rites for aborted fetuses.[1]

There's nothing at all embarrassing [about the fact that fees for posthumous names play a large role in temple finances]. It's only embarrassing when some priests think to use that money improperly.[2]

Regarding your question about a standard for donations, there is no such standard under Buddhist Law (the law of world-renouncers). But in Japan, which is a country ruled by law (worldly law), [temples] exist under the Religious Juridical Persons Law. And, I think, *danka* members have the duty to support their common property, "Religious Juridical Person xxx Temple," and to protect the temple. In that sense, there are probably some temples that have set standards. You should definitely consult [about this] with the head priest of your temple. If that is too difficult, you can always reflect on the meaning of "donation" and offer what you feel comfortable with.[3]

I have identified a variety of difficulties in maintaining a world-renouncing institution while continuing householding practices. I will now explore the difficulties of maintaining a nonsecular institution, the temple, in a secular world. Much of the criticism currently aimed at Temple Buddhism stems from the economic activities of priests. Religion and money, it is commonly assumed, should not be overly familiar partners. And yet religious organizations, like the people who create and join them, need some measure of financial stability. I begin by reviewing the history of temple funding in Japan and then go on to examine the economic activities of temples today in this chapter and the next through the lenses of taxes and death, two things even Buddhist temples in Japan seem unable to escape. An examination of the taxation of temples will demonstrate how temples have come to be viewed as businesses and touristic sites rather than as religious organizations. Such an examination leads to a consideration of the changing nature of religious association in contemporary Japan.

Approaching the temple from the perspective of death, and in particular, the granting of posthumous precept names, allows further exploration of the problems temples face today as they seek ways to remain financially solvent and to perform traditional ritual roles (despite changing perceptions of the meaning of those roles) while at the same time combating images of professionalization, privatization, and commercialization.

Critiques of Buddhist affluence are nothing new. External and internal critics abound throughout the historical record. Buddhism in China, for example, was subjected to periodic persecutions, in which wealth amassed by temples was reclaimed by the state.[4] Critiques of the economic activities of Buddhist temples also appear from early on in the record of Buddhism in Japan. The Tendai sect was not immune. In 1571, Oda Nobunaga burned the temples of Mt. Hiei to the ground and slew countless priests in an effort to erase Enryakuji's political, military, and economic power. In the Edo period, Confucian and nativist critics chastised Buddhists for their wealth, claiming it was symptomatic of religious, if not legal, corruption. During the now famous Meiji persecutions of Buddhism, negative images of corrupt and wealthy priests were used to legitimize the seizure of temple properties and the defrocking of priests.[5] In short, there is no lack of evidence that, throughout Buddhism's history in Japan and elsewhere for that matter, the economic activities of priests and temples have been questioned.[6]

Questions regarding the economic activities of temples often arise from the assumption that Buddhist priests and temples are supposed to exist removed from the mundane realm of financial matters.[7] However, priests must meet the financial requirements of their temples. Despite assumptions regarding their supramundane position, priests and temples exist in the lived world and, therefore, have fiscal and legal obligations that must be met. Ritual supplies must be purchased, land managed, and properties maintained, and even proselytizing efforts require funding. In many ways, temples today face even greater demands on their coffers than did their predecessors. Modern temple administrators must worry about fire, liability, and theft insurance and, because most temples are now connected to power, gas, and water lines, utilities bills must also be paid. Temples housing priceless works of art may need to install burglar alarms.[8] Moreover, building or maintaining classically designed structures often requires hiring expensive specialists—leaving temples to decide whether a cheap but unattractive, nontraditional cement structure might be acceptable to their *danka* members and neighbors. Then too, because most priests now marry, they must draw a large enough salary to provide for their family. And as *danka* members move farther away, or as time constraints bind, the temple may have to purchase a car. All these considerations and others make the financial management of the average temple little different from that of a family business.[9] Indeed, temples are often referred to as a form of family business. Like long-time customers, *danka* members will ask when the son will be ready to take the reins, how his schooling is going, or what his marriage prospects look like.

It is this similarity to a business that invites criticism today. Critiques regarding economic activities often assume a clear division between the sacred and profane, between world-renouncer and householder. They fail to acknowledge how thoroughly enmeshed these realms are in everyday life. Such critiques bring to light scholarly and popular assumptions about what is, or is not, properly religious or Buddhist.

Before discussing the temple as seen from the perspective of taxes, it is necessary to place the contemporary debate over the economic activities of temples in Japan within a historical context. A brief history of how temples were funded in the past will serve as background for what their major funding sources and expenditures are today. A brief introduction to the legal status of the temple as a religious juridical person will then help to clarify certain issues related to the management and taxation of temples today.

TEMPLE FUNDING PAST AND PRESENT

In the Nara and Heian periods, temples derived funding from the imperial court or court nobles. From the later Heian and into the Kamakura period, funds began to come from private estates (*shōen*) owned and operated by the temples. Temple estates became so powerful, in fact, that Kuroda Toshio describes the society and politics of medieval Japan as dominated by three groups: *kuge*, the imperial court and aristocrats; *buge*, the government (*bakufu*) and samurai authorities; and *jike*, the leading religious establishments. Each of these was organized around family-like structures and derived its wealth from estates.[10] Kuroda demonstrates how the religious and sociopolitical systems of the time were mutually dependent. For example, rites for agriculture were supported by the state because they served as the ideological basis for land taxes.[11]

In the Kamakura period, a variety of new funding sources, which may also trace their roots back further, came into play. In addition to support from noble and warrior family households and income derived from temple estates, temples also came to rely on *kanjin*, or donation campaigns, for fund-raising.[12] As Janet Goodwin notes, changes in Buddhist fund-raising practices coincided with changes in political and economic structures. The shift during the Kamakura period from seeking support from high-placed patrons to seeking it from a broader social base reflected these changing structures. In general, "The needs of the lay community informed the way the Buddhist message was promoted and received, often reshaping both message and community."[13] This point applies to Buddhism in any period, contemporary Japan included.

A wide variety of funding sources, representing the diversity of Buddhist institutions that had developed by then, is found in the Edo period. The priests of many large temple complexes received state support in the form of stipends. Smaller local temples often relied on local community members for their income. In return for ritual services, such as funerals, families made offerings to the temple. Temples that housed religious objects of renown or that were home to religious practitioners of renown might have confraternities (kō) develop around them. These confraternities would often pay for the maintenance and upkeep of the objects or individuals around which they formed to worship. The statue of Kannon at Sensōji, a temple in Tokyo, is one such example.[14] Some temples also derived income from pilgrims. Other temples derived substantial portions of their income from renting out farmland, while still others leased land to the shops that sought to accommodate pilgrims and other visitors to the temple. In addition, some temples earned income through the sale of medicines.[15] As a rule, temples relied on a mix of several such sources.

In the modern and especially the contemporary periods, sources of income display even greater variety (table 5). This variety reflects the increased strain on temple coffers that occurred when lands were lost during the Meiji and postwar periods.[16] Confraternities continue to exist and in some areas (primarily rural) play an important role by providing a web of social interaction that serves to support the temple. There are women's groups, groups dedicated to a specific image, and ritual groups (such as nenbutsu groups).[17] Confraternities and similar support groups continue to develop around famous Buddhist practitioners such as those who undergo the kaihōgyō practice of the Tendai sect. Pilgrimages are also still a major source of income for some temples today. At times, temples team up with local authorities, and also with bus and train lines, to create or reinvigorate local pilgrimages.[18] These are designed to further Buddhist proselytizing efforts while also generating revenue for temples. City planners, local businesses, and bus and train lines cooperate because pilgrimages are thought to increase consumer traffic. Just as in the Edo period, when temples developed new rituals or aggressively marketed old ones, the modern period, too, has witnessed the development of new rituals. Mizuko kuyō (rites for aborted fetuses), for example, were developed and marketed by religious organizations, including

TABLE 5
Temple Income

SOURCE OF INCOME*	PERCENTAGE OF TOTAL
Funerals	35.5
Memorial services	36.5
Prayers	7.4
Offerings	2.9
Entrance fees	1.9
Graveyard-related	4.3
Real estate	4.1
Other	7.3

Source: Zen'nihon Bukkyō Seinenkai (2003).
*The sampling is rather small (349 respondents), but the table gives a rough idea of temple income across all types of temples.

temples, in the mid-1970s to mid-1980s.[19] In addition to deriving income from rituals and confraternities, many temples have employed their remaining properties to generate income. Everything from day-care centers to parking lots to vegetarian restaurants has been attempted.[20] Another form of income available to some temples today is grants and loans from governmental offices for the maintenance and housing of objects and buildings designated as local or national treasures. Such support is often limited, but it can be of great assistance. Temple properties designated as cultural assets also draw tourists to the temple and increase the temple's name recognition. However, such support also comes with requirements, such as making the object available for public view and maintaining the object, that often cost far more than the subsidies provided.[21] Each sect also has available its own intrasect loan program, through which temples can qualify for loans to repair and maintain structures.[22]

As with donation (*kanjin*) campaigns of the past, local donation drives provide another source of income. Unlike the campaigns of the Kamakura period, however, today's donation drives invariably take place within specific *danka* for local projects and through the temples of specific sects for sect-related national projects (such as the rebuilding of storm-damaged structures on Mt. Hiei following major storms in 1997 and 1998). Contemporary donation drives, therefore, rarely afford the opportunity to proselytize beyond *danka* members, and it appears

TABLE 6
Funeral Expenses

	GENERAL FUNERAL EXPENSES	PAYMENTS TO THE TEMPLE	TOTAL EXPENDITURE*
National average	1,504,000	486,000	2,366,000
Kantō A (Ibaragi, Tochigi, Gunma, Chiba prefectures)	1,018,000	400,000	1,651,000
Kantō B (Saitama, Tokyo, Kanagawa prefectures)	1,785,000	641,000	3,130,000
Kinki (Shiga, Mie, Nara, Wakayama, Osaka, Kyoto, Hyogo prefectures)	500,000	300,000	2,392,000

Source: Japan Consumer Association (Nihon Shōhisha Kyōkai) survey on funerals, September 2003; http://www.osoushiki-plaza.com/library/index-data.html.
*This includes other expenses such as catering.

that in many cases *danka* members perceive donations less as religious acts than as a price for membership in the *danka*. Donations are often seen as acts necessary to the care and maintenance of ancestors who are buried and memorialized at the temple, rather than as funding for the promotion and support of the sect and its goals. In informal questioning, however, some priests argued that donations should be seen as a form of Buddhist practice and confided that it is a struggle to instill that motivational understanding in their *danka* members.[23]

Funerals and related services, always an important asset, grew in importance in the postwar period as social and economic conditions changed.[24] Today the average amount paid to temples (nationwide) for funerals is 486,000 yen (the national average for the entire funeral, including donations to the temple, funeral company fees, etc., is 2,366,000 yen) (table 6). There is considerable variation by locale, however; for example, the Tokyo area average paid to temples for funerals is 641,000 yen.[25] Income derived from funerals does not stop with the funeral. Donations are accepted for a series of memorial services following the funeral and for special occasions such as Obon and Higan. The average donation at such times is over 10,000 yen.[26] Assuming seven deaths in a 250-household *danka* per year, the total income from funeral and memorial services (i.e., seven funerals and twenty-one memorials [first, third, and seventh]), would be 4,025,000 yen. This figure does not include Higan and Obon services, at which time most *danka* members can be expected to donate 3,000 to 10,000 yen. It also does not include money earned by the priest when he assists other priests at such services (this last figure is practically negated by the fact that the priest must generally pay out the same amount when others come to help him). This average figure is not a great sum of money, but is on a par with the salary of low to mid-ranked businessmen. This income, however, is not the priest's; it is the temple's. The priest's salary and other temple expenses are deducted from this.

Temples also derive income from graveyards. Such income results from the sale of rights to a grave site and from grave maintenance fees. In addition, only *danka* members are typically allowed to be buried in a temple's graveyard. This means that individuals seeking a plot for a family member cannot simply purchase one; they must purchase a lasting institutional relationship with the temple, and by extension with the sect. *Danka* members are often required to donate a small sum of money annually to the temple for its support.

In the 1980s, the number of grave sites available began to fall short of demand.[27] Responding to this situation, many stonecutter firms (*ishiya*)[28] began to seek partnerships with temples. Laws governing graveyards required that public interest corporations (which most temples were and are registered as) operate them. Since *ishiya* were not so registered, they could not begin new projects on their own. Instead, they turned to temples, whose names they borrowed. Many graveyards were built in this way, with the *ishiya* managing the property and the business and paying a percentage of the gross to the temple in return for using the temple's name. In some cases, either in conjunction with an *ishiya* or on their own, temples took out loans to finance graveyard expansion. During the years of Japan's bubble economy, such loans were not difficult to obtain, especially given the assets temples had to offer as collateral—namely, temple buildings and properties. While some temples took advantage of the boom to build and fill expanded graveyards, many others arrived late to the game. The bursting of the bubble financially crippled many such latecomers. Their graveyard projects ended up creating major financial strains, rather than solving them. In extreme cases, temples have been repossessed and sold off to repay loans.

If graveyards represent the physical tie of the dead and their survivors to the temple, and thus an important and lasting revenue stream, it is the funeral that creates that tie. Until about the mid-1970s, priests were often the first person called as death approached. The priest served to guide the family through the entire death process: praying for the deceased, scheduling the funeral, acting as go-between with a funeral company when necessary, and instructing the family in the practical social relations associated with death. Today, the business of the funeral has shifted out of the hands of the priest, and with it much of the support-service roles as well. By the mid-1980s, the role of funeral companies grew from providing materials and occasional manpower assistance to scripting, implementing, and managing the funeral from beginning to end. Funeral companies became full-service providers, guiding the bereaved through all the legal and social details of the funeral, and even providing the priest. Many began to enter into referral contracts with local temples. In the cities, in particular, where a large unaffiliated population exists, funeral companies came to serve as the intermediaries between temples and bereaved families. In exchange for referrals, funeral companies generated income by taking as much as 40 percent of the donation the priest received for the posthumous name given to the deceased.[29]

Efforts by temples to generate income to support temple activities such as festivals or building maintenance have come in for criticism. However, running a temple today is not the same as popular imagination might believe it was in the past. Long gone are the times, if they ever existed, when a monk might stake out a cave, mountaintop, or grove and begin practice. Today, there are forms to be filled out (zoning laws, building permits, local registration, etc.) and bills to be paid. Moreover, although a particularly adept monk might be able to make a living begging for his daily sustenance,[30] it is doubtful that the institutions and traditions that have developed over time could survive on begging alone. (The Tendai sect's total revenue for fiscal year 1998 was 1,051,000,000, yen with total expenditures matching.)[31] Furthermore, if hundreds of monks descended upon train stations during rush hour today, begging bowls in hand, or walked through neighborhoods begging from door to door, chaos would no doubt ensue.[32]

Critiques of the income-earning activities of Japanese Buddhists often stem from the perception that begging is the proper traditional method for raising funds to support temples and priests. Such critiques, sometimes comparing images of Buddhists elsewhere in Asia to images of Japanese Buddhists, fail to take into account the social, cultural, historical, and economic circumstances elsewhere in Asia that enable begging. They also fail to take into account that begging, though practiced, has not been the primary income source in those areas for a long time (if ever). The sociocultural institutions for the acceptance of begging activities do not exist in contemporary Japan. The image of begging monks, however, remains ingrained in popular (Western and Japanese) images of true Buddhist practice. Japanese Buddhist sects themselves work to perpetuate this image. For example, training centers associated with the Zen sects continue ritualized begging as part of their practices. The Tendai sect, though lacking localized ritual begging outings as part of training, conducts an annual Tendai sect all-Japan begging (*Tendai Nihon issei takuhatsu*) fund-raising drive. This drive is led by the Tendai *zasu* and is significant for its use of the image of traditional begging to raise funds for Tendai's social welfare activities.[33]

Whether through begging or not, temples need income. Maintaining a temple, especially one that may have structures of historical value, is expensive. Funds are needed to maintain structures, including refurbishing, and to pay for insurance. Funds are needed to pay the priest, and perhaps an assistant priest, a salary.[34] Funds are required to pay for staff (at larger temples this may mean several lay assistants, while at smaller temples this usually applies only to the priest's wife). Funds must be raised to pay an annual tithe to the sect (the tithe is calculated based on the rank of the temple and the number of households in the *danka*; in the case of the Tendai sect, fees based on temple rank were between 5,000 and 126,000 yen in 1994).[35] Funds must also be raised to pay for the annual tithe a priest must pay to the sect (this is calculated based on the priest's priestly rank, 6,000 to 88,000 yen in 1994). Liability insurance often must be paid. Although Japan is not known as a litigious nation, lawsuits are not unheard of, and many more suits are resolved before the courts become involved.[36] Advice columns for priests frequently deal with questions such as "Can the temple be held responsible for food poisoning from food served after a service?" or "If the temple car is involved in an accident, can the temple be held liable?"[37] Scheduled ceremonies and festivals need funding. Such funds are often raised on a case-by-case basis through requests for donations made to *danka* members. Finally, temple supplies are not inexpensive. Quality incense can cost as much as 20,000 yen for a week's supply; a priest's robe can cost as much as 3,000,000 yen or more; and ritual implements such as prayer beads and fans also are expensive.[38]

The pressure to raise the funds needed to maintain the temple and to meet the demands of *danka* members for ritual services (primarily funerals and memorial services) often forces priests away from striking out into new realms of proselytizing or social welfare. When attempts are made at creating new, or improving old, methods of proselytizing (such as re-creating pilgrimage routes), so strong is the bias against the intermixing of money and religion that such efforts, no matter how sincerely engaged in, are often seen as little more than thinly veiled attempts at fund-raising.

LAW AND THE TEMPLE: TEMPLES AS JURIDICAL PERSONS

To understand the legal status of Temple Buddhism in contemporary Japan, we need first to discuss the peculiar nature of temples as religious juridical persons.[39] What is a juridical person? In Japan today, there are two fundamental units granted rights and responsibilities under law: natural persons (*shizenjin*) and juridical persons (*hōjin*). "Natural persons" refers to human beings. "Juridical persons" refers to other entities established under law to which rights and responsibilities are attributed. Juridical persons may be further categorized as incorporated foundations (*zaidan hōjin*) and corporate persons (*shadan hōjin*). Incorporated foundations exist to gather funds, corporate persons to gather people, for a given purpose. Religious juridical persons fall between these two types and comprise a special case. Religious juridical persons are granted maximum freedom to organize their own administrative structures.

All religious juridical persons must meet three requirements to be certified. They must promulgate religious teachings, perform rituals and observances, and educate and nurture adherents. They must also provide an accessible place of worship. A household shrine (*kamidana*) in a private home, for example, will not suffice. Religious juridical persons are granted rights and responsibilities similar to those of natural persons. However, such rights are limited to actions falling within the boundaries of the three requirements described above. Furthermore, each religious juridical person is bound by its stated purpose, which must be made clear in its bylaws. For example, the Tendai sect's rules of incorporation (*shūsei*) state the following:

> This juridical person is established based on the teachings of Dengyō Daishi, founder of this sect. With the marvelous thought of the Lotus Sutra One Vehicle teachings as its base, it will strive to make the True Law flourish, and devote itself to the sacred task of saving sentient beings. It will hold in an inclusive relationship temples and teaching centers, and labor to educate and nurture the priests, *danka* members, and adherents of these. It will contribute to the building of a Buddha land and to the realization of Buddhahood by all. In addition, it will undertake the administrative and operative duties necessary to bring to fruition the goals of this sect.[40]

Bylaws also serve as contracts either between a religious juridical person and its constituent members (i.e., *danka* members) or with other religious juridical persons with which it has relations, such as the sect in the case of local temples (as seen in the statement of purpose cited above).

In addition to the three requirements, there are three aspects of the law that are often called the three pillars of the Religious Juridical Persons Law. These are the certification system (*ninshō seido*), public announcement system (*kōkoku seido*), and responsible officer position (*sekinin yakuin*). The certification system was designed to promote freedom of religion. The previous system was a permission-based system. In a permission-based system, an applicant must receive permission directly from government authorities to incorporate as a legally recognized religion and thereby is left at the mercy of the authorities. Under the certification system, an applicant need only meet the basic standards for incorporation required by law to receive legal status as a religious juridical person. The public announcement system requires that attempts be made to make adherents and other concerned third parties aware of certain actions taken by the religious juridical person. These actions include its establishment, its amalgamation with another organization, and the establishment or disestablishment of an inclusive relationship with another organization, as well as bankruptcy, disposal of assets, or rule changes associated with any of these actions.

The third pillar of the Religious Juridical Persons Law is the responsible officer position. There are several responsible officer positions: chief responsible officer (*daihyō yakuin*), responsible officer, short-term substitute chief officer (*daimusha*), and temporary responsible officer (*karisekinin yakuin/karidaihyō yakuin*). The law requires that religious juridical persons have a minimum of three responsible officers, one of whom is the chief responsible officer. (Together they constitute the board of directors.) The chief responsible officer represents and carries out the decisions of the board of directors. In cases where the bylaws do not stipulate voting procedure, the chief responsible officer is to be elected by a majority vote of the board of directors. The officers are responsible for all nonreligious functions of the juridical person. The role of a responsible officer is described in the legal advice section of *Kōhō Tendai* as follows: determine budgets, survey properties, purchase and sell properties, negotiate loans for the temple/juridical person, plan construction, carry out general administrative duties, establish and change bylaws, and enter into contracts with other juridical persons. The law does not specify how the officers are to be appointed. In the case of temple/juridical persons, the head priest often appoints them. Bylaws of temple/juridical persons regularly state that the chief responsible officer must be the head priest.

Though the temple today is popularly imagined as a place where rituals take place or as a tourist site, it must also be understood as a juridical person. Sects such as Tendai recognize this fact, even as it is often overlooked by scholars. A representative of the Law Division of the Tendai Sect Administrative Office (Tendaishū Hōmubu) stated the following.

> We would like the priests and temple wives to undertake religious activities in keeping with the purpose of the juridical person's founding and be conscious of the fact that the temple is entrusted to them from the Daishi [Saichō] and is the property of the Three Treasures[41] and is not private property, and [we would like them] to deepen their awareness of the temple, as regards [its position in] society, as a public welfare juridical person.[42]

In 1991, the sect mailed a Ministry of Education, Religious Affairs Section, pamphlet to all temples to increase awareness among head priests of the temple's status as a religious juridical person and thereby combat the privatization of the temple, while also preventing misunderstandings between priests and *danka* members regarding proper legal management of the temple.

TAXATION AND TEMPLES

Like all other institutions, temples are subject to taxation. Taxation is not a popular subject to raise. But taxes can be a window onto the world of Buddhist temples in Japan today. An examination of how temples are taxed brings to light Buddhist roles in debates over the relationship between state and religion, temple roles in local economies, popular stereotypes of money-hungry priests, new ritual forms, and even issues regarding temple succession. Moreover, an examination of temples through the lens of the tax code reveals not only how the state, but also how Buddhists and Buddhist Studies scholars envision Temple Buddhism.[43]

Popular opinion in Japan holds that temples are not taxed and that priests, therefore, are able to accumulate wealth quickly and live an easy life. This conception, combined with movie and television images of priests driving expensive cars and drinking fine *sake* in exclusive geisha clubs, feeds a general image of priests as corrupt. Temples are, however, subject to taxes, as are priests. Priests draw taxable salary from the temple, and many of the profit-generating activities of temples are taxed. To qualify for certain tax advantages, temples must be registered as juridical persons; that is, temples must meet government definitions of a religious organization as stipulated in the Religious Juridical Persons Law.

Temples registered as religious juridical persons, along with schools[44] and places such as senior citizen homes,[45] are treated as a form of public interest juridical person (kōeki hōjin). Specifically, they are given certain tax advantages because they are supposed to be of benefit to society. These tax advantages include exemption from property tax and income taxes on both properties and activities related to the purpose of the religious organization (as defined in its bylaws) and a reduced tax rate on for-profit ventures. Defining what is, or is not, related to the stated purpose of a religious organization, however, is difficult. Doctrine and ritual, it is often assumed, are easily and correctly termed religious, or properly Buddhist, in nature. But, what about activities undertaken to support doctrinal studies or ritual practices? Early in the postwar period, most such activities enjoyed tax-free status. For example, until temples began to build upscale high-rise apartment buildings, income derived from rental properties was not subject to taxation.[46] The public outcry around what appeared to be money-making ventures led to changes in the tax code to include rental properties as one of what eventually became thirty-two business ventures that were deemed taxable (albeit at a preferred rate).[47]

Even before the making of this list, income derived from various income-generating activities was required by law to be used for the temple, the sect or organization to which it belonged, religious groups supported by the temple, or public welfare activities. In short, the law was written to forbid personal or other misuse of temple funding by the head priest or others. It was not easy to determine misuse, however, and it was not until the 1995 Aum Shinrikyō incident (Aum was found responsible for sarin gas attacks on Tokyo subways) that close scrutiny of the use of income earned by religious organizations became a major governmental concern. A 1995 survey shows that 61.5 percent of respondents believe favorable tax treatment for religious juridical persons should end altogether. This survey was conducted shortly after the Aum incident, when news programs aired nightly views of the terrifying machinery Aum was able to acquire with its tax-free wealth. A second survey conducted at about the same time found 50 percent of respondents in favor of permitting government intervention in religious affairs (another survey found 82.5 percent felt the law should be changed to allow governmental checks on religions more readily).[48] Clearly, the Aum incident had far-ranging ramifications for all religious bodies in Japan.

Growing public suspicion regarding the behavior of priests and other religious professionals is reflected in movies such as Itami Jūzō's comedy Marusa no onna II (A Taxing Woman II), in which a tenacious tax collector goes after the ill-gotten gains of a leader of a new religion, and Kitano Takeshi's *Kyōso no tanjō* (The Birth of a Founder), which traces the creation of a religious movement by a con artist. Later films such as *I Have No Grave*, in which a woman travels the country looking for a grave site and encounters one money-hungry priest after another, build on the popular image of greedy Buddhist priests engaged in questionably religious activities in their pursuit of money.

Local as well as national lawmakers and bureaucrats, starving for new forms of revenue, have encouraged greater public scrutiny of religions, especially their tax-exempt status. In the early 1980s, the National Tax Agency (Kokuzeichō), along with local tax offices, stepped up tax audits of religious organizations, including Buddhist temples. Many of these audits revealed extensive use of creative bookkeeping on the part of some priests. Such revelations only served to encourage the popular image of greedy priests. However, the majority of poorly kept books can more likely be explained by the lack of training in bookkeeping on the part of priests than by greed. Before the promulgation of the Religious Juridical Person Law, little consideration was needed or given to accounting. For example, the practice of paying of priestly salaries is relatively new (postwar). Previously, there had been no need to separate a paid managerial role from a paid ritual role. Therefore, until tax offices began aggressively auditing them, many priests saw no need to draw a salary; living expenses were drawn from donations, as were temple expenses. Questions regarding this topic appear frequently in the trade journal *Monthly Head Priest* (Gekkan jūshoku) throughout the 1980s. Furthermore, formal priestly training does not include instruction in practical managerial matters. Buddhist universities such as Taishō University offer courses on law and the temple, but these are not required of all priests.

Some activities on the current list of thirty-two taxable activities clearly appear to stray from obvious religious purposes, most notably, that of running a beauty parlor. Most temple activities, however, surrender less readily to categorization. For example, graveyards are often described as the lifeblood of Japanese Buddhism. So integral to temple ritual and financial life are funerals and graveyards that Japanese Buddhism has earned the derogatory title funeral Buddhism. Legally speaking, however, only those graveyards that are run directly by the temple, and that are sectarian in nature, qualify for tax-exempt status. Nondenominational graveyards, a popular choice among temples looking to expand their economic base today, are taxable because, although religious activities take place there, they are not tied directly to the sectarian character of the temple.[49]

Many other activities designed to support a temple financially are seen as simply cultural or habitual activities and are not often considered religious by scholars and others. For example, some temples derive a substantial portion of their income from the sale of religious objects. The purchase of protective charms and amulets, fortune lots, and the like by visitors to temples is considered by many, both scholars and the general public, merely a secular custom. In *Practically Religious*, however, George Tanabe and Ian Reader, forcefully argue that such objects are not simply part of a secular cultural tradition, but are representative of Japanese this-worldly religious practices. The Japanese tax office agrees, though a different measure is used. Such objects are judged religious and the money paid a donation because they are priced beyond a reasonable level. The money used for their purchase is considered money "thrown away," or spent without expectation of reasonable return (i.e., a donation). However, similar objects have been the point of contention in the past. In 1973, Zenkōji, a temple in Nagano prefecture, entered into a lasting conflict with local tax collectors when it began to sell prayer beads for the same price as that charged by gift-shop vendors on the temple grounds. The tax office ruled that, because the beads were similarly priced, they were simply goods for sale and that, therefore, proceeds from their sale were taxable.[50]

The line between so-called real Buddhist practice and secular or customary practice is further blurred when the tax office turns its attention to the priest. For example, as we have seen, most temples today are passed on from father to son. Father thus becomes master, and son, disciple. It might be assumed that the son's tuition and other fees for attending a Buddhist college and majoring in Buddhism could be counted as temple expenses and not as part of the priest's taxable salary because the son is the successor to the position of head priest. According to the tax collector, however, the priest as a private individual must pay a son's tuition. Any money taken from the temple for such purposes is considered taxable salary. However, expenses incurred after becoming a temple priest, such as costs incurred attending annual training courses and the like, can be deducted from temple expenses and need not be considered as taxable income. In this respect, temples are treated as business corporations. The head of a corporation cannot expect the company to pay for his child's education, even if the child is marked to take over someday. However, a company can pay for employee training, and the employees need not pay tax on the training they receive.

At the same time, this treatment of temple succession ignores the fact that in many Buddhist sects in Japan today, much of the fundamental training for the priesthood occurs at Buddhist colleges as part of the regular curriculum for young priests. For example, Buddhist colleges, not Buddhist temples, provide the setting for contemporary debates over doctrine. The idealistic image of scholar-priests debating points of doctrine in mountaintop temples lingers in the popular imagination, but intense doctrinal debate is today far more likely to be found in academic journals published by scholar-priests tenured at Buddhist colleges.

The equation of temples, understood as juridical persons, with businesses is one subtle way in which the tax code serves to conflate images of temples with images of businesses. Indeed, it is precisely at the intersection of temple economics and market society that the contemporary commercialization of religious association can be seen. The Kyoto city tourism tax case demonstrates the extreme difficulty of any attempt to cordon off the so-called purely religious from the so-called mundane as an object of either taxation or study. In particular, I will show how debates that have developed around the taxation of temples in Kyoto reveal current views of the temple as a tourist site, rather than a place of religious practice, and of priests as businessmen, rather than world-renouncers.

TAKING ON THE TEMPLES: TAXING THE RELIGIOUS

In 1999, Kyoto city officials and representatives of the Kyoto Buddhist Association (Kyōto Bukkyōkai) shook hands and smiled before press photographers. Headlines read, "Seventeen years of hostility between the city and temples ends at last," but the roots of the feud actually stretched back more than forty years, to 1956. At that time, Kyoto officials sought to construct their city as the cultural tourism center of Japan. Officials planned projects, such as the construction of a culture center, concert hall, and improved roads for tourist traffic. However, the city was in debt and was forced to hunt for new sources of income. Mayor Takayama proposed a cultural tourism facilities tax (bunka kankō shisetsuzei), which would tax visitors to popular tourist attractions (primarily temples). Temples opposed the tax, but the city council readily passed it, and the minister for home affairs approved it shortly thereafter. After one year of debate, the temples cooperated, and the tax went into effect in 1957. When it expired, the mayor (still Takayama) sought its renewal under a new rubric—special tax for cultural preservation (bunka hogo tokubetsuzei). Once again, the city council passed the tax, and the minister for home affairs approved it. However, the temples reacted much more severely than before. To placate temple protests, the mayor limited the tax to five years and signed a promise that the city would never again levy such a tax. The tax went into effect in 1964. Together, the two tax measures brought nearly 1.4 billion yen into the city's coffers.

A little over ten years after the second tax lapsed, the new mayor, Mayor Imagawa, proposed a similar tax. In 1981, Kyoto suffered from a 2.6 billion yen deficit and desperately needed income. The city lacked major industries, except tourism, so city officials once again set their eyes on the visitors flocking to temples. The proposed tax was projected to bring in 10 billion yen over ten years. Officials earmarked income generated from the tax for the preservation of cultural artifacts and preparations for the 1994 celebration of the 1,200th anniversary of Kyoto's founding.

The new tax—the Kyoto City Old Capital Support and Preservation Tax Regulation (Kyōtoshi koto hozon kyōryokuzei jōrei)—levied a tax of 50 yen on adults and 30 yen on children who entered designated temple grounds to view cultural artifacts held there.[51] The tax applied to temples that had visitors in excess of twenty thousand people per year and that charged admission. The regulation specified that the tax could not be levied on those entering temple grounds for religious purposes, defined as attending services, chanting sutras, or making ritual offerings. Elementary and junior high school students on supervised school trips were also exempted. As with the previous two tax measures, temples and shrines were made special tax collectors. The tax was added to the price of admission and collected at the time of the ticket sale. It was thus not a direct tax on temples, but the equivalent of a sales tax on admission tickets. This method also allowed the city to keep an exact count of how many tourists visited the temples each year.[52]

The Kyoto Buddhist Association, an organization representing 950 temples, stood firmly against the new tax. The city held meetings seeking to come to terms, but to no avail. To slip the tax through before the opposition grew too strong, the city announced that the tax would be proposed at a special January city council session. In response, sixty-nine temples and shrines filed suit on January 8 to halt the bill's proposal, to have the bill thrown out by the court, and to have the previous mayor's "no new taxes" pledge upheld. Despite such efforts, the bill was passed on January 18 and had only to await the approval of the minister for home affairs to go into effect. On February 1, temple representatives amended their suit to have the ordinance declared invalid.

Temple representatives' arguments against the tax were based on two points: first, the tax went against constitutional provisions for the freedom of religion; second, it broke the written promise of the previous mayor that no new taxes would be levied. The freedom of religion argument was based on the premise that temples open their grounds to the public in order to spread their teachings. Temple representatives argued that "each and every blade of grass and tree on the temple grounds is there for the purpose of spreading the Buddhist teachings. Viewing these is a religious activity. To tax this activity would be to deny its religious nature. This is an encroachment on the constitutional guarantee of religious freedom."[53] Furthermore, representatives argued that, although people went to temples for sightseeing, they also went for religious purposes, including obtaining peace of mind (anshin). Buddhist priests frequently mention obtaining peace of mind as the goal of those who visit temples. Tanabe and Reader clearly show that, in the case of the purchase of an amulet or other device related to this-worldly benefits (genze riyaku), the actual goal of the supplicant is less peace of mind than the practical this-worldly benefit associated with the charm or amulet that is purchased (e.g., traffic safety).[54] However, in the case of visiting a temple to view the gardens or sacred objects on display, it can be argued that the goal is peace of mind, since there is no other practical benefit to be had. A 1995 survey by the Public Opinion Survey Association (Seironchōsakai) found that 51.1 percent of respondents regarded religion as a matter of heart or spirit (compared to 3.1 percent for benefits [goriyaku]).[55] The importance of the search for peace of mind led temple representatives to claim that any attempt to distinguish between touristic and religious activity was impossible and intrusive. Temple representatives also argued that forcing the temples to act as officers of the state in collecting taxes crossed the state-religion divide.

However, another reason why temples were against the tax was not openly argued by temple representatives. Temple leaders did not want the city to gain an accurate count of people entering the temples. Since the tax was levied on entrance tickets, every person entering would be counted. Temple leaders feared the city could use these numbers to estimate further taxes or to gauge whether taxes currently paid were accurate. This unstated, but widely assumed, reason served to undermine the sincere arguments put forth in defense of religious freedom. By leaving the question of financial motive unaddressed, temples left it an open subject for criticism.

In response to the temples' stated reasons for protesting the tax, the city officials argued that the vast majority of people visit temples to see cultural artifacts, not to engage in religious activities. Those who might go for specific religious purposes were protected within the regulation and exempted from paying the tax. Moreover, city officials argued that temples charged entrance fees to visitors seeking out such nonreligious artifacts as gardens, teahouses, and the like. Because temples charged visitors to view the cultural aspects and not necessarily the religious aspects of their facilities, giving the temples the duty of tax collection would be no different from charging other organizations, such as art museums, with the same responsibility. As for the previous mayor's promise, city officials argued that it was just that, a promise by an individual, not a contract with the city.

The court threw out the temples' lawsuit in March 1984. First, the court determined that it could not rule on the case because the city had yet to receive the minister for home affairs' approval. Therefore, the regulation had as yet no legal standing. The court added, however, that the amount of the tax was small enough that it would not put undue burden on the faithful who might seek to visit and, therefore, did not infringe upon their religious freedom. Furthermore, it ruled that even those who visit for reasons of faith such as peace of mind are also, in most cases, visiting to see cultural artifacts. Therefore, levying a tax on that portion of visitor activity was acceptable. Finally, the court reminded temple representatives that the regulation exempted those visiting for defined religious purposes from paying the tax.

Unsatisfied, the temples filed an appeal. (The court rejected that appeal in November 1985.) In the meantime, the mayor sought permission for the tax from the minister for home affairs. On January 4, 1985, the mayor announced that the regulation would go into effect in April 1985. The anticipated revenue had been included in the budget already passed by the Kyoto city council. On January 10, 1985, the Kyoto Buddhist Association announced that affected member temples would close to the public. Priests proclaimed that the new tax regulation was the worst persecution since the Meiji period "Destroy Buddhism and throw out Shākyamuni"[56] movement, in which thousands of temples were destroyed and priests defrocked. Matsumoto Daien, the chair of the board of directors of the Kyoto Buddhist Association and head priest of Kiyomizu Temple, a famous temple that attracts nearly 2.5 million visitors annually, remarked, "Why should we priests, who have given our bodies to the Buddha, be forced to collect taxes?"[57] The closure was timed to coincide with the spring tourist season, and its announcement led to panic among members of the Kyoto Tourism Association. Kyoto attracted forty million tourists per year, and, together, the twenty-four temples that threatened to close their doors were visited by one-third of those tourists.

Because the central government was also under pressure to increase tax revenues, the minister for home affairs approved the tax after some deliberation on April 10, 1985. The tax went into effect in July. Soon after the tax went into effect, twelve of the designated temples closed their gates to the visiting public. The temples reopened after one month, in August, following a preelection deal struck with the mayor, who was facing a difficult bid for reelection because of the unpopularity of the tax affair. In this deal, the temples agreed to donate money to the city, roughly equivalent to what the tax would have generated. The offer by the temples only served to exacerbate negative image problems. Critics argued that, if temples were willing to pay the money after all, then their real reason for fighting the tax must be that they wished to hide wealth from the tax office. Paying money to the city office, in essence a bribe to keep the city at bay, would still be a breach of freedom of religion, they maintained. Shortly after gaining reelection, however, the mayor went back on his deal.[58] In response, the same twelve temples closed their gates a second time for three months, beginning in December 1985. Later, for nearly nine months in 1986, six temples closed their gates to regular traffic.

Closing their gates was the temples' trump card. Temple representatives hoped that city officials would soon cave in to the chilling effect temple closings would have on the local economy. However, the battle dragged on for years. The economic effect was severe. In 1984, when temples were open to the public, tourist-bus companies reported 670,000 customers. That number dropped to 540,000 in 1985, and 500,000 in 1986. An inn manager reported that business had decreased by as much as 48 percent.[59] Stores lining the streets in front of the major temples saw sales decline over 20 percent. Altogether, city businesses lost an estimated 30–40 billion yen in revenues during the closures. The temples also suffered. Many of the temples that closed their gates relied almost exclusively on tourist income. Ginkakuji, one of the most visited temples in Kyoto, lost virtually all of its income while closed, but was still left with annual operating expenses of nearly 100 million yen.

Throughout the dispute, the citizens of Kyoto displayed mixed feelings. Although a 1983 survey by the city found that 80 percent of respondents favored the tax,[60] a 1985 survey by *Asahi shinbun*, a nationally circulated newspaper, found 50 percent opposed to the tax, and only 36 percent in favor. Few, apparently, liked what the city was doing because they saw temples as the cultural and financial heart of the city. At the same time, however, many people had come to see the temples, especially the larger ones that attracted the majority of tourists, as money-making ventures. The entrance fees for Kyoto's temples were among the highest in the country.[61] As a *Washington Post* correspondent noted at the time, "Except for the robes and Buddha images, the scene [at temple offices] is hardly distinguishable from corporate Japan."[62] A common critique of some of the larger temples at the time was that the priests there were corrupt. "If they're not drinking in Gion [an exclusive nightlife district in Kyoto] then they're off on a trip to Europe."[63]

The city sought to capitalize on these negative images of businessmen-priests by declaring that temples received both direct and indirect city aid and, therefore, should willingly help the city collect taxes from visitors. Temple exemptions from property and city-planning taxes cost the city hundreds of millions of yen each year. By city estimates, the top nine tourist-destination temples would have to pay a total of 1.3 billion yen per year if they lost their exemptions. Furthermore, city officials noted that they spent 4.3 billion yen on cultural artifact preservation and related projects in fiscal 1982, twenty-nine times what was spent in 1964, when the previous mayor promised never to promulgate such a tax again.[64]

The affair suddenly came to a close in 1987, when the city capitulated after temple representatives played secretly taped conversations between Mayor Imagawa and temple representatives regarding the negotiations that had brought about the short-lived 1985 accord. On the tapes, the mayor revealed that he was striking the deal to get reelected, and not necessarily out of consideration for the citizens of Kyoto. The scandal caused by the public airing of the tape made eliminating the debate a top priority for the mayor. After releasing the tapes, the temples announced that they would open their gates as a goodwill gesture. The tax regulation was withdrawn soon afterward on October 17, 1987.

The effects of this lengthy feud between the Kyoto city office and the temples of Kyoto went far beyond the economic damage wreaked upon local businesses and the ruined vacations of tourists. The long battle over taxes brought questions over temple finance that had previously simmered below the surface to a boil by emphasizing already dominant images of temple priests as religiously corrupt and of temples as cultural museums.

Although the city emphasized that visiting temples was a secular activity and that temples were basically a tourist industry, the criticism of contemporary Buddhism by some, such as the following *Asahi shinbun* editorial, reveal a deeper chord of discontent, namely, anger over the commodification of Buddhism itself.[65]

> Faith and prayer are supposed to be matters of the heart, not of money. Prices [charged by temples] for posthumous names vary by rank, and those who pray [at temples], likewise, believe that they can succeed in exams or secure safety by paying for votive tablets or protective charms. This is wrong. Religion should not be a business.[66]

Thus, a debate over taxes became a forum for the discussion of the fate of Temple Buddhism in contemporary Japan. Were Buddhist temples merely secularized tourist spots, or did they reflect a new form of personalized religious practice based on commodity exchange (e.g., admission ticket price in exchange for personal ease of mind, or a fixed donation price for a protective charm good for one year)? Although temples have derived income from the sale of objects or the performance of rituals in exchange for donations throughout history, it is only in the postwar years, and especially from the 1970s, that one can speak of truly commodified practices. It is during this period that women's magazines began listing "market prices" for services such as funerals. Other mass media forms also served to create a public awareness of prices for various religious services. Moreover, during this period Japan began its shift to a modern consumer society, with large marketing campaigns aimed at the massive Japanese middle class.

In a 1998 article, Shimazono Susumu, a Tokyo University professor of religion, challenged accepted scholarly opinion, which supported the view that commodified practices were best understood as somehow not religious. Shimazono concluded that Japanese religion, including that of Buddhist temples, is best explained as a set of practices based on commodity exchange.[67] In other words, while religion in Japan is still very much a lived affair, its form has changed from devoting (consecrating) oneself to the Buddha to one-time exchanges. In his work on the contemporary festival and religion boom, Ashida Tetsurō comments on the manner in which commodification or commercialization takes place:

> The commercialization of religion tends to occur around the intersection of the ordinary and extraordinary, or rationality and mysticism. While many young people feel unable to rest easily within the world of everyday rationality, they likewise feel unable to step into the supra-ordinary world of mysticism, and wish to experience a glance at, or dabble a bit in, the world of the supra-ordinary and mysticism, while remaining firmly within the everyday world of ordinary rationality.
>
> They hope in that way to experience some degree of soul-shaking liberation, personal fulfillment, and differentiation from others, and in that sense, the religious orientation retains some utilitarian, functionalistic characteristics. In response to this demand, bookstores expand the shelf space dedicated to books on the paranormal world, television programs feature reports virtually every day on spiritualistic phenomena, and the stalls of fortune-tellers fill the street corners.
>
> ... Established religious groups have likewise prepared a variety of simplified courses in religious practice—offered for a fee—while simultaneously marketing a variety of occult products. ...
>
> As a result, while the current religious orientation is frequently transformed into a "commercialization of the soul," and thereby

reincorporated within the modern socio-economic system, there remains at the origin of that a longing for release or escape from that same commercialization.[68]

The sects of Temple Buddhism are faced with the difficult task of existing within the modern socioeconomic system while maintaining the stance that they have somehow escaped "commercialization of the soul."

This tension within commodified religious practice is seen in the view of temples as cultural artifacts. On the one hand, the city questioned the touristic nature of the temples. Temples were framed less as places where real religion could be found and more as museums home to priceless collections of artifacts designated by city, prefectural, and national governments as "cultural assets." In defense of the tax, the city argued that such artifacts, despite being the private property of the temples, were part of Japan's cultural heritage and "belonged to the citizens and, therefore, the citizens should bear some of the responsibility for their upkeep."[69] The temples countered that all cultural artifacts, and indeed "every blade of grass and tree on temple grounds," exist for the purpose of spreading the Buddhist faith. Nevertheless, the image of Kyoto's temples as museums of culture, not as sites of religious practice, remains strong. The Cultural Assets Preservation Law may contribute to this effect. Works designated as "treasures" or "assets" are thereby ideologically removed from their local and religious settings and become assets of the nation, prefecture, or city. They are made public property, and their local and religious content is packaged as part of their standing as public, cultural properties. The temples that house them thereby become museums of a shared public traditional culture.

The image of temples as museums of traditional culture is also due partly to Buddhist priests themselves because many envision themselves as keepers of tradition, a role they see as an inseparable part of their religious role in society. They consider practices such as charging entrance fees in exchange for the chance to walk through the otherworldly grounds of the temple a necessity if traditions are to be maintained. Furthermore, some of the most prominent Buddhist preachers today teach what might be termed a "religion of traditional culture." While such priests do not see themselves as museum operators, they preach that traditional Japanese Buddhist values are the key to Japan's future and that maintaining temples, gardens, and other centers of the Japanese spiritual tradition is one of their most important duties.

The debates over Kyoto's tax also focused attention on the current social role of Buddhist temples. One argument raised against the temples centers on the nature of their tax-exempt status.[70] As noted, temples that register as religious juridical persons are granted certain tax advantages because their presence is assumed to benefit the public. The battle over taxes in Kyoto, during which the temples closed their doors to the public, allowed critics to ask, "In what way do temples benefit the public?" This was part of an ongoing national debate over taxes and religion. For example, before the Kyoto incident, a member of the national Diet, who sat on a committee reviewing the tax system, commented that religion was a form of business that sold ease of mind and should be taxed on the same level as "pink salons" and "Turkish baths."[71] A commentator on the Kyoto affair later ventured the following:

> As for the temples, I wonder if they realize how many citizens hold them in respect [for their role in caring for cultural treasures across history]. There are people who visit Kyoto. There are people who come for the temples. And there are those who own shops to meet the needs of those who come. Shouldn't temples peacefully fulfill their duty as a part of the [social] structure that weaves people together?[72]

From these arguments we learn that the social role of the temple today is seen as providing ease of mind and as a community focal point—inseparably blending together religious, economic, and cultural aspects. When an imbalance between these parts occurs, as it did in the Kyoto tax affair, the whole is called into question. The social welfare activities of Tendai and other sects described in chapter 5 are one response to the critique that Temple Buddhism fails to benefit society in some tangible manner.

It is arguable that the temples were aware of the dangers of their position. Since the 1970s, a growing number of public officials had called for stricter taxation of temples, and critiques of the income-earning ventures of temples abounded. Despite negative criticism, a worsening image, and major financial hardships, however, the temples persisted in their strikes and maintained their stance that simply visiting a temple was a religious act. Moreover, in response to the criticism, some temples began to change the way in which visitors were approached for donations. Several temples eliminated entrance fees altogether. This elimination not only addressed the tax issue, since no tax could be levied if the temples did not charge admission, but also answered those critics who, holding that religion and money should remain separated, argued that if viewing temple grounds were really a religious practice, temples should not charge a fee. Other temples set out collection boxes, although minimal donations soon forced all but one to revert to charging fees. Even this one temple saw its income drop in half. It had charged 200 yen per person, but the first year it relied on donations, it received an average of 112 yen per person, the second year, an average of 102. Still other temples switched to a reservations-only system. For example, Kinkakuji allowed in only 150 people with reservations each day for a meditation and Dharma-talk meeting, for which they paid a set donation.[73] Some addressed critics further by making visitors undertake some kind of Buddhist practice, if only briefly, in exchange for admission. Usually, sutra copying was suggested. In this way, even internal critics of the temples, who had argued that the priests must meet donations of money by the faithful with donations of teaching Buddhist truths, were at least partially countered.

In the end, this case demonstrates how temples have come to be viewed in contemporary Japan. When seen against the modern history of temple funding, it clearly shows how the economic needs of temples have placed them in a difficult situation. On the one hand, they require funding in order to survive. On the other hand, income-earning ventures, even simply opening the temple for public viewing, are responsible for growing public belief that temples no longer act as religious centers. The argument that opening temple grounds to the public is a religious act found few supporters. Many priests are sincere in their belief that even the act of taking rest on temple grounds is religious and contributes to the spread of Buddhism. However, few members of the public appear willing to accept that argument unless taking rest is attached to other more overtly religious acts, such as active preaching or meditation, or unless the charging of fees, such as an admission fee, is done away with.

The tax case and examination of temple economics also shed light on the type of role many priests of Temple Buddhism see themselves as playing. They seek to defend traditional Japanese culture and a particular religious space associated with it. Temple gardens, temple architecture, and the like, priests argue, are integral to the support of traditional Japanese culture. Support of such sites goes hand in hand with the support of traditional Japanese values, which we have seen to be emphasized by the sects of Temple Buddhism.

While an examination of temples through the lenses of taxation and temple funding reveals many aspects of the debate over the place of Temple Buddhism in contemporary Japan, the primary fund-generating practice of Temple Buddhism, namely funerals and related practices, must also be examined in order to provide a more fully rounded picture. Such an examination will reveal the changing nature of religious affiliation in Japan today as well as the reaction of the sects of Temple Buddhism to the changes.

8 The Price of Naming the Dead
Funerals, Posthumous Precept Names, and Changing Views of the Afterlife

Dharma name, precept name, whatever you call it, don't try to get rich off it. There's no need for such things! We don't need graves and family altars, either. Why are sutra readings at funerals so expensive? When my dad died the sutra reading fee was 360,000 yen. On top of all that, the fees for weekly sutra readings for the first forty-nine days and the one-hundredth-day sutra reading were incredibly expensive. Can it really cost ten thousand yen for one hour of sutra reading! I just can't believe that the funeral sutra reading was 360,000 yen. That's way too expensive! How can they take that much from a grieving family! Aren't there any priests who'll do it for free?[1]

Precept names are supposed to be taken by those who seek to become disciples of the Buddha and engage in practice. Such names are granted during a ceremony in which vows are taken. If they are not taken while alive, then they are meaningless.[2]

What would happen if you had a funeral performed and didn't make an offering? Nothing really. Even if the priest gets angry, the deceased isn't going to fall into hell. I suppose the only thing that would happen is that priest won't be able to eat.[3]

I am the son of a temple [priest]. One often hears the term "funeral Buddhism." If funerals continue [to be performed] as they are now, I think that by the time those of my generation become priests people are going to say things like, "If that's the kind of funeral they're performing, I don't need one," and stop calling priests to perform. There is nothing in it to feel thankful for, it's not religious, and it doesn't do anything to care for the grief of the family.[4]

Tourism, property rentals, and the sale of religious objects are major income sources for temples, and, as we have seen, are also sources of conflicting images regarding the nature of Temple Buddhism. However, as the term "funeral Buddhism" connotes, funerals and memorial services are the primary business of

TABLE 7
Kaimyō: When Given and Donation Requirements

SECT	TIMING*	DONATIONS*
Tendai	Two characters may be given while alive, as many as six after death	No requirement noted
Kōysan Shingon	Preferably given while living, but ordination and initiation conducted at death	No requirement noted
Shingon Chizan branch	Preferably given while living, but the trend is towards giving after death	No requirement noted
Shingon Buzan branch	Given at funeral, but can be given while alive	No requirement noted
Jōdo	Promoting receiving during life, but most given in death	No requirement noted
Jōdo Shin Honganji branch	Given at the Honzan; given at local temples only for those who did not receive while alive	*Ingo* may be granted to those who have donated at the prescribed level
Jōdo Shin Ōtani branch	Given while alive; given in death only if not received in life	No requirement noted
Sōtō	Given in death for those who did not have the opportunity in life	No requirement noted
Rinzai Myōshinji branch	Should be given in life, but today most given in death	*Ingo*, etc. may be granted based on the amount donated
Nichiren	Given in life or death	No requirement noted

Source: *Jimon kōryū*, December 2001: 89.
*Data provided by the sects.

temples. While the major temples of Kyoto, Nikkō, and elsewhere are able to support themselves financially by charging entry fees and relying on donations given during New Year and other festival seasons, the vast majority of temples derive their income from funerals (see table 5). The reliance on funeral income is a major legacy of the Edo period temple registration system. The following pages give particular attention to posthumous precept names which are at the center of controversies surrounding funeral pricing and various negative images of contemporary Temple Buddhism (table 7).

Funerals, graveyards, and memorial services color the image of Japanese Buddhism to such an extent that the vast majority of Japanese claim only to associate with temples at death and, moreover, to associate temples and priests themselves with death.[5] The critique of funeral Buddhism strikes not only to the core of concerns over doctrinal or ritual degeneration, but also to the heart of concerns over contemporary temple finances. The two concerns are inseparably linked. Critics ask, "How can real Buddhists be involved in such matters as funeral rituals and ancestor worship," since these are supposedly not the true concern of Buddhist doctrine? In her work on Buddhist nuns in Japan, Paula Arai appears to take the position of her informants, whom she quotes as saying, "If there are actually any who follow Buddhist truth, they are only nuns. Monks are only concerned with ceremonies and services."[6] Such critiques also come from monks. A temple wife, distressed by the sect's lack of effort at teaching about rituals such as *mizuko kuyō* rites, complains that one priest stated, "There is no doctrine on curses!"[7] Still others argue that the alleged riches to be found in death services have corrupted the priesthood, leading priests to prefer comfortable lives as hired ritual specialists over lives as world-renouncers. As with other critiques of Temple Buddhism, these are not new to contemporary Japan. For example, Meiji critiques of Buddhism as backward or ritual-bound were numerous.

At the center of many critiques of contemporary traditional Buddhism lies the practice of granting posthumous precept names to *danka* members. The granting of such names, the money donated for their granting, and their doctrinal underpinnings have come under severe criticism in recent years (from at least the 1970s). So pervasive has this criticism become that the Japan Buddhist Federation (Zennihon Bukkyōkai), which represents all sects of traditional Buddhism, commissioned a study of the criticisms and released its findings and recommendations in early 2000.[8]

Posthumous precept names have been granted to the laity for centuries, with examples from the Kamakura period and earlier, though it was not until the 1600s that their use began to spread among the general populace.[9] In addition to the two-character precept name, which was standard until the Kamakura period, additional characters are now generally added. During the Kamakura period, the character *in*, which means "temple," and a variety of similar characters such as *ji*, *an*, and *bō* also referring to temples, began to be added to the precept name to distinguish those who contributed greatly to or were otherwise deemed thoroughly dedicated to Buddhism. As the warrior class came to power, the character *den* was added to *in*, apparently in an effort of one-upmanship by the rising class to distinguish their names from those of the court nobles. *In* and *inden* are today applied to the posthumous names of members of families that traditionally received such names and those who make exceptional contributions to the temple. In addition to the so-called *ingō* or *in* class names, *dōgō*, which were originally honorific names for high-ranking priests, were also applied to lay precept names. *Dōgō* are two characters in length. Today they are generally used to draw out an image of the deceased's life. For example, a businessman might have characters used that reflect success in business, or a tea ceremony practitioner might have characters used that relate to the tea ceremony. In addition to *ingō* and *dōgō*, a third set of characters is commonly used today as well. These are the rank name characters, or *igō*. Generally *igō* consist of two or three characters. The characters used vary from sect to sect. In addition to serving to distinguish the recipient's level of faith, donations to the temple, or service to society, these characters also serve to distinguish men from women and adults from children and, until recently, discriminated minority groups from the majority population. The general format for the whole posthumous name is *ingō-dōgō-*

TABLE 8
Posthumous Precept Name

NAME	TYPE
○	*ingo*
○	(院号)
院	
□	*dōgō*
□	(道号)
△	*kaimyō*
△	(戒名)
◇	*igō*
◇	(位号)

kaimyō-igō (table 8). Although technically only the two central characters make up the precept name, or *kaimyō*, today the full set of characters is commonly referred to as the precept name. A standard posthumous name, therefore, consists of at least six characters (*dōgō-kaimyō-igō*), and potentially many more.

Once given, the posthumous name takes on a lasting role in the life of the dead. It is carved onto tombstones, forever pronouncing to all who pass the status of the dead in life, and it is written on the memorial tablets that are placed in home altars and that play a central role in family religious practices. Memorial tablets generally are housed in the family altar until the thirty-third-year memorial service, at which point it is thought that the deceased has lost his or her individuality and has merged into the larger corporate family ancestor. The tablet is then either burned or entrusted to the family temple. The tablet is seen as a place to which the spirit of the deceased comes when family members make daily offerings or on special holidays, as the place the spirit permanently resides, or simply as a reminder to the living of the family members who have gone before them. The meaning varies. But as Robert J. Smith notes, regardless of other meanings, the memorial tablet plays a critical role in making sure that the dead are not "cut off from normal intercourse with the living members of [their] household."[10] The posthumous name marks the social status of the deceased in his or her new relationship with the living family.

Buddhist priests taught, and it was widely believed, that posthumous precept names exerted direct positive impact on the deceased's postmortem state. From early on, posthumous precept names were awarded for merit accrued vis-à-vis the temple during the deceased's lifetime (e.g., for donations or services rendered) but also for monetary donations by surviving family members. It was during the Edo period that conferring such names became a source of steady income for temples.[11] Little has apparently changed in how precept names are administered or in their role as a funding source for temples except that, as lands were stripped away from temples, income from the granting of such names and related services became critical to the survival of most temples.

A combination of two related factors has brought about severe criticism of posthumous precept names in contemporary Japan. First is the question of their necessity; namely, do they have contemporary meaning and function? The doctrinal explanations for such names, and explanations for contemporary use, including questions regarding discriminatory practices, are one source of such critiques. Second is an increasingly critical consumer society and a concomitant growth in the commodification of posthumous precept names.

DEBATING THE NECESSITY OF POSTHUMOUS PRECEPT NAMES

The Jōdo sect of Pure Land Buddhism released in August 2000 the results of a survey of the head priests of its temples throughout the country. The same sect's Chiba Prefecture Teaching District (Chiba Kyōku) also released the results of a survey of *danka* members, college students, and Internet respondents in May 2000.[12] When the results of these two surveys are set side by side, they reveal interesting aspects of the posthumous precept name debate. The fact that the majority of *danka* members (58.8 percent) responded that "posthumous precept names are necessary" is striking, given the vociferous critiques of such names in public debate. However, the proportion of *danka* members who thought posthumous precept names were necessary is still far less than the proportion that believed funerals were necessary (70 percent), suggesting some discontent with posthumous precept names. Moreover, 32.9 percent of *danka* members responded negatively regarding the necessity of such names, as did 64 percent of students, and 77.3 percent of Internet respondents, revealing clear dissatisfaction, especially among the young. Furthermore, a February 1999 survey conducted by the Japan Consumers Association (Nihon Shōhisha Kyōkai) found 57 percent of respondents selected, "I don't need a posthumous precept name, my given name is fine,"[13] and a survey by the Sōtō sect found only 10 percent of respondents believed that posthumous precept names were "absolutely necessary" (*zettai hitsuyō*). Taken together with the Jōdo sect survey, these results point to strong opposition to posthumous precept names.

The survey of head priests shows that they are aware of the popular dissatisfaction with posthumous precept names and points to what they believe are the sources of that dissatisfaction.[14] The vast majority of head priests (70.7 percent) responded, "The problem lies in the commercialization of faith, in which posthumous precept names are given in response to remuneration." Following this were those (14.6 percent) who chose, "The problem lies in the inequalities inherent in the ranking of posthumous precept names," hinting at the perceived discriminatory nature of posthumous precept names. "It is a problem of meaning, people do not understand the need for posthumous precept names," ranked third with 11.9 percent of the responses. These three can be broadly placed into two mutually influencing categories: problems of meaning and function, and the changing nature of religion in contemporary Japan (i.e., the commodification of religion). Regarding the former, there are at least three possible reasons why the meaning and function of posthumous precept names are questioned today: (1) the failure of priests to teach the laity regarding meaning and function, (2) rapidly changing views of the afterlife and salvation, and (3) the discriminatory functions of posthumous precept names.

THE SILENCE OF PRIESTS

Mizutani Kōshō, a member of the Jōdo sect, former president of Bukkyō University,[15] and member of the Japan Buddhist Federation Committee to Consider Posthumous Precept Names remarked,

> Today, particularly in the cities, posthumous precept names (kaimyō/hōmyō) are seen as something one gets when one dies, regardless of taking on the precepts or taking refuge in the Buddhist teachings. They are understood as something that is necessary and, therefore, given [at funerals]. The religious meaning of posthumous precept names is weakening.[16]

One critique leveled at the priests of Temple Buddhism is that they fail to explain the meaning and function of the ritual services they perform—that is, they fail to preach. Their failure to preach, it is argued, leads to the weakening of the religious meaning of such critical practices as the granting of posthumous precept names. Moreover, their lack of effort to expound the Buddhist Dharma is seen as evidence of their secularization or degeneration into ritual professionals. Thus, their image becomes not that of world-renouncers serving the lay community, but that of world-embracers engaged in the business of providing ritual services. Funerals and memorial services are among the rare occasions that priests enjoy a captive audience and could take the opportunity to preach. During the 1998 Regular Meeting of the Tendai Sect Diet, one priest argued that funerals were the best time to preach. He argued that Buddhists should practice spreading Buddhism through funerals, not practice funeral Buddhism.[17] Indeed, my fieldwork shows that many do take advantage of the opportunities postmortem rituals provide to discourse on Buddhist teachings in some form or other. In most instances the presiding priest dedicated the greater part of his talk to explaining the meaning of the various items used in the funeral and burial process, such as the wooden stupas (tōba) that family members place at the grave site.

There are many possible explanations for the perceived lack of preaching at funerals, including the dominant role of funeral companies in the funeral process, the belief that contact with the temple is itself a form of preaching, and the decay in temple-danka relations. In response to the critique that priests fail to preach, many priests complain that funeral companies, which today often schedule funerals down to the time allotted the priest for conducting the ritual, do not allow them time also to explain the ritual (sekkyō). However, just as many choose not to preach at these or other opportunities. At urban temples I observed, preaching was rarely conducted following regularly scheduled ritual activities, though preaching did take place at major annual events and at funerals and memorial services.[18] Rural temple priests appear more likely to engage in preaching than do their urban counterparts, perhaps because of the stronger relational bonds between priests and *danka* members in rural areas. At rural temples I observed, preaching occurred following all ritual services (scheduled ceremonies, funerals, and annual events).[19]

One possible explanation for the sporadic engagement in preaching might be that some priests believe that increasing contact with the temple itself is a form of preaching. The following, for example, is from a Tendai telephone Dharma talk.[20]

> The first thing that probably comes to mind when you think "Buddhism" is funerals. Yet the original aim of Buddhism is to spread widely the teachings of the Buddha. It is definitely not the performance of funerals. But, today, isn't it the case that through funerals, memorial services, and visits to graves, people often come into contact with temples, priests, and, therefore, with Buddhism?[21]

In an essay concerning graves, a Shingon sect priest argues that graves serve a critical role today, because people have the opportunity to visit the temple, to pay their respects before the main image (*honzon*), and, perhaps, to become interested in Buddhist teachings and to deepen their faith during regular visits to the family grave.[22]

Another factor cited in explanation of the lack of preaching is the slow decay of temple-*danka* relations. The future of temple-*danka* relations is of great concern to officials of the sects of Temple Buddhism, and most are seriously engaged in programs to reach out to *danka*. As temple-*danka* relationships weaken, and as functional relations at funerals between priest and attendees become impersonal and service based, the opportunity to encourage understanding of the religious meaning of posthumous precept names becomes limited. Relatives of the deceased are faced with a bill for 200,000–1,000,000 yen or more for a specialized portion of the funeral ceremony (the posthumous precept name) that they little understand, and this leads to mistrust.[23] Priests recognize this lack of trust; it was cited by 41.1 percent of priests surveyed as one reason for the controversies surrounding posthumous precept names.[24]

To restore meaning to posthumous precept names and, thereby, trust, members of the Japan Buddhist Federation committee and others suggest that Buddhist priests spend more time explaining the religious meaning of posthumous precept names. Most sects produce literature that seeks to explain posthumous precept names, although it is uncertain how wide the readership is (the usual pattern for distribution is to ship the product to temples, which are then responsible for passing it on to *danka* members). The following is a typical explanation, given in a Tendai sect publication for *danka* members, *Tendai Booklet*.

> It is a lot like the Christian name that Christians receive when they are baptized. In Buddhism, when you become a Buddhist, you receive the precepts. As evidence of that, you are given a precept name. Therefore, even though you might think that precept names are something that your temple head priest gives in a ceremony to someone who has passed away, originally they were to be taken while alive. It is a name for living a life of faith and pride as a Buddhist.[25]

The home pages of individual temples, essays by Japan Buddhist Federation committee members, and other sources also provide explanations. The following is from the home page of a Shingon sect temple.

> When a Buddhist believer or someone whose family religion is Buddhism dies, they receive a precept name from their temple and have a funeral performed for them. The head priest of their temple takes into consideration their character, the family's wishes, the precept names given their ancestors, and the contributions they have made to the temple, and grants them a precept name. In Shingon sect funerals, the head priest faces the main image and, there before it, takes on the deceased as his disciple, performing a ceremony to make him/her a disciple of the Buddha (i.e., a priest). Specifically, he confers the precepts upon the deceased, dresses him/her in white robes, and grants a priestly name. This is a precept name *(kaimyō)*.[26]

In the early modern period, posthumous precept names could play a meaningful role in the lives of *danka* members because such names were thought to hold considerable effective value as devices for ensuring positive postmortem salvation, whether that was rebirth in a Pure Land, rescue from rebirth in a hell, or otherwise.[27] However, many people today question their meaning, in part because of a lack of teaching on the part of priests. For example, some liken posthumous precept names to the indulgences once used by the Roman Catholic Church.[28] In a 1998 newspaper essay, Inoue Shinichi, chair of the board of directors of the Foundation for the Restoration of Buddhism (Bukkyō Fukkō Zaidan), wrote, "Posthumous precept names today are just like the indulgences issued by the Pope. In other words, if you buy this one slip of paper for a great sum of money, you can go to heaven." He notes that, like Roman Catholic indulgences, posthumous precept names sold for cash are likely to invite a protest and revolution within Japanese Buddhism.[29]

CHANGING VIEWS OF THE AFTERLIFE AND
THE RELEVANCE OF TEMPLE BUDDHISM

Attempts to teach about the meaning and function of posthumous precept names face an uphill battle. Japanese views of the afterlife, and of the role of the funeral as well, are rapidly changing. One problem suggested by these changes is that posthumous precept names no longer hold the effective meaning they once did. As expensive remnants of a little-understood ceremony, they are ripe targets for criticism and also for use in criticism of the economic activities of contemporary priests. One Tendai priest comments,

> I doubt there are too many people in today's world that fear spirits. Moreover, I don't think that talking about classical worldviews like hells and pure lands has any power of persuasion. In which case, the meaning of holding a magical service to appease the spirits [of the dead] is denied. . . . What people seek in Buddhism is a ritual to memorialize the dead and express condolences. However, the problem is that today's ritual has become a ritual for the purpose of having a ceremony. The peace of mind, which originally should be sought, is given nothing but lip service.[30]

According to the survey of *danka* members, students, and Internet respondents cited above, only 41.4 percent of *danka* members believed in the existence of a world after death, with opinions of students and Internet respondents numbering about the same (40.5 percent and 39.5 percent respectively). A different survey, conducted in 2003, found that only 16.8 percent of respondents believed in a world after death, but another 36.7 percent thought it might be possible.[31] Regarding spirits or a soul (*reikon*), 47.8 percent of *danka* members expressed belief in their existence compared with 54 percent of students.[32] For those who believe in a soul, a 2003 survey found that only 27.5 percent believed it resided in a heaven, hell, or Pure Land.[33] These numbers suggest that, for many contemporary Japanese, the granting of a posthumous precept name to assure rebirth in the Pure Land or some other form of postmortem salvation may hold little meaning. The 2003 survey found that 29.1 percent of those who believe in a soul felt that it remained in the hearts of those who survive, suggesting a strong emphasis on the living and not the dead.[34] A survey conducted by Tokyo City further confirms this. In this survey, 60 percent of respondents chose "A funeral is a custom for seeing off the deceased" and only 32.4 percent chose "A funeral is a religious act for praying for the happiness of the deceased."[35] Combined with the survey results just cited, this shows that the funeral, in which posthumous precept names play a central role, is seen by many more as a social custom designed to allow the living a moment to say farewell to the deceased than as a religious ritual designed for the well-being of the deceased in the world hereafter.

Just as views of an afterlife are shifting, so, too, are views of the family and its relationship with the dead. Ownership of home Buddhist altars, the centerpiece of household Buddhist practice (prayers for the ancestors), has dropped 10 percent in urban areas (though it has gained approximately 5 percent in rural areas) since 1985.[36] Also, the percentage of those who own home Buddhist altars is far less among the younger generations (35 percent for ages 20–40, 70 percent for age 70 and above).[37] Likewise, how the grave site is regarded points out that, while it is viewed as a site for ancestor veneration (35.2 percent, the largest single response), the focus appears to be more on specific individuals: 25.3 percent of people surveyed saw the grave as a place to remember the deceased, 8.7 percent saw it as the home after death, 17.4 percent as the place where the body is buried, 6.7 percent as evidence of one having lived. Combined, these numbers show that the majority do not relate to the grave site by way of its traditional links to ancestor veneration and the extended family. Furthermore, more than 80 percent of those polled understood the ancestors as one's closest relatives (grandparents, parents, siblings) while less than half saw the ancestors as those who make up one's family lineage from the founding generation on. This shortening of the family tree of ancestors may weaken the need felt by some to continue long-term relations with a specific temple. Finally, while 48.6 percent of males surveyed hoped to be buried in their family plot, 42.9 percent of females surveyed wished to buy a new plot with their husbands.[38] This finding suggests not only changes in how ancestors will be construed in the future, but also that the traditional family grave plot that linked *danka* members to their temple may be threatened.

Many priests recognize the public's changing view of the afterlife and of ancestors and burial, with the majority believing that alternatives to the traditional Buddhist funeral will increase and a little over 20 percent believing that people will leave Temple Buddhism altogether. In a related matter, only 28.6 percent of priests surveyed believed that bereaved family members were satisfied with the funeral.[39] Indeed, a similar but slower shift in attitudes toward the soul and the meaning of the funeral is also occurring within the Temple Buddhism priesthood. A survey conducted by the Sōtō sect found that less than 50 percent of priests were sure of the existence of a soul and less than 60 percent believed that the funeral was for the repose of the soul (while more than 85 percent believed it was for the consolation of living *danka* members). In addition, 17.9 percent believed that the granting of posthumous precepts was somehow not correct *(mujun)*.[40] Nevertheless, the sects and priests of Temple Buddhism generally remain committed to posthumous precept names because they have played a definitive role in the religious identity of Temple Buddhism for hundreds of years and because the income they generate comprises a substantial portion of overall temple income.

MEANING AND DISCRIMINATION

The meaning and function of posthumous precept names have also been called into question in recent years because of their role as means of social discrimination. The use of discriminatory posthumous precept names *(sabetsu kaimyō)*, names that mark individuals and families as members of minority or outcast groups in death as they had been marked in life, is the best-known example.[41] Such names threaten the legitimacy of both giving and receiving posthumous precept names. If a precept name were truly to signify that one had become a disciple of the Buddha, why would there be the need to segregate certain disciples out as impure? Moreover, if the purpose behind receiving such a name were to effect rebirth in the Pure Land, does discrimination continue in the afterlife?

The use of such posthumous precept names came to light dramatically in 1979 when Machida Muneo, the head representative of the Sōtō sect at an international conference on peace and religion, claimed that discrimination no longer occurred in Japan and thirty representatives of Japanese religions also in attendance clapped in response. Machida was soon called to task by members of the Buraku Liberation League (Buraku Kaihō Dōmei), which represents members of a segment of Japanese society that has been the subject of discrimination throughout the early modern and modern periods. League members pointed to the willful and continuing use in posthumous names of characters such as "beast" (*chiku*) or "leather" (*kaku*, signifying those whose ancestors worked in the "impure" trade of tanning) to mark members in death.[42]

Posthumous precept names are only the visible tip of such discriminatory scarring. Names are chiseled onto gravestones and recorded in registers of the dead kept at temples, both of which have been (and still are) used to track an individual's history.[43] Furthermore, priests have given such discriminatory names in special funeral rites designed to mediate the impurity believed to be associated with the discriminated class.

After some delay, the Sōtō sect sought vigorously to redress the problem. Discriminatory names have been removed from newer gravestones, unclaimed stones have been moved together to receive special attention, and priests are no longer permitted to share the contents of their registers with private detectives and other third parties who might use them for discriminatory purposes. Gravestones, however, were only the surface reflection of a deeper question of doctrinal support for discrimination. Sōtō officials argued that Sōtō teachings and practices were not flawed; rather it was the temple registration system of the Edo period that was to blame. This attempt to separate practices corrupted by social influences from a pure and unsullied Zen was severely criticized by the Buraku Liberation League. Critics pointed out that discriminatory practices were evident in Sōtō long before the Edo period. Others questioned the goals of the current reformation process. If the stones are erased and the records purged, will the history of discrimination be expunged from the record of Temple Buddhism? Such critics support the need to redress problems, but also hope that the memory of past discrimination will not be forgotten, lest it be repeated. Meanwhile, the process of weeding out offensive gravestones by the sect and antidiscrimination groups is ongoing, just as phone calls to temples requesting information regarding the backgrounds of individuals continue.[44]

Use of discriminatory posthumous precept names is by no means limited to the Sōtō sect. Shingon, Tendai, and other sects have also participated in such practices.[45] Not only Sōtō, but other sects, and many individual priests as well are earnestly attempting to address the problem of discriminatory posthumous precept names. They are trying thereby to restore meaning to the contemporary practice of granting posthumous precept names and to right the wrongs of their predecessors all the while restoring legitimacy to Temple Buddhism. The following example illustrates this situation.

On March 21, 1982, a rite to appease the dead was held at a small Tendai temple in Nagano prefecture. The head priest of the temple, Takahashi Shinkai, had worked as a teacher at the local junior high school, where he was in charge of a special education curriculum concerning discrimination. Upon an examination of his temple records, Takahashi found that, of the eighty-five households in his *danka*, twelve had family members who had been given discriminatory names (virtually all connoting leather workers). In consultation with the *danka* representatives, he arranged for a special service to be held at which all *danka* members would gather and he would publicly preside over a ceremony to apologize for past discrimination and to award new posthumous precept names and ritually to seek happiness for the spirits of those who had been discriminated against.

> To cut away the roots of discrimination from four hundred years ago, I, Takahashi Shinkai, [now] single-mindedly give rise to this vow. We hereby do away with the discriminatory posthumous precept names and change them. Moreover, we seek to invite to this place of practice, to join us in a memorial service, the souls of each family. We humbly implore you souls who suffered miserable discrimination in life and in death had discriminatory names carved into stone! Without a doubt, Amida's light shines throughout every corner of the other world, and Kannon's merit-power cleanses your lifetime of suffering, and the merit of this sutra chanting transmits our intentions to the other world. We hope that each of you spirits will joyfully sit atop the lotus of merit and perfection.[46]

The above was read at the ceremony and shows Takahashi's commitment to right past wrongs through ritual.

In addition to individual efforts such as this one, the Tendai sect began a Committee for the Promotion of Harmony (Tendaishū Dōwa Suishin Iinkai) in 1983. In 1996, this committee published a short piece on the history of discrimination against *burakumin* in the sect's magazine for priests (although it failed to mention discriminatory posthumous precept names, it did mention that Buddhism was "used for political purposes" in a discussion of status maintenance).

> How can we come to terms with this problem as citizens, moreover as religious of the Tendai sect? In the Tendai sect we take as our guide [the statement], "With the one-vehicle teaching of the Lotus Sutra as our base and with confidence in the universality and majesty of Buddha-nature, we undertake practices for ourselves and to enlighten others (*jigyōketa*), and make the True Law flourish. We also strive in the sacred

task of saving humanity. Further, we exhaust all efforts in developing the national culture, and endeavor so that all may realize the Buddhist path and to build a Pure Land (Tendai Constitution Article IV)." Even as we let shine forth these, the aims of our sect, we must acknowledge that it is our command and our duty as members of the Tendai sect to abolish all forms of discrimination, beginning with *buraku* discrimination, and to confirm human rights.[47]

As can be seen, the article implores Tendai sect members to bring the teachings of the sect to bear on the problem.

Discrimination by social group or race was often a one-sided process. Priests gave names that enforced discrimination to people who had little choice in the matter. However, another form of discrimination, one that is often actively encouraged by *danka* members, continues to take place today, namely, economic class discrimination. As I have mentioned, those who perform outstanding services for the temple, or donate frequently and in large amounts while alive, or whose survivors donate large sums to the temple can be awarded special prefix and suffix characters for their posthumous precept names in recognition of their role in supporting the temple. One's posthumous precept name has played and, in areas where communal bonds remain strong (generally rural areas), still does play an important social role by demarcating a family's status within the community. For this reason, certain families that have traditionally received special posthumous precept names representing past deeds of their ancestors often still seek to receive such names, even if they are no longer able to afford them.

There are few guidelines for granting special posthumous precept names. The permission of sect headquarters is usually required, but in practice the final decision is left up to individual head priests. This lack of standards for granting such names is one source of criticism. What significance can the names have, it is asked, if the standards for granting them vary from one temple to another? The Jōdo sect survey of head priests found that priests listed the following reasons for granting special posthumous precept names (multiple answers were permitted): (1) service as a *danka* representative or member of the temple board of directors (73.3 percent), (2) extraordinary contributions[48] to the temple (72.7 percent), (3) tradition of granting the family such a name (54.0 percent), (4) contributions to society by the individual or his or her family (42.4 percent), (5) by request of the individual or his/her family (42.2 percent), (6) participation in scheduled religious services, events, or service to the temple (41.9 percent), (7) participation in the *gōjūsōdenkai*[49] (32.1 percent), (8) the amount donated over time or

given through the temple support fund (22.7 percent), (9) the amount of donations given at the time of the funeral (7.9 percent).[50] This list demonstrates that,
at least among Jōdo sect priests, special names are given primarily for services
rendered to the temple. The amount of cash paid at the time of the funeral is
used far less often as a measure.[51]

Wealth remains a factor in determining special names, if a smaller one than
might at first appear to be the case. As the middle class expanded during Japan's
roaring economic recovery from WWII, more families came to have the financial wherewithal to request special posthumous precept names. In certain areas
such renaming was, and remains, nearly impossible, since local status groups
rarely accept the legitimacy of newly bought special posthumous precept names,
and priests are not inclined to upset local status relations by granting a new-
comer or newly rich *danka* member a special posthumous name. However, especially in urban areas, temples can (and do) grant special posthumous precept
names to new families. New urbanites, many of whom were beginning new
household lineages in the city, not only had the wealth to acquire such names,
but also desired to acquire what was still seen by many as a social status symbol.
There is ample evidence that many still actively seek out higher-priced names as
status symbols. For example, in 1984, family members of the deceased mayor of
a city in Ibaraki prefecture sought the removal of the head priest of their temple
because he refused to grant a special posthumous precept name.[52] The priest
argued that only those who had done outstanding acts for the temple or on
behalf of Buddhism could be granted such a name. The family argued that the
mayor had done much for the city and that for a person of his status not to have
a special posthumous precept name was embarrassing. Eventually, the priest was
forced to acquiesce when other priests cautioned him not to disturb local relationships. Causing a politically and socially powerful family to question the temple actively and, thereby, disrupting local harmony could do far more harm to
Buddhism than having weakened standards for granting such names.

Despite such examples, however, it appears that the desire for special
posthumous precept names may be waning today. Sharp-tongued critiques of
their appropriateness certainly abound. "There are even ranks in posthumous
precept names. The more money you pay, the higher ranked name you get.
What the heck is that about? It's totally nuts. Really."[53] A 1999 survey found that
46 percent of respondents could not accept that "differences in posthumous precept names could be bought for a price."[54] Much of the evidence for seeking
higher-priced names is drawn from data from the 1980s, the height of Japan's
bubble economy and a period in which family and social structures, still in flux

today, had perhaps yet to change to the extent they have now. The social meaning of posthumous precept names may therefore be changing in line with changes in family structure. The shift to nuclear families correlates with a decreased interest in ancestor veneration or lineage-supporting rituals such as the granting of posthumous precept names. Community structure has also changed from communal to individual relational networks that are not confined to a local area. All of these changes weaken major incentives (social status, filial piety, lineage maintenance) for acquiring a special posthumous precept name.

COUNTERMEASURES: PRECEPTS FOR THE LIVING

Lackluster teaching efforts, especially as concerns postmortem care, combined with changing attitudes toward the afterlife and salvation contribute to the growing impression that, if not corrupt, Temple Buddhism is at least out of touch, a collection of form-only practices. The granting of lay precepts to the living is one means under consideration by some members of Temple Buddhist sects to repair this image.[55] To emphasize the precepts as a moral guide for the living would counter criticisms, while also creating a modern religious meaning for the sects of Temple Buddhism. Given the changing views of the Japanese public toward the role of the funeral, this move to shift meaning to the living might seem an effective route for reform. However, though this may be possible, shifting from posthumous to living precept names may also be exceedingly difficult, for the posthumous granting of precept names has become associated less with taking on a set of moral prescripts to guide one in a life of faith as a Buddhist than as a once-effective device for ensuring the postmortem salvation of the deceased. Changing this association of precept names with death to an association with leading a moral life while alive requires changing basic assumptions about association with the temple: the temple must shift from a place one joins only in death to a place one actively associates with in life, from a place that centers on ensuring the welfare of the dead to one that centers on activities to encourage the living to explore and practice Buddhist teachings.

The difficulty involved in shifting from relations based on postmortem rites to relations based on rites for the living is demonstrated by the often inconsistent and unsure steps toward implementing lay precepts that the various sects have attempted. Although most sects now allow for the taking of precepts by laity, none has well-advertised and supported programs, though most produce literature on the subject.[56] Furthermore, none has taken on such a program as a primary part of its proselytizing efforts. This lack of effort, noted by Japan Buddhist Federation committee members, weakens the viability of precepts for the living as a method for reforming and giving meaning to precept names for the dead, or for taking the more radical step and shifting to precepts for the living only.[57]

The lack of effort to implement precepts for the living may stem from the critical role posthumous precept names play in temple finance. Posthumous precept names account for most of the income derived from funeral services. Even if a current head priest could financially afford to institute a program for granting precepts to *danka* members while alive, the priest who followed him might find his financial base undermined because donations requested for the granting of a precept name while alive are generally about one-tenth to one-twentieth of the amount requested for posthumous precept names. Not only would income from funerals be considerably lower than it has been, but income from memorial services that are conducted on the 49th day and the 100th day and on the 1st, 3rd, 7th, 13th, 17th, 25th, 33rd, and 50th anniversaries of death would also drop significantly since the amount donated for memorials is generally linked to the amount donated for and the rank of the posthumous precept name. The effect on temple finances is a major concern. However, because the living precept name consists of only the two-character *kaimyō*, temples would still be assured of income from granting the remaining characters at death (*ingō*, *dōgō*, etc.).

The granting of precepts to laity while living is a difficult path for the sects of Temple Buddhism to embark on because it would exacerbate the debate over priests and precepts in contemporary Japan. Questions concerning precept maintenance or lack thereof by priests play a major role in the debate over the very legitimacy of the Temple Buddhism priesthood. Encouraging the formal taking and maintaining of lay precepts among one's *danka* members would not only require a priest to explain the meaning of lay precepts, but might also require an explanation of priestly precepts by way of comparison. This, in turn, could lead to a demand for stricter maintenance of the precepts on the part of the priests themselves or could even call into question their current lifestyles. Moreover, precept maintenance serves to distinguish professional Buddhists and lay Buddhists within the sects of Temple Buddhism (with the exception of the Jōdo Shin sect, which openly distanced itself from precept maintenance in the Kamakura period and has always had a married priesthood).[58] Encouraging lay precepts might raise the issue of the meaning of the distinction between lay and professional, casting further questions on the legitimacy of the professionals.

Despite lack of effort on the sect level, many individual priests do encourage the holding of lay precepts as part of their teaching efforts. The following is an example taken from a Tendai sect collection of Dharma talks (sermons) that is available at some temples in the Tokyo area. In a piece titled "Lifestyle Guidelines for the Tendai Faithful," the writer comments, "All members of the Buddhist faith must hold to the five precepts. The five precepts are (1) not to take life, (2) not to steal, (3) not to have improper sexual relations, (4) not to tell lies, (5) not to drink alcohol."[59] In this case, however, whereas the precepts are used to teach proper moral behavior, they are not tied to the formal taking of precepts.

Implementing a precept program for the living is difficult not simply because of priestly concerns, but also because of lay concerns. Until recently, *danka* members have rarely been called upon to take as specific and active a step as taking on precepts and a Buddhist name. A recent Sōtō sect survey suggests, however, that sect efforts to encourage laity to take the lay precepts has met with some success; 30.4 percent of respondents claimed to have attended a lay precept ceremony.[60] Also, Yamada Etai, the head priest of the Tendai sect from 1974 to 1994, believed the precepts to be an important part of lay and priestly practice and conducted numerous mass precept ceremonies during his tenure. One of the greatest challenges to Temple Buddhism sects is the conversion of *danka* members from people who look to the temple as a place only for postmortem practices into active believers in the tenets of the Buddhism expressed by each sect.

TO HOLD THE WAVES OF COMMODIFICATION AT BAY

As the sects and individual priests of Temple Buddhism work not only to reinterpret and reapply posthumous precept names but also to make amends for past discriminatory practices, they must face a further hurdle as well, namely, the changing nature of religious affiliations in Japan. As I have shown, many changes in contemporary Japanese religions are due to a growing consumerism on the part of adherents and a concomitant trend to viewing religious practices as commodities. Within such an environment, posthumous precept names may no longer hold the religious or social meaning they once did and may become an increasingly difficult service to sell.

While the meaning of posthumous precept names is frequently questioned, the initial cause for questioning often derives from what are perceived to be exorbitant prices. Articles about some aspect of posthumous precept names and high prices appear in newspapers and weeklies regularly, and many individuals "know of someone" who has been asked to pay, or has paid, large fees for a posthumous precept name.[61] Part of the dissatisfaction with high prices might be linked to a consumer mentality. People expect that the product they have purchased will work as advertised, especially if they have paid a premium for it. In the case of posthumous precept names, for which results cannot be seen or experienced in this life, dissatisfaction can easily result, especially in the absence of full faith inspired by the salesperson in the product. As such names lose their meaning within contemporary society, if the salesman (priest) fails to pitch his product (preach) effectively, full faith wanes.

One approach taken by some priests has been to turn questions regarding price setting into opportunities to expound upon the spirit of donation. For example, one priest writes,

> In Japan today, most people think donations are what "you give a priest when he chants a sutra for you." Why must one give money? It's only natural as an offering of gratitude in exchange for the labor of chanting a sutra. But if that's the case, it's much higher than the average market-rate wage. It's a big mistake to think of donations in this manner. Shakyamuni left us these words: "The joy of giving alms, to forget the self, to forget the other, and to forget the gift. This is the greatest form of giving alms." There might not be anyone capable of giving like that, but the true meaning of giving alms was originally to give without seeking reward.[62]

The attempt to shift the debate away from the use of such terms as "labor," "exchange," and "market wage" and toward the use of terms such as "almsgiving" is one way some priests choose to fight the growing commodification of their labor and to teach Buddhism as they understand it.

Another method is to combat dissatisfaction over pricing. Members of the sects of Temple Buddhism often rightfully point out that priests who charge exorbitant fees and those who take advantage of a family's suffering to extort extra money for the granting of special prefixes and suffixes represent only a small minority. For example, 56.4 percent of the Jōdo sect priests surveyed responded that they relied strictly on donations and never used fees. Another 29.6 percent said they rely on donations for standard posthumous precept names but do set a fee for granting special posthumous precept names. However, the fact that some priests are able to continue to create an image problem, while also further commodifying posthumous precept names, shows the lack of control sects have over individual priests. Especially after the Religious Juridical Persons Law passed in 1951, head priests of individual temples registered as separate juridical persons have enjoyed substantial leverage upon sect headquarters. Moreover, the fact that apparently little has been done until recently to present openly a counterimage to that generated by rogue priests indicates a complicity of silence in the system of pricing posthumous precept names.

The consumer mentality can be seen in other aspects of the acquisition of posthumous precept names as well. First, people can now shop for prices. As family structure shifts to nuclear families and as the job market switches from one in which individuals live where they grew up to one in which they may live far from their hometown, or may even move several times in their lifetime, many families find themselves in the market for a new temple affiliation when a close family member dies and is in need of a funeral. Such individuals may have leeway to search for a temple that offers a product at an affordable price, or the individual may seek out a famous temple, preferring association with a quality "brand name." More than likely, they will be introduced to the temple by their funeral company representative, who will also instruct them regarding market prices for the posthumous precept name. Such market rates can also be found on the Internet (the current rate is 300,000 to 3,000,000 yen or more, with 3–5 percent of the primary mourner's annual salary said to be a rough gauge for the basic name).[63] Under these conditions, donations to temples for posthumous precept names are understood not as donations, but as fees for services rendered and for a product delivered.

Second, recurrent calls for making temple finances, and the structures for pricing posthumous precept names in particular, transparent illustrate an emerging commercial mind-set. Consumers (*danka* members and others in need of religious services) demand to know why the product they are purchasing is priced as it is, and shareholders (*danka* members) demand to know how the company (temple) keeps its books. Related to this are calls for making posthumous precept names free. If they are truly religious in nature, the argument runs, then there should be no need for money to change hands. Countering this, some argue that they are not to be priced in the first place. Money given is a donation, which is itself a form of practice. However, these arguments are fighting against the tide of change. That such monies are no longer perceived as a donation by most, but are rather expressed in the common terms "fee" (*ryō*) and "market price" (*sōba*), further points to the commodification of the act. Recognizing this, 60.3 percent of priests surveyed responded that the source of current posthumous precept name problems is "the social trend toward believing everything can be solved with money."[64] In a separate survey, 70.7 percent of head priests responded, "The problem lies in the commercialization of faith, in which posthumous precept names are given in response to remuneration."[65]

Once the practice has been commodified, taking the giving of posthumous precept names off the market, as it were, may not be so easily accomplished.

Third, as we have seen, priests are increasingly viewed as professionals offering a service. For this reason, those seeking their services expect "service for what they paid for and no further relationship."[66] This view of the priest is influenced by the fact that growing numbers of people are now introduced to priests through funeral companies and interact with the priest as a one-time service provider. The priest is hired not for his ability to effect postmortem salvation for the deceased, but to play a role in the funeral ceremony.[67] The advent of robot priests at some memorial parks is a telling sign of how the role of priests has come to be viewed. These lifelike wonders, true "chanting machines," will chant the appropriate sutra at the push of a button.

Finally, new funeral options are appearing. Of particular interest is the natural funeral (shizensō) movement.[68] This movement calls for such funeral options as burial at sea, scattering of ashes in mountains, and the like. There is little role allowed for the services of a priest unless those services can be meaningful in some way to the surviving family members. One way of understanding this movement is as a reaction to a service provider (temples) that fails to deliver a product (funeral) that satisfies (plays an effective emotional, social, or religious role). This movement, while receiving support from a limited number of priests, is more often the target of criticism by priests. One cynical reaction to priestly complaints is to point out that natural funerals obviate the need for graves and, thereby, pose a potentially devastating threat to the economic survival of Temple Buddhism. However, the following passionate critique by a Tendai priest shows that, for some priests at least, natural funerals are more than simply a threat to temple finances: they are a threat to the very moral foundations of Japanese culture.

> If we recognize the majesty of human life, it should be clear that the body cannot just be thrown out. Whatever excuse one uses for scattering remains, it comes down to throwing them out. Usually, one visits the grave thinking of the parents. What do people who throw out the remains do? Visit the mountains or forest? . . . The extended family has already collapsed. But I don't think it is all right to destroy parent-child relations as well. Even in a nuclear family, parent-child relations are authoritative. They are tied to good neighborly relations. We should reaffirm the fact that the family line is extended through the grave. . . .

The lack of an ethical view is a major problem. Ethical views begin in the family. . . . Set the mind straight, train the body, support your family, govern the country, make all equal under heaven. Are these just too old-fashioned? I think reaffirming the importance of the family and the importance of community relations will shed light on the antisocial nature of scattering remains.[69]

The author also describes what he feels must be done by priests to combat this practice—to give precepts to as many as possible through funerals and to live exemplary lives as priests.

The teachings of Tendai are the One Buddha Vehicle and the possession of Buddha-nature by all. All people will equally become Buddhas in the future. That being the case, the precept ceremony allows the faithful their first step as Buddhists. Precept ceremonies should be conducted one after the other. I hear that in the cities the time allotted for funerals is limited. [If that's the case,] then explanations and preaching can take place at the memorial service. Being a priest to whom *danka* members and the faithful feel they can safely entrust their parents' funeral, that's something nurtured through daily contact. Good preaching and a good lifestyle are what is needed. If we start from there, there will no longer be people who think to have natural funerals or to scatter remains.[70]

Both priests fighting to reconstruct a meaningful role within traditional boundaries and those pushing for new roles such as providers of social welfare services must construct their strategies within a changing world. Priests as service providers, competition, calls for clear pricing schemes, and price comparison all illustrate a commodification of Buddhist services. The conclusion of the Japan Buddhist Federation that the term "fee" must never again be used by priests lest it encourage a commodified view of posthumous names and contribute to a negative view of priests as business-oriented is itself clear evidence of the trend toward the commodification of Temple Buddhism. For all this, these observations apply more strictly to urban areas and, within urban areas, to individuals establishing new relationships with a temple. In temples where a family has had a long relationship or where, as in rural areas, individuals are more likely to have relationships with the temple outside of funerals (festivals, local meetings, etc.), priests are far less often viewed as merely funeral company employees or as one-time hired professionals. To this extent, therefore, it would be less accurate to claim that religion has been fully commodified than only that the trend is toward commodification.

THE FUTURE OF POSTHUMOUS NAMES

Contemporary constructions of Temple Buddhism as empty of meaning, compounded by critiques of a corrupt priesthood, profiting from death, shape the scholarly, popular, and sectarian images of Temple Buddhism today. At the heart of such critiques lies the reliance of the priests and sects of Temple Buddhism on postmortem care for their financial stability and as their primary social role. At least three factors ensure that priests will be increasingly unable to justify the cost of the postmortem care they deliver. First, they fail to instill meaning in their actions through preaching. Second, views of the afterlife and postmortem salvation held by the larger society are no longer in accord with the traditional views put forth by the sects of Temple Buddhism. Third, social disputes regarding the inequity of Buddhist postmortem care call into question the very purpose of that care. The commodification of religious practice in contemporary Japan represents a formidable challenge to Buddhist insistence on traditional forms of religious affiliation. Commodified (one-time, short-term, individual, price-based) relations with *danka* members and others threatens not only the traditional (repeated, long-term, family- or community-based, oblation-based) forms of religious activity still sought out by Temple Buddhist sects, but also the *danka* member system that such relations support and the financial stability that system represents.

Finally, changing views of the afterlife and the commodification of religious activities may reflect the expectations of younger generations. These are the very generations that the sects of Temple Buddhism must turn to in the future for the next generation of laity and priests. As the sects continue to press for traditional functions, such as funeral and memorial services, they risk further alienating those who have yet to commit to a temple, primarily younger urbanites. Japanese youth, though interested in subjects such as spirits and ghosts, do not seek traditional relationships with religious institutions, but rather, as witnessed by the rise of the new new religions, personal, introspective religious experiences. If the leaders of the sects of Temple Buddhism are to reach out to the coming generation of Japanese, they will first need to address the religious needs of Japanese youth. Facing the changing nature of society at the turn of a new century, the sects of Temple Buddhism have attempted to construct and implement plans to cope with the new realities, such as social welfare programs and committees on issues such as discrimination, the environment, and proselytizing. Furthermore, as the creation of the committee to study problems with posthumous precept names shows, the sects of Temple Buddhism are actively investigating the roots of their current unpopularity. It remains to be seen whether such measures will assure their survival in their current form into the twenty-first century.

CONCLUSIONS

I have noted the many difficulties temples face as they attempt to fund their activities. Temples are viewed as businesses, juridical persons, tourist sites, actors in local status structures, funeral centers, and more. An examination of temple activities through the lenses of taxes and death has shown that the sects of Temple Buddhism today face a changing society and new demands. As the nature of religious association shifts from communal to private, from long-term relationships to one-time exchanges, the demands placed on temples change. As commodification continues, temples and the sects of Temple Buddhism are forced to adapt. As we have seen, they have generally not adapted, but have rather held fast to traditional practices, such as funerals, and to traditional roles, such as world-renouncer and householder, while excoriating contemporary developments such as natural funerals.

As they continue to press for traditional functions, they risk further alienating those who have yet to commit to a temple. Their defense of traditional roles often relies on a rhetoric of conservative values. The emphasis on filial piety, care for the ancestors (as seen in chapters 2 and 3), and maintaining traditional culture (as seen in the Kyoto tax affair) suggest that sect leaders are appealing to an older audience. If the leaders of the sects of Temple Buddhism are to reach out to the coming generation of Japanese, they will need to address the religious needs of Japanese youth.

A basic barrier to successfully overcoming the hurdles represented by changing patterns of religious affiliation is the divide between world-renouncers and householders that is constructed by the sects of Temple Buddhism. Moreover, business or touristic images of Temple Buddhism serve to undermine the image of the practicing world-renouncer that the sects wish to maintain as a source of their religious authority and legitimacy. Contemporary economic circumstances require temples to raise funding by renting out properties or by charging admission to view sacred objects. Finally, the practice of relying on income from funerals, and in particular the granting of posthumous precept names that has continued from the late 1600s, has come into question in postwar Japan. As the funeral services offered become increasingly viewed through the lens of commodification, priests come to be seen not as world-renouncers, but as salaried professionals. The sects of Temple Buddhism today are trapped between financial necessities, traditional postmortem ritual roles, and their desire to be seen as sincere Buddhist practitioners. Breaking free from this dilemma represents one of their greatest hurdles as they enter the next century.

Epilogue
The World of Householding World-Renouncers

The sun shone hot and bright on the clearing between the Light Up Your Corner Hall and a grove of trees overlooking Konponchūdō, one of the great halls on Mt. Hiei. A couple of hundred chairs sat empty in the scalding heat as those gathered to attend the annual Gathering to Pray for World Peace, held in commemoration of the religious summit meeting on Mt. Hiei, slowly drifted in but still lingered in the shade under the eves of the hall or the outstretched limbs of the tall pines. The director-general of the Tendai sect, clad in black robes, stood, sweat glistening from his bald pate, in front of a microphone to announce the beginning of the thirteenth annual gathering. Slowly, attendees made their way to their seats. The priests manning the reception table offered them hats from two large cardboard boxes.

Once seated, the director-general offered an opening speech in which he reminded members of all faiths that it was their duty to care for the suffering of humanity and that they had to act out of respect for the sanctity of human life. Soon thereafter, more than one hundred participants from the Tendai Youth Gathering on Mount Hiei (Tendai Seishōnen Hieizan no Tsudoi) marched to the stage led by troop leaders carrying Tendai banners. As each member reached the stage, he or she hung a prayer for peace on the stage wall facing the audience.

Those in attendance represented members of many different faiths, including Christianity, Buddhism, Shinto, and Islam. They gathered to offer a prayer for world peace and to listen to speeches by leaders of Japan's religious communities. The gathering has been held each year in commemoration of the original religious summit meeting on Mt. Hiei held in 1987.

The original summit was a triumph of ecumenical cooperation and has been a point of pride for the Tendai sect. A link to photos of the 1997 tenth anniversary of the religious summit meeting on Mt. Hiei is displayed prominently on the sect's home page.[1] In 1987, the original religious summit meeting drew more than fifteen hundred participants from around the world, representing a wide array of religious affiliations. Participants attended meetings and activities for two days on Mt. Hiei and in the Kyoto area. The summit, which was based on an even larger event held in 1986 by the Vatican, served to place the Tendai sect at the center of efforts by Temple Buddhist sects to shift attention away from local problems and negative stereotypes and toward an image of

Temple Buddhist priests as engaged at the international level in the struggle for world peace, environmental protection, and care for the needy. The association of the priests of Temple Buddhism with Vatican representatives, for example, (prominently displayed and noted in Tendai literature ever since), served a legitimating function by showing Buddhist priests recognized as concerned religious professionals by an institution widely regarded as legitimately religious.[2]

The summit was a success in large part due to the strong friendship between Yamada Etai, then the head priest of the Tendai sect, and Niwano Nikkyō, then the head of the Risshō Kōseikai, whose strong international ties helped bring together the participants. Later Tendai sect leaders, however, have not been as aggressive as Yamada and have lost some of the early momentum. The 2000 gathering, described above, as well as the previous gatherings, now serve a more ceremonial than proactive agenda, though every few years a larger-scale and more proactive gathering is still held.

When the speeches of the thirteenth annual gathering were finished, the sun-scorched participants filed down to the parking lot to catch a bus either to the local train station to go home or to take them to the reception for drinks and conversation. The entire ceremony lasted a little over one hour.

As with the Light Up Your Corner Movement, the open call for priests, and the temple wife ordination ceremony, the religious summit and the Gathering to Pray for World Peace demonstrate a clear desire on the part of Tendai sect leaders to create new roles or to re-create old ones to meet the needs of contemporary Japanese and to maintain their religious authority and legitimacy. These attempts, however, also shed light on the difficulties still confronting the sects of Temple Buddhism today. The Tendai sect, like all sects of Temple Buddhism, is faced with weak central control, regional variations, the conflicting interests of individual priests, clerical marriage, the need to expand opportunities for further involvement of *danka* members in sect activities, and negative images surrounding temple finances. Each of the previous chapters has shown how Tendai and the other sects of Temple Buddhism are pulled in different directions as they seek to negotiate traditional priestly and *danka* member roles, the commodification of religion and related changes in how people affiliate with temples, and the presence of temple families, while all the while upholding their traditional rhetoric of renunciation.

The examination of the Light Up Your Corner Movement in chapter 3 demonstrates the Tendai sect's efforts to create a new relationship with *danka* members. It also shows that the sect has simultaneously attempted to reconfirm old relationships. In the end, the sect remains trapped between differing visions of how it should proceed in a society where potential *danka* members have considerable choice in selecting religious affiliation. Because of legally mandated temple affiliation in the early modern period, sects had little incentive to develop active roles for *danka* members and others within administrative or religious structures, and they have maintained a strong lay-clerical hierarchy within the sect itself, envisioned as a community of world-renouncers. Responding to contemporary demands, the Tendai sect sought to re-create the (passive) role of *danka* members by supplementing the role of recipient of postmortem-related services with that of moral citizen. Priests would still lead, but *danka* members would be given the opportunity to work alongside priests in social welfare efforts, rather than to associate with the temple only through death. At the same time, however, the Tendai sect also sought to emphasize the traditional passive role of *danka* members by teaching the value of ancestor veneration, in which *danka* members rely on priests for ritual services and instruction. The inability of the sect leadership to move beyond passive roles and to integrate *danka* members into active roles is due in part to the continued reliance on *danka* donations given for postmortem services as the financial underpinnings of the temple and, thereby, the sect as well. Moreover, the sect is still construed by many priests as a community of priests, or a world-renouncing institution, in which trained renunciate priests see to the religious needs of the *danka,* whose place, in turn, is to support the priests.

At the same time, this examination of the priesthood has shown how the world-renouncer image has been weakened by widespread images of Temple Buddhism priests as ritual professionals. The Tendai sect's open call is a clear attempt to overcome negative images of the priesthood. However, the young priests who graduate from it are still faced with a dearth of economically viable temples because of a de facto system of temple inheritance, itself a direct result of clerical marriage. All priests, too, must face the demands of a *danka* member system that, despite growing discontent, is based on a (memorial) service-centered relationship and often leaves them little room for innovation. There is scant evidence at this point that such a small transfusion of new blood will bring about the desired changes in the patient.

This discussion has also shown that priests today live trapped between images of an ideal, such as true Buddhism (philosophical, cosmopolitan) and true priests (world-renouncing, learned, engaged in ritual or compassionate practices), and images of a corrupt reality, such as funeral Buddhism (ritualistic, local, income generating) and corrupt priests (secularized, not engaged in true Buddhist practice). Priests are forced to walk an uneasy path between traditional roles as real priests who maintain their religious authority[3] as they also serve the needs of certain constituencies (primarily established *danka* members) and modern roles that address contemporary changes in modes of religious affiliation and social engagement.[4]

Chapter 6 demonstrates that the rhetoric of renunciation used by the Tendai sect to establish legitimacy faces one of its greatest challenges from the practice of clerical marriage. The Tendai sect has attempted to bridge the gap between rhetoric (renunciation) and practice (clerical marriage) with the temple wife ordination system. Sect leaders had planned to incorporate temple wives into the sect and its worldview through ordination. Had this been accomplished, problems revolving around the place of temple wives in the sect, privatization of the temple, and economic support for temple wives following the head priest's death would have been resolved. Temple wife ordination designed to span the gap between the rhetoric of renunciation and the reality of clerical marriage is similar to the Light Up Your Corner Movement, which seeks to reconfirm the traditional *danka*-temple relationship against contemporary changes in the basis of temple affiliation. In the case of the Light Up Your Corner Movement, as in the case of temple wife ordination, success has yet to be achieved because sect leaders are forced to maintain the rhetoric of renunciation for the purpose of legitimation even as this rhetoric works against their own efforts to recognize clerical marriage or to expand the role of *danka* members.

Both support for temple families and the rhetoric designed to encourage traditional family structures among *danka* members serve to reveal that the world of Temple Buddhism is built atop the family. To strengthen this base, the sects of Temple Buddhism have engaged in efforts to maintain the traditional family system. Sect leaders have also sought to create a strong base for teaching family values and to provide temple wives with an authoritative basis to act as a role model for the family, thereby securing a place for temple wives within the religious and administrative structures of the sect and strengthening *danka* families. However, these actions have worked against the rhetoric of renunciation, and they serve to demonstrate that Temple Buddhism consists of two inseparable yet antagonistic halves: that of renunciate priests who seek to maintain traditional practices and images (world-renouncers), and that of priests who live a more secularized life and seek to serve the needs of their local communities (*danka*-temple priests).

Finally, I have shown that the sects of Temple Buddhism face a variety of issues related to temple economics, including the commodification of religion, and that these have served to change patterns of affiliation and to reinforce images of the secularization of the priesthood. The examination of the taxation of temples demonstrates that temples are often viewed as businesses and touristic sites rather than as religious organizations, and this perception has in turn revealed widespread views of what does, or does not, constitute religious activity. It has also illustrated how religious affiliation in contemporary Japan has become more and more commodified. The topic of death and, in particular, the granting of posthumous precept names, has provided an avenue for exploring further sources of the problems temples face today as they seek ways to remain financially solvent and to perform traditional ritual roles while still combating images of secularization, privatization, and commercialization.

As the nature of religious association shifts from communal to private and from long-term to one-time exchanges, the demands placed on temples change accordingly. Traditional practices, such as the granting of posthumous names, are called into question. As commodification continues, the priests and sects of Temple Buddhism are forced to adapt. Frequently, however, they hold fast to traditional practices, such as funerals, and to traditional roles, such as world-renouncer, while lambasting those who support recent developments (e.g., natural funerals).

The issues raised in each of these chapters point the way for future research on Buddhism in modern and contemporary Japan. Perhaps our work can spark a larger debate and further investigations. Chapter 3 raises the topic of social welfare programs and their role in the sects of Temple Buddhism. The importance of these social welfare programs to contemporary Temple Buddhism, their similarity to those of the new religions, and the early history of Buddhist social welfare in Japan all beg further investigation.

Chapters 2, 7, and 8 also draw attention to the wide variety of local practices at temples and the manner in which they create networks of support for the temple. Further ethnographic examination of these practices would reveal even more about how temples operate and serve their various constituencies. For example, pilgrimage confraternities, *nenbutsu* confraternities, and women's groups all serve to connect local temples to local society and to other regional temples. Likewise, the system of Dharma-relatives among temples, which functions to connect individual priests as well as temples, plays an important role in temple life today.

Each of the chapters has touched in some way on the topic of law and religion in Japan. This is a field virtually untouched in English-language literature, especially as concerns law and the formation of religious practices and institutions in modern Japan. Moreover, even in Japanese scholarship, the study of law and its role in shaping Temple Buddhism has yet to be integrated into traditional Buddhist Studies.

Chapters 4 and 5 lead to questions concerning the current institutional structures of Temple Buddhist sects, especially regarding the training and status of priests.[5] To my regret, the scope of this project did not allow for an in-depth examination of nuns in the Tendai sect and other sects that lack major training facilities for nuns. The status and training of nuns in contemporary Tendai, as well as in earlier periods, require further investigation. Similarly, the divide between lay-born and temple-born priests, which is reflected in the differences of opinion held by male (generally temple-born) and female (generally lay-born) priests regarding clerical marriage, is an additional topic in need of further examination.

Chapter 6 raises questions of how precepts are understood today. Work needs to be done to trace the development in Japanese Buddhist thought regarding the role of precepts, especially from the early modern period onward. This chapter also raises questions regarding the role Temple Buddhist priests play in perpetuating certain gender stereotypes and what conscious role, if any, they have played over time to support state-imposed gender relations (such as the prewar Good Wives, Wise Mothers campaign).

Chapters 7 and 8 focus on the economic dimensions of the temple and open a number of possibilities for further research. The role of tourism in Temple Buddhism is one topic for exploration. The function of the temple in local economies is another, as is the relationship between temples and traditional crafts. For example, the demand for kimono, *geta* (clogs), and other priestly accoutrements plays a substantial role in supporting these crafts. Another area of research open to further discussion is the study of *ishiya*, the stonecutters who play a major role in the grave site industry, maintain close connections with local temples, and catalogue local and national traditional and modern trends in burial and religious statuary. Likewise, the larger economic changes that have shaped contemporary Japanese values must be explored in relation to the commodification of religion in Japan today. Finally, the role the government plays in temple finance through the establishment of cultural properties laws and in the creation of a civic religion of traditional culture represents a rich field for further investigation.

The great diversity of possible subjects for study reflects the endless variety found within the complex structures and relationships within Temple Buddhism as well as in how scholars, practitioners, *danka* members, and the public at large view Temple Buddhism. As I have shown, one source of this variety is the central dilemma of Temple Buddhism, something not seen in the new religions or elsewhere within Japanese religion, namely, that the sects of Temple Buddhism are trapped between an image of world-renunciation and demands and practices that do not correspond to it. Priests, *danka* members, temple families, and other members of Temple Buddhism still face a wide variety of difficulties, and understanding the complexities of these difficulties represents the greatest challenge for scholars. Scholars must come to terms with the complex reality of the temple, which is simultaneously a bastion of tradition, home to the ancestors of the *danka* members, home of a temple family, a place of business, a site of practice, a tourist site, a public space, part of a sect, and part of something larger called Buddhism.

Notes

Throughout the notes there are references to *Dainanajūyonkai tsūjō shūgikai giji hōkoku* or some variant thereof (*Daihachijūkai tsūjō shūgikai giji hōkoku, Daihachijūhahikai tsūjō shūgikai giji hōkoku,* etc.). These refer to the Tendai Diet minutes listed in the bibliography as (*Tendaishū*) *Tsūjō shūgikai giji hōkoku,* 1986–2000.

Introduction

1. The Tendai sect relies on the performance of the esoteric fire ritual as a form of legitimation of religious authority. Other sects, such as Rinzai and Sōtō Zen, rely on such images as priests sitting meditation in weeklong winter retreats.

2. Buswell Jr. (1992:17).

3. Bunkachō (1999). These statistics can be used only as a rough estimate because of reporting procedures. The government relies on numbers provided by Buddhist organizations, and these numbers are often inflated or out of date. "New religions" refers to religious organizations founded during the modern period (1850–present).

4. "New new religions" is a term coined by Nishiyama Shigeru and widely used by the Japanese press and refers to those religious groups that formed from the 1970s onward that reflect a more introspective and individualistic worldview than the so-called new religions, which are more oriented toward traditional Japanese family values. Although differences warrant a distinction with the "new religions," the term itself leaves much to be desired.

5. The number 157 comes from the Japanese Ministry of Education and includes all Buddhist sects or branches that are registered as comprehensive religious juridical persons (*hōkatsu shūkyō hōjin*). In prewar Japan there were 13 sects and 56 branches recognized by the government. The wartime Religious Organizations Law forced amalgamations, bringing the total to 28 sects or branches. With the liberalization of laws concerning registration of religious organizations in the postwar period, many groups that had been forced to amalgamate during the war separated, and many powerful temples broke off from their sects to form their own sect or branch, resulting in the current 157. Throughout this work I use the term "sect," rather than "school," to translate *shū.* "School" may be a more accurate translation for the medieval period and earlier, but it does not reflect the strong sectarian divisions that have developed since the early modern period.

6. The exception is Ōbaku Zen, founded in Japan in 1654.

7. The Japanese term for a Buddhist priest, *obōsan,* is generic and can be applied alike to those practicing exclusively in monasteries (i.e., monks, *sōryo, sō,* or *nansō*) and to those living and working among the laity. Japanese female priests are popularly referred to as nuns (by the generic term *amasan* and by the term *nisō,* "female monastic") regardless of

whether or not they are monastics. I use "priest" throughout to refer to both male and female priests, unless otherwise specified. Although the terms "monk" and "nun" are traditionally used within Buddhist Studies to refer to those who renounce the worldly life and take priestly precepts, the distinction between monastics and those religious living a more secularized way of life is fast disappearing in modern Japan.

8. The Tendai sect discussed here is the comprehensive religious juridical person Tendai sect. The Tendai sect, founded in 805 by Saichō, split into three sects: the Tendai sect, Tendai Jimon sect (993), and Tendai Shinban sect (1495). These three were amalgamated forcibly under the 1939 Religious Organizations Law. Under the postwar (1951) Religious Juridical Persons Law, they separated once again. The Tendai sect claims five times as many adherents and almost fifteen times as many temples as the Jimon sect, which is larger than the Shinban sect. The Tendai sect is also heir to Mt. Hiei and the famous temples and practices thereon. It has special relationships with more than a dozen sects and branches that also broke from it in the postwar period.

9. See, for example, Reader (1983) and Williams (2000).

10. The allure of Zen in the West is evidenced by the numerous "Zen and the Art of…" books.

11. Tendai studies in the West are slowly advancing, led by scholars such as Paul Swanson (Chinese Tendai), Paul Groner (Japanese Tendai), and Jacqueline Stone (Japanese Tendai, and Tendai-influenced schools). Recently Kiuchi Gyōo, a well-respected scholar of Tendai, has begun investigations into modern-period Tendai. See, for example, Kiuchi (1999a:23–34 and 1999b:177–209).

12. Covell (1993).

13. Some refer to this self-contradictory nature as schizophrenic. While by nature Temple Buddhism appears schizophrenic, the term schizophrenia as a general label is avoided here because in contemporary parlance it invokes images of an illness marked by deterioration and degeneration.

14. See Stone (1999:100). As James Laidlaw points out, we must allow for the possibility that individuals (and, I would argue, by extrapolation, the institutions they create) may not always act consistently and may even simultaneously hold contradictory value systems. Laidlaw (1995:1–21).

1 Temple Buddhism Today

1. See Covell (forthcoming a).

2. Ketelaar (1990).

3. Anesaki (1963:146).

4. This definition is based upon the one used by Shimazono Susumu. Shimazono (1981:213).

5. The following discussion is based on Hayashi and Yamanaka (1993:207–228).

6. Ienaga (1965:39).

7. Recently, the issue of Buddhist responsibility in World War II has begun to be addressed. See, for example, Daitō (1994), Endō (1995), and Victoria (1997).

8. Yasumaru is similarly discussed in Shimazono (1981:207–223).

9. Shimazono (1992) and Tsushima et al.(1979:139–161).

10. Davis (1992).

11. Paul Watt offers a brief introduction to "corruption theory"; see Watt (1984: 188–189).

12. Tsuji (1942:546).

13. Ibid., 516.

14. Tsuji uses the term *kaikyū seido* (class system) to refer to the *mibun seido* (status system).

15. Tsuji (1942:517. On status and the priesthood, see Vesey (2003).

16. Ōno (1961:248–249). Emphasis added.

17. Watanabe (1964:59).

18. Tamamuro Taijō (1963:1).

19. Ibid., 2.

20. Tamura (2000:214).

21. Matsuno et al. (1972:22–23).

22. Tamamuro Fumio (1999:227).

23. Ibid., 4.

24. See, for example, Habito (1995:83–101), Hur (2000), Schopen (1997), and Stone (1995:17–48).

25. For secularization theory as it relates to Japan, see Davis (1992), in particular his chapter on secularization. See also Tamura (1979:89–113). The arguments of Davis (1992) and Tamura provide the basis for the explanation provided here. See also Davis (1980:261–285).

26. Cooke (1974b:272–273); see also Cooke (1974a:18–34).

27. Cooke (1974b) discusses three lay groups as "signs of life": the Zen-based F.A.S. Society, the Jōdo-based Zaike Bukkyō Kyōkai (Laymen's Buddhist Association), and the Shingon-based Daishikō (Daishi Confraternity). The first two of these groups represent generally intellectual movements in search of true Buddhist practice, whether that be sitting *zazen* or critically reevaluating Buddhist practices in Japan (Watanabe Shōkō, who is cited above in the discussion of corruption theory, was a founding member of the

Laymen's Buddhist Association). Cooke's signs of life therefore ignore direct efforts on the part of the sects of Temple Buddhism, implying that the sects themselves may lack any such signs of life.

28. Ienaga (1965:1–41).

29. Eger (1980:7–24).

30. Iijima (1995:60–61). Iijima's position, and that of others involved in the debate over how best to understand this-worldly benefits, is discussed in Reader and Tanabe (1998: 71–106).

31. Minami (1998:99). Cited in Kumamoto (forthcoming).

32. Gombrich and Obeyesekere (1988:446). The following list is partially derived from Bunnag (1973).

33. Wilson (1996:19).

34. Kieschnick (1997:140).

35. Sekiguchi (1990:14). Translation is mine.

36. For more on early monastic clothing, see Wijayaratna (1990:32–55). For a look at monastic clothing in contemporary Japan, see Riggs (2004).

37. Dutt (1960).

38. Kieschnick (1997:66).

39. Ibid., 110.

40. Ibid., 141.

41. Lopez Jr. (2001:136).

42. The Tendai, Rinzai, Jōdo, and Sōtō sects do not permit inherited succession of the main temple or other major temples. Morioka (1986:96).

2 Laity and the Temple

1. *Jimon kōryū*, November 2001:12.

2. *Jimon kōryū*, December 2001:18.

3. The literal meaning of *danka* is donor household. It can refer to a household or all households supporting a temple. "Donor household" no longer reflects the nature of the relationship (it has not done so since sometime in the early modern period). The standard translations used in the field of Japanese Religious Studies are "parishioner" and "parish." I have chosen not to translate the term to avoid misunderstandings based on the Christian term "parish." When referring to households belonging to *danka*, I use the term "*danka* member."

4. See chapter 7 for more on financing a temple.

5. Tamamuro Fumio (1971, 1987, 1999) and Tamamuro Taijō (1963).

6. This document, of which numerous copies with slight variation exist, could be called the smoking gun of Temple Buddhism's corruption. Those working on Edo-period Buddhism frequently cite it. See, for example, Tamamuro Fumio (1971:183–187) (here he makes the argument that this was not an official government document); idem (1999: 183–184); Tamamuro Taijō (1963:265–266); and Shimada (1994:120–121). For an example in English, see Williams (2000). The translation here is based upon Williams' translation.

7. See Williams (2000) and Hur (2000).

8. Tamamuro Fumio (1990a:44).

9. The first national family registration law was developed in 1871 and it was promulgated in 1872. It was abolished in 1873. In 1886, registration was required under a Ministry of Home Affairs ordinance. In 1898, family registration became part of civil law (minpō). Laws regarding family registration were changed following World War II from requiring multigeneration registration to nuclear family registration.

10. Meiji-period developments are discussed in detail below. See also chapter 3. Relevant works include Collcutt (1986:143–167), Grapard (1984:240–265), Hardacre (1989), Ikeda (1976, 1996), Kashiwara (1990), Ketelaar (1990), Kishimoto (1955), and Oguri and Nakamura (1972).

11. Tamamuro Fumio describes an incident in which one man was struck from the temple records for failing to pay the proper donations to the temple and for failing to attend the required services (1999:203). He also details an incident in which one group of danka members sought to break off relations with their temple because the priest was caught having an affair with a villager's wife upon whom he had forced himself under threat of striking her family from the temple register (208–218). Despite their efforts, and despite the nature of the priest's actions, the danka members were not able to break away. They were, however, able to force the head priest's transfer.

12. Tamamuro Fumio (1999:227).

13. Edicts limiting the scale of burials and memorials can be found from early on in Japanese history. Tamamuro Taijō describes such edicts occurring as early as 646 C.E. (1963: 94–95). He also notes efforts to control grave marker size throughout the Edo period (154). Such measures were to control not only lavish spending, but also status (i.e., each status group's marker could only be of a certain size).

14. Shimada (1994:124).

15. As the case cited in note 11 demonstrates, there were limits to the power of danka members. Average danka members could rarely effect change. Leading danka members, if persistent, could effect the removal of the head priest if evidence of corruption was overwhelming.

16. Takemura (1981:84–86).

17. Although this bill, and a similar one in 1929, failed to pass the Diet and become law, many of its provisions were instituted as ordinances.

18. Despite their decreased legal standing, *danka* members are still capable of effecting major changes, including the sacking of the head priest. For more on law and temples in the contemporary setting, see Covell (2000:7–23).

19. The Meiji government's stance was also due to pressure from Western countries to lift the ban on Christianity.

20. Ikeda (1996:45); see also idem (1976).

21. For an example of an influential novel from this period, see Kurata (1917).

22. Government efforts to quell Ōmotokyō eventually failed. The religion rose again and continues to exist today. For more, see Garon (1986:273–302), Hardacre (1990:47–62, 1992:215–241), Nadolski (1975), and Ooms (1993). See also Morioka (1994:281–310). Regarding the postwar period, Morioka describes the manner in which Risshō Kōseikai was attacked in a series of articles by an influential national newspaper. Today, attacks on new and new new religions as representing a danger to society continue to appear regularly in newspapers and magazines.

23. Moving graves, plots, urns, and other remnants of their relationship with the temple was not logistically a feasible option for most until recently. It was expensive and required permission from authorities.

24. Reader (1983). Although sect affiliation appears to matter little, it is not entirely forgotten. Continuance of sect affiliation as a form of paying respect to one's ancestors continues to play an important role in people's selection of a temple. Urbanites in search of a new temple to affiliate with generally seek to maintain affiliation with the same sect of their original family temple not because they prefer the teachings of Tendai over Sōtō or Jōdo over Shingon but because that is the tradition in which their ancestors have been cared for over generations. For example, in 1995, the head priest of a temple in rural Chiba prefecture sought to officially relinquish his position. In order to do so, he was obligated to find a replacement. He chose a priest to replace him who was ordained in a different sect. Traditionally, temple affiliation changes with the head priest's affiliation; thus the *danka* members were faced with having to switch their sect of affiliation. The *danka* members were angered by the priest's decision and refused to accept his choice for the new head priest. In the end, the original head priest was forced to leave, his replacement was not accepted, and the *danka* members asked the sect headquarters to appoint someone for them.

25. Tamamuro Fumio (2000).

26. See Reader (1991a) and Reader and Tanabe (1998).

27. See Xian (1980:12–15).

28. Those temples that held on to their forest lands were later able to develop them into mountain graveyards, parks, and the like. Temples that sold such properties were finan-

cially hobbled in the long run. For example, a temple in rural Chiba prefecture, where I served two years as the weekend priest, is one such case in point. The temple sold off all the property surrounding it, leaving it only a small patch of land for *danka* member graves. Years later, as the area began to be developed into a bedroom community for Tokyo, the temple leaders began to consider buying back the land they had sold off years before in order to build a larger graveyard to service the growing community.

29. See chapter 7.

30. See LaFleur (1992) and Hardacre (1997).

31. Yamaori, Kakehashi, and Sasaki (1993:10–12).

32. This complex is related to more than the performance of funeral rituals. Problems such as married clergy, which are based on interpretation of priestly precepts, also exacerbate the complex. See chapter 7.

33. On occasion, a *danka* representative, who lived near the temple at which I was staying, would stop by with a bottle of Chinese gin to share as he told me about how corrupt he thought Buddhism in Japan had become. Once, he passed me the book *Mistake-Filled Buddhism* (Akizuki Ryōmin, *Gokai darake no Bukkyō: shindaijō undō no ikkan toshite* [Tokyo: Hakujūsha, 1993]).

34. Families informally questioned on this topic disclosed that they looked forward to moving their family grave to the city. However, the move is not always easy to accomplish. For example, one family in the Tokyo area was forced to spend considerable time and money to move their family grave to Tokyo. The priest of the temple where the family grave had been argued that they should not move it. Because his cooperation was necessary to get the proper paperwork completed for the city office, the priest was able to delay the process until the family met his fee for moving their plot.

35. One priest commented to me that she would like her own temple, but one without a *danka*, because an established *danka* would run her life and leave her little time for practice.

36. See the Japanese public television special on the disappearance of rural temples for an especially good account of this. NHK (1990).

37. It is not uncommon to see letters to the advice column regarding this topic in *Gekkan jūshoku* (The Monthly Head Priest).

38. For more on this, see Covell (2000), Hasekawa (1994), Ōie, ed. (1985), Wakahara (1981, 52–78), and Yasutake (1979:223–232, 1985:158–178).

39. The obvious conflict of interest that this creates can lead to disputes and clearly blurs the secular-religious division sought by those who designed the law.

40. Xian Jian claims that the Religious Juridical Persons Law actually allowed greater *danka* member roles than before. He argues that previously, under the Religious Organizations Law (1939–1945) and the Religious Corporations Ordinance (1945–1951) *sōdai* were relegated to advisory roles only, whereas under the new law they were given the

opportunity to control temple management. Although technically the case, in actual practice, as discussed here, *danka* members were often totally excluded from temple management by shrewd board of director membership selection on the part of the head priest and by a strict reading of the law by the courts, which made determination of legal standing vis-à-vis the temple for *danka* members extremely difficult.

41. For example, in 1981, the Supreme Court of Japan handed down a verdict against a couple that sued Sōka Gakkai seeking the return of their donations. They demanded a refund of their donations when it was determined that the object of worship their donations helped to buy was a fake. Moreover, the building it was to be housed in, to which they also donated, failed to be built. The court ruled that, although the suit could be interpreted as a straightforward fight over rights and obligations connected to the donation, the donation was based on a matter of faith, and the problem of the quality of the fake object of worship as an object of faith was a doctrinal matter and therefore out of the court's power to decide. Hasekawa (1994:172–173).

42. See chapters 4 and 5 for more on inheritance of the position of head priest.

43. The extent to which this is the case varies by locale. However, it is rapidly becoming the norm in urban as well as rural areas. Funeral supply companies also play a major role in flattening out regional differences. Such companies, driven to keep profit margins adequate, favor product standardization and mass production techniques.

44. The priest recommended by the funeral company was from a different sect. The grave marker, therefore, stood out starkly against the other markers in the graveyard.

45. Sekizawa Mayumi draws on survey results to show that in 1990 professionals were involved in bathing the body of the deceased ten times as often as in 1960, and they selected the burial clothing three times as often. Sekizawa (2002).

46. Other critical practices such as the *honeage* (bone-lifting ceremony) still remain. In this ceremony, close relatives gather around the still warm cremated remains and, in pairs, lift the few remaining chalklike bones into the urn. (This is why it is impolite to lift food or other objects together with someone else at the dinner table in Japan.) Changes in death practices are similar throughout the developed world and reflect the modernization of the death process (e.g., death in hospitals, advanced cremation techniques).

47. At either the wake or after the funeral proper, priests will usually give a short talk. The content of the talk varies from priest to priest, but most often it centers on explaining the funeral ritual and the afterlife.

48. See chapter 8.

49. Some women also take up natural funerals as a form of resistance to the traditional patriarchal grave system (in which the wife is buried in her husband's family grave). See Rowe (2003:85–118).

50. Hikita (1991:92).

51. Ibid., 84.

52. This survey is conducted every five years. See Sōtōshū Shūsei Chōsa Iinkai (1984) and Sōtōshū Kyōka Kenkyūjo Sōritsu Nijū Shūnen Kinenkai (1975).

53. Hikita (1991).

54. Shimazono (1998:183).

55. Ibid., 186.

56. See chapter 8. See also Reader and Tanabe (1998:183).

57. See Shimazono (1992).

58. Although this structure reflects Tendai's developmental history over centuries, it is also due in part to the 1951 Religious Juridical Persons Law, which put sects and their temples on equal legal footing.

59. One method used with some success by the Hō no Hana group (the leadership of which was put on trial for fraud for nonrelated reasons) involves inserting postcard questionnaires into publications. Individuals who took the time to fill out and send in such questionnaires would soon receive calls and visits from representatives of Hō no Hana.

60. See, for example the Zen-based F.A.S. Society (founded in 1944) and the Jōdo Shin–based Zaike Bukkyō Kyōkai (Laymen's Buddhist Association, founded in 1952). Cooke (1974b:267–330).

61. See chapter 4.

62. See, for example, Tanabe (2004).

63. See the following Web sites for links to the home pages of most Temple Buddhism sects, as well as to new and new new religion home pages and the home pages of other religious groups: www.otera.net, www.jtvan.co.jp, www.jiin.net, www.evam.com. There were 425 books on Buddhism published in 1999. The total number of books on religion was 931 (combining the categories of religion [shūkyō] Shinto, Buddhism, and Christianity). There were 81 different magazines (monthly, bimonthly, weekly, etc.) on the topic of religion. Shuppan Nenkan Henshūbu (2000:308–318).

64. Reader and Tanabe (1998:233).

65. Ibid., 232.

66. Ibid., 233.

67. The first scene in the Mt. Hiei 1,200th anniversary video is of a kaihōgyō practitioner walking in the deep woods of Mt. Hiei. That is also the first scene in the Tendai sect's promotional video for its social welfare campaign. Likewise, a recent book on Tendai in Korea, China, and Japan produced by the Tendai sect features a kaihōgyō practitioner prominently on the cover (Media Bankusu 1999). Tendai has also begun a yearly one-day kaihōgyō course open to the public. This one-day experience allows those who would know more of the practice an opportunity to experience, for one day, what the practitioners must go through for one thousand days. The one-day program is also an opportu-

nity to advertise the Tendai sect through the *kaihōgyō*. Members of the mass media take part and write short essays on the experience (see, for example, *Sapio*, August 27, 1992; and *Kyoto shinbun*, August 24, 1998). The *kaihōgyō* is what Tendai wants the public to associate with the Tendai sect: rigorous, traditional, powerful, and alive.

3 Trying to Have It Both Ways

1. Helen Hardacre and William LaFleur held a debate concerning the nature of rites for aborted fetuses. Hardacre argues that it is a completely new invention, while LaFleur maintains that it has roots that can be traced back to at least the Edo period. Both sides have valid points: the rites themselves may be new, but the performance of rituals for the dead (*kuyō*) is one with deep roots. Just as blessings for cars and pet funerals may be new, the practice of empowerment through prayer (*kitō*) and ritual offerings to the dead (*kuyō*) have long and rich histories.

2. Interestingly, temples that sell trendy talismans must learn marketing. One temple at which I worked part-time during festival seasons found itself with unmovable stock when it overstocked a talisman that had been popular the previous year, but had since fallen out of favor.

3. There are no statistics available on how many people opt against becoming *danka* members of temples. Given the rise in interest in alternative funerals, the increased use of nondenominational graveyards, and the apparently declining number of individuals who continue memorial services past the 13th year, it is safe to say that at least some potential *danka* members are seeking other options and that many current *danka* members affiliate less through a sense of belonging to a religious community than through a need to secure a grave site. Japanese government statistics help little. The government survey of 1939 showed 1,897,134 *danka* members (*danto*) and faithful (*shinto*), and a 1999 survey found 1,531,498 faithful (*shinja*, which in this case does not discriminate between affiliated *danto* and nonaffiliated *shinto*). This would indicate a decline of nearly 20 percent. However, because the measurements vary, it is difficult to discern whether a decline actually occurred or not. The survey in 1950, for example, found only 333,393 faithful, the 1997 survey, 613,295. Moreover, the totals remained consistent to a person over several years at a time (between 1979 and 1989, for example), raising suspicion regarding accuracy. (Bunkachō, 1939–1999). Furthermore, individual temples often underreport the number of households in their *danka* in reports to the sect because the tithes exacted by the sect on temples are based, in part, on the number of *danka* member households.

4. Nara (1980:3).

5. Light Up Your Corner home page (originally, www.biwa.ne.jp/~ichigu/main/ichigu.html; now www.tendai.or.jp/ichigu/index.html). This home page has undergone changes and may no longer contain some of this material. I have printouts from fall 1999.

6. Light Up Your Corner home page.

7. See below for more on the textual source and development of it within the Light Up Your Corner Movement. The Tendai sect, like many other sects, divides the country into

teaching districts, which are administrative units. The physical boundaries of the teaching districts do not correspond to prefectures.

8. Ichigū Wo Terasu Undō Tokyo Honbu (1999:43). The leader's name is Tani Genshō.

9. The following discussion is based on the succinct summary of this debate in Okubo (2000:96–110).

10. Ichigū Wo Terasu Undō Tokyo Honbu (1999:37).

11. Ibid., 47.

12. Ibid., 46.

13. One aim of the sect, according to a movement leader (Tani Genshō), is to use the movement as a "unifying theme" for the sect. Ichigū Wo Terasu Undō Tokyo Honbu (1999:52–53).

14. *Eizan jihō*, December 8, 1999:2. The leader goes on to conclude that it is, and must be, all of the above.

15. Light Up Your Corner bylaws, articles 3 and 4: in Yamada (1996:961).

16. This is a collection of Saichō's petitions to the court to permit Tendai yearly ordinands. At Saichō's time (early ninth century), the court strictly limited the number of monks allowed to ordain each year. For an in-depth discussion of the history of this text, see Groner (1984).

17. Light Up Your Corner home page.

18. Ibid.

19. Ibid.

20. Ichigū Wo Terasu Undō Tokyo Honbu (1999:94–95).

21. Mukhopadhyaya (2001:19–34).

22. The Tendai sect nun Kōno Jikō, for example, ties Saichō's teaching to the Buddhist saying "wanting little and knowing satisfaction." This, she says, is the key to a happy life. Kohno (1998:128).

23. *Eizan jihō*, March 8, 2000:1.

24. Ibid., May 8, 1999:4.

25. Buddhist groups throughout the world have been actively relating Buddhist teachings to environmental causes. The Japanese sects of Temple Buddhism are part of a larger trend within contemporary Buddhism. Within Japan, new religions such as Risshō Kōseikai have made caring for the environment a major part of their efforts to engage society. Garbage collecting and volunteer clean-up activities are encouraged and organized by the Brighter Society Movement. Internationally, there are the Sarvōdaya Sramadāna movement in Sri Lanka, the international Tiep Hien (Interbeing) movement (founded by the famous Vietnamese monk Thich Nhat Hanh), the Wildlife Fund Thailand, the Ladakh

Ecological Development Group, and the efforts of the Dhalai Lama to establish Tibet as a "zone of nonviolence." Harvey (2000:179–185).

26. *Eizan jihō*, January 8, 2000:8.

27. Light Up Your Corner home page and various leaflets.

28. *Eizan jihō*, May 8, 1999:3.

29. The practice of giving up one meal and donating the money that might otherwise have been spent on it to assist those in need is common. In 1974, for example, Risshō Kōseikai began a program called the Donate a Meal Campaign (Ichijiki Wo Sasageru Undō, www.kosei-kai.or.jp/heart-frame.html). Funds collected through Risshō Kōseikai's program are donated to the Fund for Peace and Development of the Japan Committee of the World Conference on Religion and Peace (WCRP). A search under "Donate a Meal" on Yahoo! (U.S.A) found over half a dozen similar programs with Web addresses, including UNICEF's Donate One Meal Campaign and several by Christian or community groups in the United States.

30. *Kōhō Tendai*, May 1997:24–25.

31. *Chūgai nippō*, February 19, 2000:4. The *Chūgai nippō* is Japan's oldest and largest religion newspaper.

32. Light Up Your Corner home page.

33. *Eizan jihō*, November 8, 1999:4.

34. Ibid.

35. *Eizan jihō*, April 8, 2000:5. A leader of the movement tells the story of a young woman who went to live with her husband's family in the countryside. The point of the story was that the grandparents, people of a bygone era, teach the young woman how to live properly by always saying thank you, always giving thanks for the food one receives, and always saying the name of the person from whom the gift of food was received before eating it to express gratitude.

36. Ichigū Wo Terasu Undō Tokyo Honbu (1999:98–99).

37. Ibid., 102–103.

38. Ibid.

39. *Eizan jihō*, March 8, 2000:4.

40. Ibid. This theme is prevalent in the writings of Tendai priests. The following is from a famous Tendai practitioner of mountain asceticism, Mitsunaga Kakudō. See Mitsunaga Kakudō (1996:221).

> Even though you wake up today, there is no guarantee that when you go to bed tonight, you will wake up the next morning. You could be cold and dead the next morning. That we are able to go to sleep without a worry is, to me, a mystery. To wake up and think "Ah! I am alive another day!" is how it really should be. Give

thanks that you are alive, and if you are given life, think what you can do that day. First, face your ancestors and give thanks that you are able to wake up and be there. Then, the rest of the day should be spent thinking how you can repay that gratitude. To give thanks to your ancestors and build up [merit] little by little each day is truly returning the debt of gratitude.

41. Ibid., 5.

42. Hardacre (1986:189).

43. Tsushima et al. (1979:139–161) and Reader (1993b:237).

44. Ooms (1993:33–44). See also Yasumaru (1974), Murakami and Yasumaru (1971), and Davis (1992).

45. Davis (1992:113–151).

46. Monbukagakushō (2002:30).

47. Ichigū Wo Terasu Undō Tokyo Honbu (1999:38).

48. Ibid., 46–47.

49. In business terms, temple-sect organizational relations in the Tendai sect can be pictured as a franchise business. The home office controls basic product guidelines, uniforms, and employee training, thus guaranteeing some unity in product. Each store, however, is individually owned and operated and has leeway to cater to local needs.

50. During my stay in Japan, I was able to attend three conventions: the Tokyo branch's thirtieth anniversary convention in 1999, the Tokyo branch's year 2000 convention, and the Saitama branch's year 2000 convention. The convention described here took place on June 10, 2000, in Tokyo.

51. The presence of the Korean choir is due to recent Tendai efforts to establish links with Chinese and Korean Tendai. Japanese Tendai seeks to position itself as the rebuilder of Tendai Buddhism in China and Korea, the countries whence Tendai in Japan originated. This positioning, in turn, works toward supporting the legitimacy of contemporary Japanese Tendai.

52. The *shamisen* performance may also be seen as part of the move to construct an atmosphere of traditional Japan.

53. This rhetoric is similar to that used by the sects of Temple Buddhism regarding temple wives (see chapter 6) and within the various new religions. On women in the new religions, see Hardacre (1986).

54. For more on charismatic Tendai priests and their teachings, see Covell (2004a).

55. Ichigū Wo Terasu Undō Tokyo Honbu (1999:59).

56. The contemporary work of the sects of temple Buddhism abroad, such as aiding in international relief efforts, building schools, or financing the reconstruction of temples in China, as well as the efforts of the sects to establish themselves on the international stage

through participation in international religious conferences or by sponsoring such conferences, is the subject of a work I am currently writing.

57. Ichigū Wo Terasu Undō Tokyo Honbu (1999:54–55).

58. A spate of relief efforts, including assistance for the back-to-back 1999 earthquakes in Taiwan and Turkey, seriously strained the ability of temple priests to solicit donations from *danka* members. The sect headquarters usually generates relief money by putting out a general call for donations. Each teaching district is given a target amount to collect, that amount is collected from individual temples within the district. Temples sometimes opt not to press *danka* members for donations and instead make the donation out of operating expenses because, in addition to meeting sect and movement demands for donations, temples must also seek donations for their own needs, such as rebuilding halls.

59. Mukhopadhyaya (2001).

4   The Contemporary Priesthood

1. The vows of a young Saichō, founder of the Tendai sect in Japan, written shortly after climbing Mt. Hiei to begin twelve years of secluded practice. Taken from the *Ganmon* (Vows). Translation is Groner's. Groner (1984:28–29).

2. Matsunami (1996:127–128). Poem written by a contemporary Hōkke-sect priest.

3. In addition to inexpensive and widely available forms of print media (newspapers, magazines, *manga* (comics), and paperbacks), television and film, in particular, sway large audiences.

4. Kuroda (1996a:313). In the Nara period (710–794), Emperor Shōmu ordered the construction of a network of Buddhist temples throughout Japan, each tied to the central temple in the capital. This national temple *(kokubunji)* system served to link the center to the periphery through a physical network of temples that symbolized imperial rule.

5. Most founders of new schools of Buddhism in Japan made similar appeals.

6. Kuroda (1996b:271–286). Prayers for the protection and well-being of the imperial household continue today.

7. Dobbins (1996:223–224).

8. Buddhists were expelled from their coveted state roles for other reasons as well. First, Shinto activists were in a position to promote Shinto over Buddhism. Second, the leaders of the fledgling state sought to create a modern state, which was understood at the time to be one in which state and religion were separate. See Hardacre (1989), Ketelaar (1990), Collcutt (1986:143–167), and Grapard (1984:240–265).

9. Ikeda (1996:25).

10. Grand Council of State (Dajōkan) Law 133, 1872.

11. See Kiuchi (1999b:185), Hikita (1991:284), and Jaffe (2001). Jaffe provides an extensive examination of this and related subjects.

12. See the discussion of secularization theory in chapter 1.

13. See Ketelaar (1990) and Staggs (1983:251–281).

14. See Collcutt (1986); Grapard (1984); Murakami, Tsuji, and Washio (1925–1929); Murata (1999); and Yasumaru (1979).

15. Fridell (1973:154), Hardacre (1989:44), and Ketelaar (1990:98).

16. Ketelaar (1990:98).

17. Cited in ibid.

18. Jaffe (1998:53).

19. Ketelaar (1990:105).

20. For a fascinating history of this temple, see Hur (2000).

21. Taishō Daigaku Gojūnenshi Hensan Iinkai (1976:99). Regarding Meiji laws governing sects, see Kiuchi (1999b) and Ikeda (1998:13–17).

22. Thelle (1987:49).

23. Akazawa (1985:109–110).

24. Ikeda (1996:76–78).

25. Ibid., 91–93.

26. Ibid., 98.

27. The kanchō system was an administrative organizational structure in which each school was required to appoint one representative as the chief officer (kanchō) of the school. The Buddhist bill sought to imbue the position with vast powers to enforce centralization and prohibit internal difference. The kanchō system was initially established in 1872 and underwent various changes during the early years of the Meiji government. It forged the modern organizational structure of the sects of Temple Buddhism, placing each under the administration of a single leader (the kanchō). See Ikeda (1998:16–18) and Jaffe (2001).

28. The committee consisted of three Shinto representatives, eight Buddhists, two Christians, eight government officials, six scholars (also contracted by the government), and twelve members of the Diet. For more on this debate, see Abe (1968–1970:268–338, 57–97, 181–203, 27–53, 54–79, 223–296).

29. Akazawa (1985:116–118). See also Bunkachō Bunkabu Shūmuka (1983a).

30. The bill was criticized for many reasons. The powers given to the Minister of Education, the nationalization of religious instructor standards, and the kanchō system were especially singled out for attack. Religious groups lodged the majority of the complaints. Christians complained that the kanchō system was based on Buddhist organizational structures and, therefore, was inappropriate. They also strongly objected to the strictures against teaching by noncertified instructors. This, too, they claimed infringed

on their organizational structures, which they considered as an integral part of their religious faith. Buddhists were generally receptive of the bill. Sect Shinto (Kyōha Shintō) officials fretted over the possibility of losing their special status as part of the de facto state religion and sought extralegal guarantees of that status. The new religions did not voice any strong opposition to the bill because, Akazawa contends, the new religions viewed state and religion as inseparable and because they possessed a weak sense of human rights. He argues that they instead focused their efforts on currying favor from the nobility and the bureaucracy. To apply this logic to the new religions alone is questionable. Some Buddhist and Christian leaders may have argued for the right to freedom of religion, but their role in the development of this bill demonstrates that their primary interest was in securing their own protection and benefit. And they were aggressively engaged in political machinations toward that end. In fact, Akazawa notes that the Christians were slow to respond because they at first understood the bill as regulating new religions only. Akazawa (1985:123).

31. Taishō Daigaku Gojūnenshi Hensan Iinkai (1976:383–394).

32. Ibid., 364.

33. Ibid., 377–412.

34. Yamada (1980a:26–27). This conversation also appears in a recent biography of Yamada Etai. See Nagao (2002:206–207).

35. Victoria (1997:138).

36. Koike, Nishikawa, and Murakami (1978:81–116).

37. Ishikawa (1998:87–116).

38. *Kōhō Tendai*, October 1995:6.

39. Ibid., 4.

40. *Chūgai nippō*, September 14, 2002:1.

41. Although the new constitution forbade state support for religion, the ruling Liberal Democratic Party consistently, and often successfully, pushed the boundaries of the law through semiofficial donations and official visits to Shinto shrines. See O'Brien and Ohkoshi (1996). Buddhist temples are rarely the object of such direct political support today because they do not have the same cache as national religion that state Shinto earned during the prewar and war years. However, Buddhist temples do receive some state funding. Artifacts (buildings, paintings, statues, etc.) deemed national treasures are eligible for funding to support their upkeep.

42. *Mainichi Daily News*, September 19, 1999. Online edition "Top News" (http://mdn.mainichi.co.jp).

43. *Daily Yomiuri*, February 4, 1994:2.

44. Ibid., April 16, 1995:2.

45. "Mahayana" means "greater vehicle" and is the term used to describe the form of Buddhism that developed in India centuries after the Buddha's death and flourished in East Asia. The bodhisattva precepts that Saichō introduced existed in China but were taken on top of the full precepts by priests or were taken by lay members. Saichō's innovation was to use the bodhisattva precepts for priestly ordination, something that was not done in China. Saichō permitted the taking of the full precepts only after a period of twelve years of training under the bodhisattva precepts. See Groner (1984).

46. Stone (1999:17-19). See also Minowa (1999) and Groner (1984).

47. Ikeda (1996:7).

48. For more on Jiun, see Watt (1984:188–214).

49. Ikeda (1996:7–8).

50. Jaffe (1998:56).

51. Ikeda (1998:20).

52. Morioka (1986:74).

53. Ibid., 78–79.

54. *Tendai shūhō*, May 1994:82.

55. *Bukkyō Times Weekly*, December 7, 2000:1. See chapter 6 for more on clerical marriage today.

56. During fieldwork I often witnessed *danka* members plead with priests to accept drinks. The more the *danka* members had to drink, the more forceful the measure taken to fill the priest's cup. As a vegetarian, I was often forced to explain why I didn't eat meat dishes offered. In defense of their own meat eating, priests regularly lectured me on early Buddhist practices of meat eating.

57. This response was common enough that I began to believe it must be taught to priests today, though I have not yet found a specific source (class, contemporary instructions to priests, etc.). There is textual evidence within Buddhism to support the assertion by contemporary Japanese priests that meat eating is acceptable. Harvey, for example, cites extensive evidence for the acceptance of clerical meat eating in early Buddhism. However, Harvey also cites evidence (*Mahāparinirvāna Sūtra, Lan'kāvatūra Sūtra*) of prohibitions against eating meat in later Buddhism (Mahayana), especially as it appeared in China. See Harvey (2000:159–165).

58. One young priest I encountered always turned down offers. However, he was forced to repeat himself at each new occasion, even among the same people. His most effective tool was to say that he was the designated driver.

59. Nakasato Tokukai, director-general of the Tendai sect, in Yamada Etai (1980a: foreword).

60. Ibid., 5–6.

61. *Kōhō Tendai*, May 1997:10.

62. Yamada Etai (1980a:30–39).

63. The Tendai sect produces several lay-oriented publications including *Tendai Booklet* and *Tomoshibi*. Various teaching districts also produce material such as *Tendai koyomi* and temple newsletters.

64. I have little evidence of wide-scale success.

65. Eleven of these, however, completed the *kaihōgyō* in the postwar period.

66. Bessatsu Takarajima Henshūbu (1995:263).

67. *Chūgai nippō*, March 28, 2000:6. Some argue that religious organizations now are no different than secular organizations: They have health plans, retirement plans, etc.

68. *Jimon kōryū*, August, 2002:77.

69. *Daily Yomiuri*, May 25, 1995:7.

70. These robots cost 30,000,000 yen each. *Aera*, February 9, 1993: 70.

71. Yamaori, Kakehashi, and Sasaki (1993:23).

72. *Bukkyō Times Weekly*, December 07, 2000:1, quoting Suzuki Kōkan.

73. Matsunami (1996:81).

74. For more politics and Buddhist debate in the Heian period, see McMullin (1989).

75. Jōnin Henshū Iinkai (1980:521–530).

76. Ketelaar 1990, esp. chapt. 5. See also Ikeda (1996:100–103).

77. Stone (1990:217–233).

78. Yamaori, Kakehashi, and Sasaki (1993:11).

79. *Gekkan jūshoku*, July 1990:60.

80. Ibid., 61.

81. *Daikyūjūsankai tsūjō shūgikai giji hōkoku* (1999:29). Tendai sect officials note that the inheritance of temples is not a matter of policy (ibid., 31).

82. See chapter 7.

83. Priests wishing to change temples or to move up from assistant head priest to head priest must wait long years for vacancies to appear. This is true not only of those from lay backgrounds, but also of those from smaller temples. Regarding the succession problem faced by Tendai, for example, one priest voiced his concerns at the 1999 sect Diet meeting regarding the fact that even major temples were now passed on to sons, whether qualified for such a position or not, and that sons of smaller temples, therefore, have little chance of moving on to such a position (*Daikyūjūsankai tsūjō shūgikai giji hōkoku* [1999:24]). During fieldwork in the Tokyo area, I was witness to the advancement of one

such priest. The priest had been the assistant head priest at a temple in the Tokyo area. He was not entirely satisfied with that position because it left little time for him to pursue his own studies, and his relationship with the head priest was strained. When a mid-sized temple, also in the Tokyo area, opened up, he was asked to step in and chose to accept. The position, however, was vacant for a reason. First, the previous head priest was still there, though mentally unstable (and, thus, no longer the acting head priest), and living in an apartment across from the temple. His older sister, however, continued to live at the temple. She was in good graces with the *danka* and was not willing to move out. A previous replacement had died before he could overcome arguments with the *danka* representatives, who had come to wield a great deal of control, and with the sister of the ill head priest. A well-respected priest was then asked to look after the temple in addition to his own. He dutifully did so but was frustrated with interacting with the *danka* members and wanted out. This is what created the "opportunity" for the young priest to become the head priest of his own temple.

84. *Gekkan jūshoku*, July, 1990:61.

85. Bessatsu Takarajima Henshūbu (1995:140–146).

86. *Gekkan jūshoku*, July 1990:61.

87. Tokuzō Betsuin, http://www.d1.dion.ne.jp/~tokuzo/text/94con.txt, now at http://www.nichiren.net/tokuzaji.

88. Ibid.

89. Bessatsu Takarajima Henshūbu (1995:193).

90. Ibid., 194. I took care of a small temple while conducting fieldwork and training as a priest. During my stay at the temple, I had to adjust my regular schedule to that of the *danka* members. One man regularly stopped by at 5:00 in the morning on weekends, opened the door to the living quarters (where I lay sleeping) and plopped a sack of fresh vegetables on the floor while saying "Good morning!" Others would stop by to visit their family graves, and one would drop by in the evening to sit and talk. While my presence as a foreigner may have brought about extra curiosity and thus visits, my observations at other temples and conversations with other priests led me to conclude that my experience was not unique. Temple family homes are expected to be open for business at all hours.

91. Bessatsu Takarajima Henshūbu (1995:195).

92. An acting head priest *(kenmujūshoku)* is responsible for his own temple and may also oversee one or more additional temples that have no full-time head priest.

93. *Chūgai nippō*, February 15, 2000:2.

94. *Gekkan jūshoku*, April 1982:72–74.

95. Ordination is the first step to priesthood. For example, in the Tendai sect, anyone who undertakes priestly ordination is considered a priest (*sōryo*, literally, "monk" or "nun"). However, that status is insufficient to allow one to officially preside at ceremonies

and rituals. One must complete a two-month training course on Mt. Hiei. Further initiations are required if one wishes to perform certain more advanced ceremonies.

96. Risshō Kōseikai, for example, grew from 1,413 members in 1945 to 399,806 members in 1960.

97. See Metraux (1999) and Reader (2000). For more on Aum, see also Hardacre (1995), Kaplan and Marshall (1996), and Reader (1996).

98. Nichan neru, http://mentai.2ch.net/soc/kako/972/972443085.html.

99. *Chūgai nippō*, March 23, 2000:6.

100. I witnessed these events during fieldwork in 1995.

101. *Jimon kōryū*, February 2000:12.

102. Ibid.

103. Ibid., April 2004:6.

104. Kōmyūji, http://www.komyoji.com/jyuku/.

105. As of 2001, twenty-five students had chosen the Tendai sect course.

106. See, for example, Hongō (1999).

107. Bessatsu Takarajima Henshūbu (1995:61).

5   New Priests for New Times?

1. Kimura Eishō, Kansai University professor and Jōdo Shin sect priest. Comments made at the symposium "The Modern Debate over Priests." Cited in *Chūgai nippō*, March 27, 2003:1.

2. Sugitani Gijun, director-general of the Japan World Conference on Religion and Peace, previously director-general of the Tendai sect. Ibid.

3. Yamaori Tetsuo. Ibid.

4. The program is called Gakuryō because that is the name of a previous study and training center on Mt. Hiei. The previous Eizan Gakuryō had fallen into disrepair, but it was once the Tendai sect's center for training disciples of monks from the provinces. Eizan Gakuryō had been in operation since the mid-Shōwa era. Hirano Takaai (2000:122).

5. The call was not open to women. The official reason was that avenues for laywomen seeking to become priests already existed.

6. These items are given to all applicants to the priesthood. I received a similar set upon my ordination in 1994.

7. *Kōhō Tendai*, January 1996:15.

8. Ibid.

9. *Jimon kōryū*, July 2000:104.

10. Kashiwagi Masahiro (1997:318–329).

11. For example, welfare doctrine, aid techniques, social education, counseling, etc.

12. See Covell and Rowe (2004).

13. *Saga shinbun*, September 1, 1996; www.saga-s.co.jp.

14. Ibid., January 6, 1996; www.saga-s.co.jp.

15. Kiyohara Eikō, a leading Tendai priest on Mt. Hiei, called for the addition of course work at Eizan Gakuin for all monks enrolled in the three-year mountain seclusion practice. See *Chūgai nippō*, January 22, 2000:12.

16. Hirano Takaai (2000:76–79).

17. Inoue Enryō, "Nikujiki saitai ron," *Zenshū* 35:25–29. Cited in Jaffe (1998:72). Inoue Enryō (1858–1919) was an influential Meiji-period Buddhist intellectual. He was a critic of Christianity but also of the Buddhist institutions of his time (he was raised in a Jōdo Shin sect temple). He was trained in Western philosophy and used his training to expound a scientific, rational Buddhism.

18. Ishikawa Tōkaku (1997:248).

19. Hikita (1991:298).

20. Japanese Buddhist involvement in welfare activities is divided by Ikeda Eishun into five periods: (1) from medieval times to early modern, (2) from the development of industrial society to the Taishō democracy, (3) the Pacific war, (4) early postwar, (5) the period of high growth postwar. Ikeda (1980:368–370).

21. Ishikawa Tōkaku (1997:250–251).

22. Prince Shōtoku (Shōtoku Taishi) was an early supporter of Buddhism in Japan and is credited by many for its early adoption and spread within Japan. He is said to have written commentaries on sutra, incorporated Buddhist doctrine into the seventeen-article constitution he drafted, which outlined proper relations and actions, and to have generally sponsored the spread of Buddhism.

23. Sakagami (1997:147–154).

24. Yoshida and Hasegawa (2001:31–33).

25. Ibid., p. 51.

26. Ibid., pp. 64–65.

27. Ibid., pp. 85–88.

28. Ibid., pp. 89–91.

29. Morinaga (1980).

30. Yoshida and Hasegawa (2001:117).

31. Sōma (2000:176).

32. Umehara and Hasegawa (2000:226–240).

33. Ketelaar (1990:132–133).

34. Morinaga (1980:371).

35. Yoshida (2000:24).

36. Kikuchi (2000:159).

37. Sōma (2000:179).

38. Morinaga (1980:372).

39. Ibid., 372.

40. The SVA was begun in 1979 as the Japan Sōtōshū Relief Committee, which was formed in response to the Indo-Chinese refugee problem. The name was changed to the Sōtō Volunteer Association in 1981. In 1999, the organization became independent and the name was changed to Shanti Volunteer Association. See http://www.jca.apc.org/sva/index.html.

41. Ueda (2004).

42. Kindergartens, child care, and related activities comprised almost 62 percent of Buddhist social welfare activities in 1951. A 1965 Sōtō sect survey found a little less than 40 percent of facilities to be child-care related; a 1971 Nichiren sect found almost 80 percent. Morinaga (1980:371–374).

43. The Tendai sect supports local scout troops through the Tendai Sect Scout Federation Cooperative (Tendaishū Sukauto Rengō Kyōgikai), which is affiliated with the sect.

44. *Jimon kōryū*, August 2000:48–53. In a sign of the directions in which Temple Buddhism is pulled, the article immediately following this is on how to build a funeral center capable of holding large numbers of mourners on temple grounds.

45. See Mizutani (1996) and Tashiro (1999).

46. See Wöss (1993:191–202).

47. Many thanks to Takahashi Yumi for bringing these to my attention. For an in-depth exploration of religion and aging in Japanese society, see her forthcoming master's thesis, "Being Old in an Aging Society: The Meaning of Old Age in Contemporary Japan" (Western Michigan University, Kalamazoo, Michigan).

48. Reader (1995:7–8).

49. Matsunami (1996:69). Here Matsunami is responding to the question "Why don't you just quit the priesthood, if you find the life of temple priest so difficult?"

50. *Chūgai nippō*, March 23, 2000:6.

51. Yamaori, Kakehashi, and Sasaski (1993:26–27).

52. Sugitani (1980:258–261).

53. *Kinki* is a term for the western region of Japan.

54. *Eizan jihō*, August 8, 1999:9.

55. Covell (2004).

56. *Kōhō Tendai*, May 1996:27.

57. Tendai, for example, in its initial aid efforts for the volcano victims in Hokkaidō, donated 500,000 yen through the Light Up Your Corner Movement head office to the *Hokkaido Newspaper* relief effort fund. *Chūgai nippō*, April 18, 2000:3. The Tendai sect also began a relief drive for Taiwan following the earthquake there in 1999. The Tendai sect donated over 1,000,000 yen from its emergency relief funds and added Taiwan relief aid to the call for aid it made after the earthquake in Turkey earlier that year. *Bukkyō Times Weekly*, September 30, 1999:1.

58. Hyōgo is the name of a prefecture.

59. *Kōhō Tendai*, October 1995:10–13, and May 1996:25. The Kobe experience laid the foundation for future relief efforts. For example, in January 1997, a Russian oil tanker sank off the coast of Shimane prefecture. Tendai set up a response center in the area and put out a call through its youth associations for volunteers to clean oil from the beaches. *Kōhō Tendai*, May 1997:20.

60. The first official board of directors meeting was August 5, 2000. The center was officially begun in March 2000.

61. *Chūgai nippō*, February 1, 2000:2.

62. Ibid., March 14, 2000:4.

63. Ibid., March 3, 2000:15.

6   Coming to Terms

1. Matsunaga Hakuei quoted in "Daikyūjūyonkai tsūjō shūgikai giji hōkoku," in *(Tendaishū) Tsūjō shūgikai giji hōkoku* (2000:42–43).

2. *Gekkan jūshoku*, April 1979:2. Statement by a priest and member of the Kōyasan Shingon sect Diet regarding a case in which, after three years of negotiation, the wife and daughters of a priest who died before an heir could be found reached a settlement with the sect to be paid 40,000,000 yen on the condition that they leave the temple premises.

3. *Gekkan jūshoku*, April 1979:8. This statement is by the eldest daughter of the deceased head priest.

4. Kawahashi (1995a:175).

5. *Tendai no fujin*, no. 26 (January 1998): 6.

6. For Meiji legal changes affecting clerical marriage, see chapter 4.

7. *Chūgai nippō*, January 22, 2000:6. See also Kawahashi (1995a:161–183).

8. Jaffe (1995:18). For an in-depth discussion of the history of clerical marriage in Japan, see Jaffe's dissertation as well as Jaffe (1998:45–86).

9. Cited in Stone (1999:139).

10. Ihara (1969:150).

11. Morioka (1986:89).

12. Interview, January 15, 2001.

13. The yen to dollar exchange rate in December 2004 was 105 yen to 1 dollar.

14. This case appears in *Jimon kōryū*, January 2001:22–29.

15. Not her actual name.

16. Few jobs open to middle-aged or older individuals in Japan pay a living wage. This is especially so for women, and even more so for individuals with little or no job experience.

17. This is common to all Temple Buddhism sects except Jōdo Shin, though the situation is slowly changing.

18. This gender ideal is not a traditional aspect of Japanese culture. It is the direct result of governmental policy applied aggressively from the Meiji period through to today. Creighton (1996:192–220).

19. Roberts (1996:224). See also Creighton (1996:215).

20. Awaya and Phillips (1996:244–270).

21. Japan's lengthy recession, however, has drastically limited their job opportunities.

22. Upham (1987:125).

23. Long (1996:156–176).

24. Upham (1997:128).

25. Hardacre (1986:192).

26. Nakamura (1997:87–120).

27. There is overwhelming evidence that such "traditional" female roles are a modern creation. Kathleen Uno, for instance, argues that Meiji educational policies, together with industrialization and increasing middle-class wages, led to the advent of the professional housewife. Government policies after the turn of the century, as reflected in the slogan Good Wives, Wise Mothers, sought to encourage this new "traditional" gendered bifurcation of household roles. Uno (1991:17–41).

28. *Tendai no fujin*, January 2000:1.

29. Ibid., January 1997:2.

30. Tendai Constitution, Article 48, *"jizoku"* (Temple Families); and Temple Family Bylaws, Article 12, *"Jiteifujin"* (Rights and responsibilities of temple wives). Yamada (1996:12, 560). Morioka (1986:88–91).

31. *Jimon kōryū*, August 2002:76.

32. The Chizan branch of Shingon and the Sōtō sect in 1952, the Myōshinji branch of Rinzai in 1963, the Tendai sect in 1967, the Buzan branch of Shingon and the Kōyazan Shingon sect in 1969, and the Nichiren sect in 1971. The extent to which each sect recognized temple wives varied. Some were recognized in the sect constitution, some in bylaws, some in both.

33. Priests are those who have taken the priestly precepts. In most sects of temple Buddhism, there are a variety of ranks within the priesthood. Doctrinal instructors are generally those who have completed the basic training and initiations required of those who seek to become head priests. Ranking as a doctrinal instructor allows one to perform ceremonies.

34. Interview, November 2000.

35. Kagamishima Mariko argues that urbanization also put a greater demand on the services of temple wives. She argues that those who might have worked for the temple left for the cities. She blames this exodus on a changing value system in which economics took precedence over faith. Kagamishima (1999:175). In 1992, the Ōtani branch of the Jōdo Shin sect permitted women who had ordained as priests to become head priests, but only if there was no appropriate male heir. In 1997, the sect amended the rules again to remove this restriction. *Kyoto shinbun*, June 11, 1996 (Web archive version; http://www.kyoto-up.co./jp).

36. *Tendai no fujin*, January 1997:7. On cleaning as practice, see Reader (1995:227–245).

37. *Tendai no fujin*, January 1998:1. Fuji Kōgen, then director-general of the Tendai sect.

38. Hardacre (1986:192).

39. See Jaffe (2001) and Kawahashi (1995a).

40. Kawahashi (2000:151). See also Kawahashi (1995b:194–198).

41. Interview, January 15, 2001.

42. Related to this view of the temple family, one priest notes, "That is why they [*danka* members] say things, meaning them as compliments, like 'You've come to look just like the previous head priest' or 'You sound just like him.'" Here the "previous head priest" he refers to is his father. Inoue and Kokusai Shūkyō Kenkyūjo, eds. (1995:258).

43. In reality few priests live up to the image of so-called real priests. Tendai sect ascetics, some Zen monks, and a few others strive to meet this image and are encouraged in their efforts by the sects because of the legitimating effect of their practice on the sect as a whole. Sōtō sect nuns, as Paula Arai demonstrates, often pride themselves on main-

taining strict codes of conduct and traditional practices. And many, she notes, believe they are the only real priests still practicing in Japan. Arai (1999).

44. Sōtōshū Shūsei Chōsa Iinkai (1984:174–175).

45. Kawahashi (2000:150).

46. *Tendai no fujin*, January 1998:1.

47. Ibid., 2. Kobori Setsuko, then advisor to the Temple Wives Federation.

48. Ibid.

49. Interview, December, 2001. According to *Jimon kōryū*, 25.3 percent of temple wives report being from temple family backgrounds (August 2002:75). Many temple daughters also attend sectarian universities to look for potential mates.

50. Unfortunately, I have not yet found any studies of family businesses from the point of view of gender studies. Family businesses would provide the closest possible comparative sample for temple family structures and relationships. The typical middle-class household, the standard object of study, is not comparable to temple families. Therefore, comparisons to the "education mother" syndrome are not possible here. Middle-class mothers fall into the syndrome because Japan is an "educational achievement society" (*gakureki shakai*). In short, one's success in school from as early as kindergarten determines one's future. Although temple mothers must consider their children's schooling, the education mother syndrome may not play a role in child rearing at temples because the future of at least the eldest son is determined (or at least planned and hoped for) from birth. Moreover, for most temple sons, and for those temple daughters raised to marry into temple households, gaining a degree at the sect-sponsored university often is seen as optimal. This is especially so for male heirs in the Tendai sect because education achievement at the sect university, and particularly in Buddhist Studies, is directly tied to priestly ranking. However, if the education mother syndrome is considered as a social acceptance syndrome, comparisons can be made. In the case of temple mothers, social success within temple society is determined by their success or failure to raise (educate) a successor to the temple.

51. *Jimon kōryū*, August 2002:75.

52. *Tendai no fujin*, January 1997:1. Sugitani Gijun, then Tendai sect director-general.

53. The four noble truths and eightfold path are early Buddhist teachings recognized by most Buddhist as central tenets of the Buddhist faith. The four noble truths are suffering (the effect), craving (the cause), nirvana (the cessation of suffering achieved through extinguishing craving), and the path (the method to achieve cessation of suffering). The eightfold path consists of the following: right view, right thought, right speech, right action, right livelihood, right effort, right mindfulness, and right concentration.

54. Interview, December 2001.

55. This system was also used to raise funds for the federation by charging a small fee for copying practice and instruction.

56. Uko (1999:133).

57. Chieko Kuriki, *Chicago Tribune*, January 14, 1990: zone 6, 7.

58. Uko (1999:133).

59. Kuriki (see n. 57). A temple wife interviewed for Kuriki's article states, "In reality discrimination against [temple wives] is wors[e] than against ordinary women. [Temple wives] are viewed as temple property, not as human beings."

60. Kawahashi (2000:156). This does not appear to be the case in the Tendai sect.

61. *Chūgai nippō*, January 22, 2000:6.

62. Interestingly, this is in opposition to a small but growing trend among secular wives willfully to seek out a grave plot separate from their husbands. Where temple wives seek burial with their husbands for purposes of recognition of their identity as wives, secular wives seek separate burial for recognition as individuals.

63. See, for example, Kagamishima (1999).

64. *Jimon kōryū*, August 2002:79; Kawahashi (1995).

65. *Chūgai nippō*, November 20, 1999:6. Originally appeared in October 30, 1999, issue.

66. This network is the leading transsectarian association for temple wives, nuns, and other concerned Buddhist women to discuss issues regarding gender and Buddhism in Japan.

67. *Chūgai nippō*, November 20, 1999:6.

68. *Dainanajūyonkai tsūjō shūgikai giji hōkoku* (1992:28).

69. Ibid.

70. Ibid., 25.

71. In such instances, the temple often loans the priest money to build the house, with the understanding that the house will become temple property when the priest leaves.

72. Tendaishū Jiteifujin Rengōkai (1997: attachment 3–4).

73. *Bukkyō Times Weekly*, November 2, 2000:1.

74. See Arai (1999).

75. Ibid., 140.

76. Aoyama (1998:228–230). Cited in Kumamoto (2004).

77. Interview with Setouchi Jakuchō, June 17, 2000.

78. There is a definite preference for male priests at local temples. See below for further discussion of this matter.

79. *Gekkan jūshoku*, May 1979:7.

80. *Jimon kōryū*, August 2002:78.

81. Ibid., 76.

82. *Dainanajūyonkai tsūjō shūgikai giji hōkoku* (1992:48). I do not have access to the original report. Therefore, I cannot ascertain which temples were included in the survey. If temples without resident priests are included, the actual percentage of temples with temple families could be significantly higher.

83. *Tendai shūki*, 559.

84. Morioka (1986:102).

85. *Dainanajūyonkai tsūjō shūgikai giji hōkoku* (1992:25).

86. Unfortunately, Chiyoda Life Insurance was one of several large companies to recently experience severe financial difficulty in Japan. Although the matter is still before the courts at the time of writing this, it appears that those who invested in Tendai's policy through Chiyoda will get only a small portion of their investment back. This development represents a major blow to temple wife support as well as to the financial resources of some priests. Luckily, the system was only relatively recently (1984) adopted, so the amounts invested were not as significant as they might otherwise have been.

87. *Chūgai nippō*, November 20, 1999:6.

88. Ibid.

89. Morioka (1986:102). *Jimon kōryū*, August 2002:78.

90. Kawahashi (2000:154).

91. *Jimon kōryū*, December, 2001:19.

92. Interview, January 15, 2001.

93. *Bukkyō Times Weekly*, January 18, 2001:3.

94. *Jimon kōryū*, December 2001:18.

95. There are cases where the mother of the deceased or absent head priest, not the wife, ordains to care for the temple until an acceptable male family member can replace her.

96. *Chūgai nippō*, March 16, 2000:7.

97. *Bukkyō Times Weekly*, January 11, 2001:3. Many younger male priests seem to favor the position of temple wives. Therefore, it is possible that this attitude will change in the future as those who are young today gain seniority within the system. The average age of the respondents was over fifty-five (76.4 percent were between the ages of fifty-five and seventy-four).

98. Watanabe Noriko (1999:113).

99. Ibid., 123.

100. Interview, October 1, 2000. Those priests who are critical of the sect, however, often support their wives' demands for reform.

101. Ōka Jakujun, head of the Juridical Person Division. *Daihachijūrokukai tsūjō shūgikai giji hōkoku* (1996:38).

102. *Kōhō Tendai*, May 1996:7.

103. The three precepts of refuge are vows to take refuge in the Buddha, the Dharma, and the Sangha. The bodhisattva vows are, "However innumerable sentient beings are, I vow to save them; however inexhaustible the passions are, I vow to extinguish them; however limitless the dharmas [teachings] are, I vow to study them, however infinite the Buddha-truth is, I vow to attain it." *Japanese-English Buddhist Dictionary*, rev. ed. (Tokyo: Daitō shuppansha, 1991), 304.

104. According the 2001 survey of temple wives, 45.8 percent of Rinzai and Ōbaku sect temple wives had taken the lay precepts *(jūkai)* and 12.2 percent had undergone ordination *(tokudo)*. *Jimon kōryū*, August 2002:78.

105. *Daikyūjūgokai tsūjō shūgikai giji hōkoku* (2000:30–31).

106. This is an esoteric Buddhist ceremony (Tendai is considered a sect of esoteric Buddhism). In this ceremony the initiate establishes a special connection with a deity.

107. *Kōhō Tendai*, September 1996:3.

108. *Tendai no fujin*, January 1997:1.

109. Individuals who undertake priestly ordination are required by sect bylaws to complete certain practices on Mt. Hiei and to continue training indefinitely. Those who undergo the temple wife ordination are not required to train as priests, but are required to attend study retreats.

110. Temple wife and priestly ordination are clearly separated in other sects as well. For example, in the Sōtō sect one cannot be registered in the temple wife registry if one takes the priestly precepts. Seno (1999:156). Lay ordination is free for those who take it on Mt. Hiei at prescribed times. Lay ordinations conducted at local temples often require a donation. *Daikyūjūgokai tsūjō shūgikai giji hōkoku* (2000:33).

111. *Tendai no fujin*, January 1997:4. These are comments by a temple wife reflecting on a lecture given by a priest to temple wives gathered on Mt. Hiei.

112. Tendaishū Jiteifujin Rengōkai (1997:20).

113. *Daikyūjūsankai tsūjō shūgikai giji hōkoku* (1999:39).

114. Tendaishū Jiteifujin Rengōkai (1997:18).

115. *Kōhō Tendai*, September 1996:2. Tendaishū Jiteifujin Rengōkai (1997: attachment 5).

116. Tendaishū Jiteifujin Rengōkai (1997:20).

117. Ibid., 19.

118. *Tendai no fujin*, January 1997:13.

7 Money and the Temple

1. *Asahi shinbun* (Tokyo), evening edition, June 6, 1995:7. "Aum" refers to Aum Shinrikyō, the new religious movement found responsible for the 1995 sarin gas incident on Tokyo subways.

2. *Asahi shinbun* (Tokyo), morning edition, June 21, 1997:4.

3. Tendai Busseinen (Tendai Young Buddhist Association) home page: http://www2t. biglobe.ne.jp/~tendai/cgi-qa/renlst.cgi; a response from a priest to someone writing to the "Q&A" section of the home page; accessed February 7, 2000. New address: http:// www.tendai-yba.com).

4. See Gernet (1995).

5. An 1868 survey found 459,040 temples extant; a survey four years later found only 51,245 temples extant. Although the counting procedures and quality undoubtedly differed, the surveys still show a significant drop in temple numbers. Bukkyō Nenkan Hensan Iinkai (1969:526).

6. See Harvey (2000) and Sizemore and Swearer (1990).

7. Of course, local and national politics, as well as economic rivalries, have always played a part in how and when such rhetoric is used.

8. Some early modern temples installed burglar alarms as well: the so-called nightingale floors. These were floors designed to creak loudly when walked across.

9. Larger temples are more like foundations than family businesses. They generally have several priests on staff and often lay employees as well.

10. Dobbins (1996:217–232). Kuroda (1996a) calls the society of this period *shōen shakai* (estate society).

11. Taira (1994:257–301).

12. See Kuroda (1996a:287–320).

13. Goodwin (1994:142). In this sense, Goodwin gives a more nuanced analysis of Buddhism and the economy than Gernet. Gernet's assertion that Buddhism collapsed under the weight of its own economic success fails to account for the continued flourishing of Buddhism in China. However, Gernet does provide valuable insights as well. Echoing the situation in contemporary Japan, Gernet asserts that the Buddhist economy—and Buddhism itself—began its collapse in the Tang with the advent of new social structures and relationships that broke the web of interpersonal relationships upon which the Buddhist economy relied.

14. Hur (2000).

15. See Williams (2000:chap. 4).

16. One rural priest asked me to be sure to note that postwar land reforms were directly imposed by MacArthur and that the current dire financial straits of many temples, in which priests are often forced to take on outside work, can be directly blamed on MacArthur. However, it is clear that land reform measures had been proposed by Japanese bureaucrats since before the war and that those proposals meshed well with Occupation aims.

17. At one rural temple observed, members of a local women's group (*fujinkai*) request the services of the priest to pray for ease of childbirth. This rite is called *inukuyō* (memorial for dogs). The women bring a Y-shaped stick to the priest, on which he inscribes a prayer for the positive rebirth of any dog that should happen by the stick. In return for making this offering for the salvation of dogs, the women hope for a doglike childbirth (dogs are seen as having especially easy births). *Rokuza nenbutsu* groups, though rare today, are one example of a *nenbutsu* group. *Rokuza nenbutsu* is a form of Buddhist practice based on chanting *nenbutsu* (i.e., chanting the phrase, "Namu Amida Butsu" or "I put my faith in Amida Buddha"). During my fieldwork, I was allowed the opportunity to observe and film one group active in the Chiba area. For more on this practice, see Ichishima (1997:41–48).

18. Reader (1987b). For material on pilgrimage in Japan, see Reader and Swanson (1997).

19. Hardacre cites a survey demonstrating that 47.5 percent of temples marketing *mizuko* rites began to advertise such rites between 1975 and 1984. Nearly half (47.9 percent) of those temples charged a fee for the service ranging from 5,000 to 20,000 yen. For most temples, this is only a supplementary source of income. The survey cited by Hardacre shows 59.5 percent of temples surveyed had ten or fewer clients per month. Hardacre (1997:94–95). For more on *mizuko kuyō*, see Brooks (1981:119–147), Hoshino and Takeda (1993:305–320), LaFleur (1992, 1995:185–196), Tanabe Jr. (1995:197–200), Werblowsky (1991:295–354), and the collection of articles in the *Journal of the American Academy of Religion* 67, no. 4 (December 1999).

20. An imperial nunnery in the Tokyo area is now renowned for its vegetarian restaurant. The restaurant was started as one measure (running a kindergarten was another) to support the temple. The temple even has produced an English-language cookbook, *Zen Vegetarian Cooking* (Yoneda and Hoshino, 1982). Nunneries such as this previously relied almost entirely on the support of the imperial household. The Meiji government cut such support, and lands were stripped away in the postwar period. This situation left such temples in desperate financial situations because they had no *danka* to rely on and because nuns are not traditionally called upon to perform ritual services for the dead.

21. The year 2000 marked the fiftieth anniversary of the Cultural Artifacts Law (Bunkazai hogohō, promulgated in May 1950). This law was a revised form of prewar laws regarding the preservation of national cultural assets. Most local cultural preservation laws are based on it. The law provides for the designation of certain physical or abstract properties (such as works of art or the skills of a master craftsman) as national cultural

assets or treasures. Objects so designated become eligible for funding to support their preservation. *Chūgai nippō*, November 23, 2000:1–2 and 8–9. See also Bunkachō Bunkabu Shūmuka (1983a:432–436) and Sayre (1986:851–890).

22. The Tendai sect fund is called the Temple and Teaching Center Promotion Fund (Jiin Kyōkai Shinkō Shikin) (*Daihachijūkai tsūjō shūgikai giji hōkoku* [1994:42]). Total expenditures in 2000 were 80,100,000. *Tendai shūhō*, no. 213 (May 2000):25.

23. Donation is one of the six *pāramita* (*ropparamitsu*), which are one way of framing traditional Buddhist practice. The six are as follows:(1) donation/charity (*fuse*), (2) taking/observing the precepts (*jukai*), (3) forbearance (*ninniku*), (4) assiduousness (*shōjin*), (5) meditation (*zenjō*), (6) wisdom (*chie*). These six represent the most common formation of the Mahayana Buddhist path.

24. In a recent survey, 62 percent of priests responded that they believe income from funeral and related services will decrease in the future. Zen'nihon Bukkyō Seinenkai (2003:154–155).

25. From the September 2003 Japan Consumer Association (Nihon Shōhisha Kyōkai) survey on funerals. See Osōshik Puraza, http://www.osoushiki-plaza.com/library/index-data.html

26. From the May 1995 Sanwa Bank survey, "Survey of Relations from the Point of View of Money." See http://www.osoushiki-plaza.com/library/index-data.html.

27. In 1987, there were fourteen thousand applicants for 750 new plots at a memorial park in Hachioji, a suburb of Tokyo. In 1992, Tama Memorial Park (Tama Reien), a publicly run memorial park in suburban Tokyo, added 300 new plots. There were over five times as many applicants as plots. Such circumstances led to extensive competition to find plots. Tour companies teamed up with memorial parks to bring potential customers to view the available sites. Bukkyō Nenkan Hensan Iinkai (1988:28). Images of such tours can be seen in the film *Ohaka ga nai* (I Have No Grave).

28. *Ishiya* are those who make gravestones. However, with the advent of public memorial parks, they came to provide a variety of other services as well.

29. *Asahi shinbun* (Tokyo), evening edition, January 19, 1999:6. This is one possible reason for the postwar rise in posthumous name prices. Priests passed the cost of the kickback on to the consumer.

30. Some individuals, many of whom are not ordained monks, earn their living begging in major train stations, such as Shinjuku in Tokyo.

31. *Daikyūjūgokai tsūjō shūgikai giji hōkoku* (2000:10). See also *Tendai shūhō*, no. 213 (May 2000):16. Of this amount, the majority (697,700,000) was derived from sect fees (including tithes on temples and fees for priests), fees paid for ordination and various promotions (133,050,000), and transfers from a maintenance endowment (158,500,000). The largest expenditures were for sect personnel (366,330,000) and for education and proselytizing (216,070,000).

32. Training temples are an exception.

33. The year 2000 was the fifteenth anniversary of the beginning of this event. In 1999, a total of 10,326,596 yen was generated. This money was used for the social welfare projects of the Tendai sect's Light Up Your Corner Movement, as well as for local efforts at social welfare.

34. Few temples have more than one priest on full-time staff. However, many pay other local priests to assist them at funerals and other events that require more than one priest (such as the *goma* fire ritual at Tendai temples). The current standard pay in Tokyo for such assistants is 30,000 yen (more for senior priests). The tax office encourages priests to draw salaries. The income of priests is taxable, therefore, failure to draw a salary leads tax auditors to the assumption that the priest is taking money from the temple for personal expenses and not reporting it as earned income.

35. *(Tendaishū) Tsūjō shūkishū* (1996).

36. See Haley (1991). See also Hamilton and Sanders (1992).

37. *Kōhō Tendai*, September 1996, and January 1999. For instance, one priest relates the example of a temple that was forced to be sold to pay for liabilities incurred when the branch from a tree on temple grounds fell onto a car and killed the driver. *Daihachijūhachikai tsūjō shūgikai giji hōkoku* (1997:38).

38. Further work must be done on the relationship between traditional handicrafts and temples. Kimono, sandal, prayer bead, incense, even traditional umbrella industries rely on temples for a substantial amount of their business. Prices charged for their products are often high because of the amount of time and care put into their making. However, prices can also be maintained at artificially high levels because suppliers know that in many cases it is not an individual but an organization (the temple) that is paying the bill; thus, like Ginza nightclubs, they are able to charge more because the bill is being charged to an expense account. With the prolonged recession, however, many such industries are facing financial crisis. Donations to temples have dropped, leaving temples little extra money. The result is that some purchases must be forgone, and, when purchases are made, low-end products must be chosen. The future of traditional arts and crafts in Japan, therefore, is linked to the future of temple Buddhism.

39. This section appeared previously as Covell (2000).

40. *(Tendaishū) Tsūjo shūkishū* (1996:42).

41. The Three Treasures refers to the Buddha, the Dharma (the teachings), and the Sangha (the community of priests).

42. *Daihachijūkai tsūjō shūgikai giji hōkoku* (1994:43).

43. Neil McMullin and Jamie Hubbard exchange thoughts on this issue including the question of how the object of study is constructed. See McMullin (1989:3–40), Hubbard (1992:3–27), and McMullin (1992:29–39). This topic is easily expanded if we include Ian Reader and George Tanabe's *Practically Religious*, in which they argue that this-

worldly benefits are the heart of Japanese religion and offer evidence that doctrine and practice must be read in an integrated fashion. See also Anderson (1991), and Reader (1991).

44. Educational juridical persons (*gakkō hōjin*).

45. Social welfare juridical persons (*shakai fukushi hōjin*).

46. Changes were made as part of the April 1971 tax code revisions. In an early postwar case, the tax office sought to tax income from a parking lot owned by a shrine. Shrine officials argued that the lot was there so they could bless the cars parked in it. To prove their point, they walked the lot blessing cars. The tax office lost the battle. When the law was later revised, parking lots were added to the list of taxable ventures. Yazawa (1980: 215–216).

47. *Gekkan jūshoku*, January, 1982:41. The rates circa 1980 were 40 percent for large companies and 28 percent for small companies compared to 23 percent for religious juridical persons. Moreover, 30 percent of profits could be donated, pretax, to the juridical person. Yazawa (1980:215).

48. Ishii (1997:157–158).

49. An article discussing this appears in *Kōhō Tendai*, May 1996:26.

50. Hasekawa (1994:265–266).

51. The tax also designated several shrines and one castle. The temples, however, led the fight against the tax.

52. Under the national Law Governing Local Taxation, the tax was a nonstatutory ordinary tax (*hōteigai futsuzei*), which meant it had to be approved by the minister for home affairs and could be sought only when necessity could be proven. (It was not an ordinary statutory tax [*hōtei futsuzei*] or a purpose-oriented statutory tax [*hōtei mokutekizei*].) Nonstatutory ordinary taxes can be used for any purpose; therefore, to avoid foreseeable complaints that the funds raised would be used to pay off city debt, city officials added a line to the effect that proceeds had to be used for the preservation and maintenance of historically valuable cultural assets. Because the minister for home affairs cleared the two previous versions of this tax, officials believed this tax, too, would quickly win approval. However, because the tax could be defined as purpose-oriented, some argued that it should be categorized as a nonstatutory purpose-oriented tax, which would be illegal under the Law Governing Local Taxation.

53. *Asahi shinbun* (Tokyo), morning edition, July 17, 1986:4.

54. Reader and Tanabe (1998:17–21).

55. Ishii (1997:152).

56. Shakyamuni is the historical Buddha.

57. *Gekkan jūshoku*, March 1985:11.

58. Temple representatives began bargaining at 50 percent but settled on paying 70 percent of the projected amount. *Asahi shinbun* (Tokyo), morning edition, January 13, 1987:3.

59. *Asahi shinbun* (Tokyo), morning edition, May 1, 1987:3.

60. *Gekkan jūshoku*, January 1983:16.

61. Kyoto temples charged on average 300–400 yen, approximately 100 yen higher than the Nara average and 200 yen higher than the Kamakura average.

62. *Washington Post*, December 21, 1985:A16.

63. *Gekkan jūshoku*, January 1983:17.

64. Ibid., January, 14. The actual amount directly received by temples was considerably less. The city gave approximately 30,000,000 yen annually to help temples maintain cultural artifacts in their possession through the Kyoto City Cultural Tourism Maintenance Fund Foundation (Kyotoshi Bunkazai Shigen Hogo Zaidan). *Jurisuto sōgō tokushū*, March 1983:30.

65. For more on the topic of commodification of religion in Japan see Reader and Tanabe (1998) and Shimazono (1998).

66. *Asahi shinbun* (Tokyo), morning edition, October 27, 1985:4.

67. Shimazono 1998.

68. Ashida (1994:193–194).

69. *Asahi shinbun* (Tokyo), evening edition, March 7, 1985:3.

70. *Gekkan jūshoku*, January 1982:19.

71. Ibid., 5.

72. *Asahi shinbun* (Tokyo), morning edition, January 16, 1987:5.

73. Today Kinkakuji charges an entrance fee and is open to the public. However, its most famous halls require reservations and an additional fee to view.

8   The Price of Naming the Dead

1. *Jimon kōryū*, February 2000:64. A quote from a Japanese male, age forty-three, Hyōgo prefecture.

2. Ibid., p. 65. A quote from a Japanese male, age sixty-five, Chiba prefecture.

3. Tendai Busseinen home page. Q&A section. Response by a priest to an inquiry regarding donations (see chap. 7, n. 3).

4. Ueda (2004:8).

5. When questioned about this during informal conversation, one priest jokingly responded that patients who see a priest enter their room at a hospital in robes tend to say, "Not yet, not yet, I'm not dead yet!"

6. Arai (1999:139).

7. *Jimon kōryū*, August 2000:113.

8. The Japan Buddhist Federation is the 1957 incarnation of the Dainippon Bukkyōkai (same translation), which in turn had been the Nippon Bukkyō Rengōkai (same translation). These federations, in turn, had their roots in the Bukkyō Konwakai (Buddhism Society), which was founded in 1900. Its home page is www.jtvan.co.jp/~jbf/. The posthumous precept name debate has even been reported in the U.S. mass media; see, for example, Sakurai (1999).

9. See Tamamuro Fumio (1999) for more on the topic of posthumous precept name ranks. Katoh Eiji claims that posthumous precept names were in wide use by the general populace by the mid-eighteenth century. *Jimon kōryū*, July 2000:84–87.

10. Smith (1974:66).

11. See Williams (2000:chap. 6). For an in-depth discussion of the history of posthumous precept names in English, see Bodiford (1996).

12. Results of the *danka* member/student/Internet–based survey can be found in *Chūgai nippō*, May 9, 2000:12. Those for the head priest-based survey can be found in *Jimon kōryū*, August 2000:86–89.

13. Cited in *Jimon kōryū*, September 2000:81.

14. Some 84.8 percent responded that they had heard or read of it in the mass media, 45.8 percent had heard directly from people other than *danka* members, and 20 percent had heard about it directly from *danka* members. *Jimon kōryū*, August 2000:86.

15. Bukkyō Daigaku is affiliated with the Jōdo sect.

16. *Jimon kōryū*, April 2000:44.

17. *Daikyūijūgokai tsūjō shūgikai giji hōkoku* (2000:34, 36).

18. One informant, for example, told me that sermons are almost always conducted at rites for aborted fetuses, at least at her temple.

19. Samplings from observations are too small and in the future must be backed with broader survey results.

20. Various Buddhist groups, sectarian and transsectarian, offer telephone Dharma talks. There are several varieties. For example, individuals seeking advice from priests may call in to speak with a priest. Other services offer prerecorded talks on specific subjects.

21. Kanagawa Bukkyū seihenkai, http://tendai.room.ne.jp/~kanagawa/index.html.

22. Komuro (1998:218).

23. The market price in some areas is based on the deceased's earning power while alive, generally one month's salary. Kichijōji home page, www.dokidoki.ne.jp/home2/kisyoji/index.htm (see under the *kaimyō* question).

24. *Jimon kōryū*, August 2000:87.

25. *Tendai Booklet*, no.19, 18–19. See *Jimon kōryū*, May 2000:77–78, for similar explanations offered by the Shingon sect Chizan branch, the Jōdo sect, and Jōdo Shin sect Otani branch.

26. Kichijōji home page, July 22, 1999: www.dokidoki.ne.jp/home2/kisyoji/index.htm or see www.dokidoki.ne.jp/home2/kisyoji/QA.htm.

27. The effect understood to result from the granting of a posthumous precept name varied from sect to sect, though today it appears most laity understand it to mean rebirth in a Pure Land.

28. Tendai Busseinen home page, Q&A section, February 7, 2000 (see chap. 7, n.3). See also Katō Eiji, *Jimon kōryū* July 2000:88.

29. *Mainichi shinbun*, November 19, 1998.

30. Takigawa (1998:184).

31. Survey conducted by Suzuki Iwayumi of Tōhoku University in 2003. Cited in *Jimon kōryū*, January 2004:92. More results from this survey can also be found in *Jimon kōryū*, November 2003:72–81. Another survey, conducted by Shūkyō to Shakkai Gakkai in 1996, found that 15.9 percent believed in a world after death, and 38.8 percent thought it might be possible. Cited in Ishii (1997:85).

32. Surveys conducted by national Temple Buddnewspapers (*Asahi shinbun, Mainichi shinbun, Yomiuri shinbun*) show the numbers to be in flux during the postwar period but rarely exceeding 50 percent. See *Jimon kōryū*, January 2004:92. The stronger numbers shown by youth reflect the growth in interest in the occult, afterlife experiences, and the like among Japanese youth. Whereas sects of Buddhism tend to promote traditional values and culture, Japanese youth are showing more interest in experiential religion. Bukkyō Nenkan Hensan Iinkai (1988:22–23)

33. *Jimon kōryū*, January 2004:93.

34. Ibid.

35. A 2003 survey conducted by Suzuki Iwayumi found that 38 percent saw the funeral as a ritual to see the dead off to the afterlife. *Jimon kōryū*, December 2003:74.

36. *Asahi shinbun* survey (September 23, 1995), cited in Ishii (1997:68). Between 1981 and 1995, ownership nationwide has dropped from 63 to 59 percent.

37. *Jimon kōryū*, January 2004:97.

38. Ibid., August 2002:83–85.

39. Zen'nihon Bukkyō Seinenkai (2003:159). This number is the average taken from responses from priests aged 20–69.

40. Sugawara (2002).

41. There are many studies on this subject in Japanese. In English, see Bodiford (1996) and Williams (2000).

42. Bodiford (1996).

43. On occasion, private detectives are hired to determine the social background of individuals by families negotiating a wedding and by companies seeking to know the background of a prospective employee. Individuals from status or race groups that are subject to discrimination (such as Koreans or burakumin) are selectively denied permission to marry or employment based on such background checks.

44. A 1999 Asahi shinbun article claims that a priest in Nagano reported at least two such phone calls recently (Asahi shinbun [Tokyo], morning edition, December 16, 1999:27). And a 1996 article examines the on-going process in Saga prefecture of searching for and processing gravestones and temple registers of the dead with discriminatory posthumous precept names recorded in them.

45. Gekkan jūshoku ran a series of articles dealing with discriminatory practices by the Shingon sect (Gekkan jūshoku, April–June 1983), and a follow-up series (December– February 1994), and Jimon kōryū ran a series on discriminatory remarks by a Jōdo Shin sect priest and the subsequent sect-level meetings.

46. Gekkan jūshoku, May 1983:36–37.

47. Kōhō Tendai, January 1996:18–19.

48. Here "contributions" does not necessarily mean money. It can also mean contributing one's time to temple projects or working to promote or aid the temple.

49. A Jōdo sect ceremony that lasts from five to seven days in which participants take part in a fivefold transmission of Jōdo sect teachings. A lay ordination takes place during the ceremony.

50. Jimon kōryū, August 2000:88.

51. This conclusion fits well with information related to me by several priests following an academic conference in Tokyo. Although they admitted that they are delighted when a danka member donates a large sum of money in return for a special name, they claimed they do not ask for a set amount, nor do they require a set amount. For special names, they remarked, service to the temple is the foremost deciding factor.

52. Gekkan jūshoku, July 1984:21–26.

53. Tendai Busseinen home page, Q&A section, February 7, 2000 (see chap. 7, n. 3).

54. Japan Consumers Association survey cited in Jimon kōryū, September 2000:81.

55. The turn to precept reform is nothing new. Calls to reform priestly adherence to precepts have been made throughout history in Japan, and calls to have laity adhere to lay precepts have also been made on occasion. See, for example, the precept reform movement of Jiun Sonja.

56. See, for example, *Tendai Booklet,* no. 27 (November 2002), which was dedicated to a discussion of the precepts.

57. *Jimon kōryū,* August 2000:90–91.

58. Here, and throughout this work, "precept maintenance" refers to adherence to the precepts (or lack there of). However, clerical marriage, more so than consumption of alcohol or other infractions, serves to define much of the debate over precepts today.

59. Interestingly, the author notes, "I won't say that 'Not to drink alcohol' means to not touch a drop as in the Hinayana, but too much alcohol can upset one's mind so it should be had only to warm the heart and purify one a bit." *Tendai koyomi kangyōkai,* 86.

60. Sugawara (2002).

61. Indeed, a family friend whose husband had unexpectedly passed away once phoned me about trouble she was experiencing with a priest. The priest, she told me, was requesting 200,000 yen for a regular posthumous precept name but told her she could have a more effective special posthumous precept name for 1,000,000. Such priests, however, are exceptions to the rule. Of the many priests I met during fieldwork, I know of none who has engaged in such practices.

62. Tendai Busseinen home page, Q&A section, February 7, 2000 (see chap. 7, n. 3).

63. See, for example, PHP Kenkyūkai, eds., Ina to iu toki okane wa ikura hitsuyōka (Tokyo: PHP Kenkyūkai, 1998): http://ekitan.com/biz/handbook/data/1011400.htm or Sōsai manna-:Manna-Q&A.sūshiki at Minsō.com, at http://www.minso.com/sougi/m-kaimyo.htm.

64. *Jimon kōryū,* July 2000:92.

65. Ibid., August 2000:86–89.

66. Ibid., 87.

67. A more radical example is that of the "Christian" priests who perform weddings at some wedding chapels in Japan. Many are not ordained; they are merely foreigners (white) who look the part and can read the Bible in English.

68. See, for example, Rowe (2003:85–118).

69. Sakamoto Kōhaku, director of studies at Eizan Gakuin in *Kōhō tendai,* September 1998:12–13.

70. Ibid.

Epilogue: The World of Householding World-Renouncers

1. Hieizan Web site; see http://www.hieizan.or.jp/enryakuji/jcont/access/mother/summit.html. See also Nihon Shūkyō Daihyōsha Kaigi (1987).

2. Many of the sects of Temple Buddhism and many new religions as well seek to maintain public contact with the Vatican.

3. The Hieizan home page greets one with a picture of Saichō sitting in meditation; the next screen is of priests clad in elegant robes walking in the early morning mist of Mt. Hiei to the sound of chanting. The text at the bottom of the picture begins, "A holy place of silent beauty and strict discipline, Enryakuji may at first glance seem uninviting." See http://www.hieizan.or.jp/enryakuji/jcont/index3.html.

4. See, for example, the Light Up Your Corner Movement home page.

5. The education of Buddhists and Buddhist education more broadly are the focus of my current research. See Covell and Rowe (2004).

Sources Cited

Abe, Yoshiya. 1968–1970. "Religious Freedom under the Meiji Constitution. Parts 1–6." *Contemporary Religions in Japan* 9:268–338; 10:57–97, 181–203; 11:27–53, 54–79, 223–296.

Akazawa Shirō. 1985. *Kindai Nihon no shisā dōin to shūkyō tōsei*. Tokyo: Azekura Shobō.

Akizuki Ryōmin. 1993. *Gokai darake no bukkyō: shindaijō undo no ikkan toshite*. Tokyo: Hakujusha.

Anderson, Richard W. 1991. "What Constitutes Religious Activity?" *Japanese Journal of Religious Studies* 18 (4): 368–372.

Anesaki, Masaharu. 1963. *History of Japanese Religion: With Special Reference to the Social and Moral Life of the Nation*. Original edition 1930. Rutland, Vt.; and Tokyo: Charles E. Tuttle.

Aoyama Shundō. 1998. *Michi haruka nari tomo*. Tokyo: Kōsei Shuppansha.

Arai, Paula Kane Robinson. 1999. *Women Living Zen: Japanese Sōtō Buddhist Nuns*. New York and Oxford: Oxford University Press.

Ashida, Tetsuro. 1994. "The Festival and Religion Boom: Irony in the 'Age of the Heart.'" In *Folk Beliefs in Modern Japan*, edited by Inoue Nobutaka. Tokyo: Institute for Japanese Culture and Classics, Kokugakuin University.

Awaya, Nobuko, and David P. Phillips. 1996. "Popular Reading: The Literary World of the Japanese Working Woman." In *Re-Imagining Japanese Women*, edited by Anne E. Imamura. Berkeley: University of California Press.

Bessatsu Takarajima Henshūbu, ed. 1995. *Obōsan to isshō*. Bessatsu Takarajima, vol. 218. Tokyo: Takarajimasha.

Bodiford, William M. 1996. "Zen and the Art of Religious Prejudice: Efforts to Reform a Tradition of Social Discrimination." *Japanese Journal of Religious Studies* 23 (1–2): 1–27.

Brooks, Anne Page. 1981. "*Mizuko Kuyō* and Japanese Buddhism." *Japanese Journal of Religious Studies* 8 (3–4): 119–147.

Bukkyō bunka jōhō. http://www.evam.com.

Bukkyō Nenkan Hensan Iinkai, ed. 1988. *Bukkyō nenkan '88*. Kyoto: Hōzōkan.

———, ed. 1969. *Bukkyō dai nenkan: The Buddhist Almanac*. Tokyo: Bukkyō Taimusu Sha.

Bunkachō. 1939–1999. *Shūkyō nenkan*. Tokyo: Gyōsei.

Bunkachō Bunkabu Shūmuka, ed. 1983a. *Meiji ikō shūkyō seido hyakunenshi*. Tokyo: Hara Shobō.

———, ed. 1983b. *Shūkyō hōjin no kanri unei no tebiki dainishū: shūkyō hōjin no jimu*. Tokyo: Gyōsei.

Bunnag, Jane. 1973. *Buddhist Monk, Buddhist Layman: A Study of Urban Monastic Organization in Central Thailand*. Cambridge: Cambridge University Press.

Buswell Jr., Robert E. 1992. *The Zen Monastic Experience: Buddhist Practice in Contemporary Korea*. Princeton, N.J.: Princeton University Press.

Collcutt, Martin. 1986. "Buddhism: The Threat of Eradication." In *Japan in Transition: From Tokugawa to Meiji*, edited by Marius B. Jansen and Gilbert Rozman. Princeton, N.J.: Princeton University Press.

Cooke, Gerald. 1974a. "In Search of the Present State of Buddhism in Japan." *Journal of the American Academy of Religion* 42 (1): 18–34.

———. 1974b. "Traditional Buddhist Sects and Modernization in Japan." *Japanese Journal of Religious Studies* 1 (4): 267–330.

Covell, Stephen G. Forthcoming. "Funerals, Posthumous Names, and the Image of Buddhism in Japan Today." In *Death Rituals and the Afterlife in Japanese Buddhism: A Historical Perspective*, edited by Makiko Walters and Jacqueline Stone. Honolulu: University of Hawai'i Press.

———. 2004a. "Learning to Persevere: The Popular Teachings of Tendai Ascetics." *Japanese Journal of Religious Studies* 31 (2): 255–287.

———. 2004b. "Opening the Lotus: Yamada Etai and Modern Japanese Buddhism." Paper presented at the International Lotus Sutra Conference, Toronto.

———. 2000. "The Temple/Juridical Person: Law and Religion in Japan," *Asian Cultural Studies* 26:7–23.

Covell, Stephen G., and Mark Rowe, eds. 2004. "Round-Table: The Current State of Sectarian Universities." *Japanese Journal of Religious Studies* 31 (2) 429–464.

Creighton, Millie R. 1996. "Marriage, Motherhood, and Career Management in a Japanese 'Counter-Culture.'" In *Re-Imagining Japanese Women*, edited by Anne E. Imamura. Berkeley: University of California Press.

Daitō Satoshi. 1994. *Otera no kane wa naranakatta*. Tokyo: Kyōikushirio Shuppankai.

Davis, Winston. 1992. *Japanese Religion and Society: Paradigms of Structure and Change*. Albany: State University of New York Press.

———. 1980a. *Dōjō: Magic and Exorcism in Modern Japan*. Stanford, Calif.: Stanford University Press.

———. 1980b. "The Secularization of Japanese Religion." In *Transitions and Transformations in the History of Religions: Essays in Honor of Joseph M. Kitagawa*, edited by Frank E. Reynolds and Theodore M. Ludwig. Leiden, The Netherlands: E. J. Brill.

Dobbins, James C. 1996. "Editor's Introduction: Kuroda Toshio and His Scholarship." *Japanese Journal of Religious Studies* 23 (3–4): 217–232.

Dutt, Sukumar. 1960. *Early Buddhist Monachism*. Bombay: Asia Publishing House.

Eger, Max. 1980. "'Modernization' and 'Secularization' in Japan: A Polemical Essay." *Japanese Journal of Religious Studies* 7 (1): 7–24.

Fridell, Wilbur. 1973. *Japanese Shrine Mergers, 1906–1912*. Tokyo: Sophia University Press.

Garon, Sheldon. 1986. "State and Religion in Imperial Japan, 1912–1945." *Journal of Japanese Studies* 12 (2): 273–302.

Gernet, Jacques. 1995. *Buddhism in Chinese Society: An Economic History from the Fifth to the Tenth Centuries*. Translated by Franciscus Verellen. Studies in Asian Culture. New York: Columbia University Press.

Gombrich, Richard F., and Gananath Obeyesekere, eds. 1988. *Buddhism Transformed: Religious Change in Sri Lanka*. Princeton, N.J.: Princeton University Press.

Grapard, Allen G. 1984. "Japan's Ignored Cultural Revolution: The Separation of Shintō and Buddhist Divinities in the Meiji and a Case Study: Tōnomine." *History of Religions* 23 (3): 240–265.

Groner, Paul Sheldon. 1984. *Saichō: The Establishment of the Tendai School.* Berkeley Buddhist Studies series, vol. 7. Seoul, Korea: Po Chin Chai.

Habito, Rubin L. F. 1995. "The Logic of Nonduality and Absolute Affirmation: Deconstructing Tendai Hongaku Writings." *Japanese Journal of Religious Studies* 22 (1–2): 83–101.

Haley, John O. 1991. *Authority without Power: Law and the Japanese Paradox.* New York: Oxford University Press.

Hamilton, V. Lee, and Joseph Sanders. 1992. *Everyday Justice: Responsibility and the Individual in Japan and the United States.* New Haven, Conn.: Yale University Press.

Hardacre, Helen. 1997. *Marketing the Menacing Fetus in Japan.* Twentieth-Century Japan, 7. Berkeley: University of California Press.

———. 1995. *Aum Shinrikyō and the Japanese Media: The Pied Piper Meets the Lamb of God.* Institute Reports. New York: East Asia Institute, Columbia University.

———. 1992. "Gender and the Millennium in Ōmoto Kyōdan: The Limits of Religious Innovation." In *Innovations in Religious Traditions,* edited by M. A. Williams, Collett Cox, and Martin Jaffee. Berlin: Mouton De Gruyter.

———. 1990. "Gender and the Millennium in Ōmotokyō, a Japanese New Religion." *Seri Ethnological Studies* 29:47–62.

———. 1989. *Shintō and the State: 1868–1988.* Princeton, N.J.: Princeton University Press.

———. 1986. *Kurozumikyō and the New Religions of Japan.* Princeton, N.J.: Princeton University Press.

Harvey, Peter. 2000. *An Introduction to Buddhist Ethics: Foundations, Values, Issues.* Cambridge: Cambridge University Press.

Hasekawa Masahiro. 1994. *Jiin un'ei no hōritsu nyūmon.* Tokyo: Dōhōsha.

Hayashi, Makoto, and Yamanaka Hiroshi. 1993. "The Adaptation of Max Weber's Theories of Religion in Japan." *Japanese Journal of Religious Studies* 20 (2–3): 207–228.

Hiezan Enryakuji. http://www.hieizan.or.jp.

Hikita Seijun. 1991. *Bukkyō shakaigaku kenkyū.* Tokyo: Kokusho Kankōkai.

Hirano Takaaki. 2000. *Sōryo nyūmon.* Tokyo: Tōhō Shuppan.

Hongō Enjō. 1999. *Teinen washō: sarariman ga obōsan ni natta!* Tokyo: Nikkei BP Shuppan Sentā.

Hoshino, Eiki, and Dōshō Takeda. 1993. "Mizuko Kuyō and Abortion in Contemporary Japan." In *Religion and Society in Modern Japan,* edited by M. R. Mullins, Shimazono Susumu, and Paul L. Swanson. Berkeley: Asian Humanities Press.

Hubbard, Jamie. 1992. "Premodern, Modern, and Postmodern: Doctrine and the Study of Japanese Religion." *Japanese Journal of Religious Studies* 19 (1): 3–27.

Hur, Nam-Lin. 2000. *Prayer and Play in Late Tokugawa Japan: Asakusa Sensōji and Edo Society.* Harvard East Asian Monographs, 185. Cambridge and London: Harvard University Asia Center.

Ichigū Wo Terasu Undō Tokyo Honbu, ed. 1999. *Ichigū wo terasu undō sanjū shūnen kinenshi.* Tokyo: Shōbunsha.

Ichijiki Wo Sasageru Undō. www.kosei-kai.or.jp/heart-frame.html.

Ienaga, Saburo. 1965. "Japan's Modernization and Buddhism." *Contemporary Religions in Japan* 6: 1–41.

Ihara Saikaku. 1969. *The Life of an Amorous Woman and Other Writings*. Edited and translated by Ivan Morris. Norfolk, Conn.: New Directions.

Iijima Yoshiharu. 1995. "Genze riyaku no kami to wa nani ka." In *Nihon no kami*, vol. 2, edited by Yamaori Tetsuo. Tokyo: Heibonsha.

Ikeda, Eishun. 1998. "Teaching Assemblies and Lay Societies in the Formation of Modern Sectarian Buddhism." *Japanese Journal of Religious Studies* 25 (1–2): 11–44.

———, ed. 1996. *Zūsetsu Nihon Bukkyō no rekishi: kindai*. Tokyo: Kōsei Shuppan.

———. 1980. *Bukkyō fukushi to ha nani ka? Fukushi rinen no rekishi teki na tenkai*. In *Gendai Bukkyō wo shiru daijiten*, edited by Gendai Bukkyō wo Shiru Daijiten Henshū Iinkai. Tokyo: Kinkasha.

———. 1976. *Meiji no shin Bukkyō undō*. Tokyo: Yoshikawa Kōbunkan.

Inoue Nobutaka and Kokusai Shūkyō Kenkyūjo, eds. 1995. *Shūkyō kyōdan no genzai: wakamono kara no toi*. Tokyo: Shinyōsha.

Ishii Kenji. 1997. *Deta būku: gendai nihonjin no shūkyō: sengo gojūnen no shūkyō ishiki to shūkyō kōdō*. Tokyo: Shinyōsha.

Ishikawa, Rikizan. 1998. "The Social Response of Buddhists to the Modernization of Japan: The Contrasting Lives of Two Sōtō Zen Monks." *Japanese Journal of Religious Studies* 25 (1–2): 87–116.

Ishikawa Tōkaku. 1997. "Fukushi shakai ni okeru Bukkyō fukushi kadai." In *Bukkyō no ningengaku II: 21 seki bukkyō wa dō aru bekki ka?* edited by Taishō Daigaku Tokyo: Michi Shobō.

Itami Jūzō. 1988. *Marusa no onna II*. Film. Itami Productions.

———. 1984. *Osōshiki*. Film. Itami Productions.

Jaffe, Richard Mark. 2001. *Neither Monk nor Layman: Clerical Marriage in Modern Japanese Buddhism*. Princeton, N.J.: Princeton University Press.

———. 1998. "Meiji Religious Policy, Sōtō Zen, and the Clerical Marriage Problem." *Japanese Journal of Religious Studies* 25 (1–2): 45–86.

———. 1995. "Neither Monk nor Layman: The Debate over Clerical Marriage in Japanese Buddhism, 1868–1937." Ph.D. dissertation, Yale University.

Japan Buddhist Federation. http://www.jtvan.co.jp.

Jiin komu. http://www.jiin.net.

Jōnin Henshū Iinkai, eds. 1980. "Shūgaku." In *Gendai bukkyō wo shiru daijiten*, edited by Gendai Bukkyō wo Shiru Daijiten Henshū Iinkai. Tokyo: Kinkasha.

Kagamishima Noriko. 1999. "Jiin ni okeru jōsei no kūkan." In *Bukkyō to jendā*, edited by Josei to Bukkyō Tōkai-Kantō Nettowāku. Osaka: Toki Shobō.

Kanagawa Tendai Bukkyō Seinenkai, http://tendai.room.ne.jp/ ~kanagawa/index.html.

Kaplan, David, and Andrew Marshall. 1996. *The Cult at the End of the World*. New York: Crown.

Kashiwagi Masahiro. 1997. "Daigaku ni okeru sōryo yōsei no kadai." In *Bukkyō no ningengaku II: 21 seki bukkyō wa dō aru bekki ka?* edited by Taishō Daigaku. Tokyo: Michi Shobō.

Kashiwara Yūsen. 1990. *Nihon bukkyōshi: kindai*. Tokyo: Yoshikawa Kōbunkan.

Kawahashi Noriko. 2000. "'Seisabetsu shinai bukkyō' wa kanō ka?" In *Gendai shisō— bungaku to bukkyō: bukkyō wo koete*, edited by Kobayashi Takasuke, Furuta Shōkin, Mineshima Hideo, and Yoshida Kyūichi. Tokyo: Heibonsha.

———. 1995a. "Jizoku (Priests' Wives) in Sōtō Zen Buddhism: An Ambiguous Category." *Japanese Journal of Religious Studies* 22 (1–2): 161–183.

———. 1995b. "'Jizoku'—atarashi moderu no kōzō ni tsuite." *Kyōka kenkyū* 38:194–198.

Ketelaar, James Edward. 1990. *Of Heretics and Martyrs in Meiji Japan: Buddhism and Its Persecution.* Princeton, N.J.: Princeton University Press.

Kieschnick, John. 1997. *The Eminent Monk: Buddhist Ideals in Medieval Chinese Hagiography.* Kuroda Institute Studies in East Asian Buddhism, 10. Honolulu: University of Hawai'i Press.

Kikuchi Masaharu. 2000. "Senzen no fukushi kyōiku to Bukkyō." In *Fukushi to bukkyō: sukui to kyōsei no tame ni*, edited by Ikeda Eishun, Kiba Akashi, Sueki Fumihiko, Serikawa Hiromichi, and Tanaka Kyōshō. Tokyo: Heibonsha.

Kishimoto Hideo, ed. 1955. *Japanese Religion in the Meiji Era.* Vol. 2: *Japanese Culture in the Meiji Era.* Tokyo: Ōbunsha.

Kiuchi Gyōō. 1999a. "Kyōjishō ni tsuite." *Sange gakkai kiyō* 2:23–34.

———. 1999b. "Tendaishū no kindaika ni tsuite." In *Bukkyō kindaika no shosō: dentō to sono saihyōka*, edited by Taishō Daigaku "Bukkyō Kindaika no Shosō" Kenkyūkai. Tokyo: Taishō Daigaku Gakujutsu Joseikin Iinkai.

Kohno, Jiko. 1998. *Right View, Right Life: Insights of a Woman Buddhist Priest.* Tokyo: Kōsei Publishing.

Kōhō Tendaishū. 1995–2000. Ōtsu, Shiga Prefecture: Tendai Shūmuchō Sōmubu.

Koike Kenji, Nishikawa Shigenori, and Murakami Shigeyoshi, eds. 1978. *Shūkyō dan'atsu wo monogataru.* Tokyo: Iwanami Shoten.

Komuro Yūjū. 1998. "Bochi ni kansuru koto: atarashii bochi no arikata wo." In *Jiin no genzai*, edied by Hokushindō. Tokyo: Hokushindō.

Kōmyōji. http://www.komyoji.com.

Kumamoto, Einin. 2004. "Shut Up, Zen Priest: A Review of Minami Jikisai's *The Zen Priest Speaks* and Other Works." *Japanese Journal of Religious Studies* 31 (2): 465–487.

Kurata Hyakuzō. 1917. *Shukke to sono deshi.* Tokyo: Iwanami Shoten.

Kuroda, Toshio. 1996a. "Buddhism and Society in the Medieval Estate System." *Japanese Journal of Religious Studies* 23 (3–4): 287–320.

———. 1996b. "The Imperial Law and the Buddhist Law." *Japanese Journal of Religious Studies* 23 (3–4): 271–286.

LaFleur, William R. 1995. "Silences and Censures: Abortion, History, and Buddhism in Japan: A Rejoinder to George Tanabe." *Japanese Journal of Religious Studies* 22 (1–2): 185–196.

———. 1992. *Liquid Life: Abortion and Buddhism in Japan.* Princeton, N.J.: Princeton University Press.

Laidlaw, James. 1995. *Riches and Renunciation: Religion, Economy, and Society among the Jains.* Oxford Studies in Social and Cultural Anthropology. Oxford: Clarendon Press.

Light Up Your Corner. www.biwa.ne.jp/~ichigu/main/ichigu.html (currently, www.tendai.or.jp/ichigu.index.html).

Long, Susan Orpett. 1996. "Nurturing and Femininity: The Ideal of Caregiving in Postwar Japan." In *Re-Imagining Japanese Women*, edited by Anne E. Imamura. Berkeley: University of California Press.

Lopez Jr., Donald S. 2001. *The Story of Buddhism: A Concise Guide to Its History and Teachings.* New York: Harper San Francisco.

Matsunami Kōdō. 1996. *Nihon bukkyō kaikakuron.* Tokyo: Yūzangaku.

Matsuno Junkō, Murakami Shigeyoshi, Kasahara Kazuo, and Nakamura Hajime. 1972. *Gendai Bukkyō: shinkō no jiyū to Bukkyō,* edited by Nakamura Hajime, Kasahara Kazuo, and Kanaoka Shūyū. Vol. 9: *Ajia bukkyōshi nihon hen.* Tokyo: Kōsei Shuppan.

McMullin, Neil. 1992. "Which Doctrine? Whose 'Religion'? A Rejoinder." *Japanese Journal of Religious Studies* 19 (1): 29–39.

———. 1989. "Historical and Historiographical Issues in the Study of Pre-modern Japanese Religions." *Japanese Journal of Religious Studies* 16 (1): 3–40.

Media Bankusu, ed. 1999. *Chūgoku, Kankoku, Nihon sankoku Tendai kokoro no tabi.* Tokyo: Common Sense.

Metraux, Daniel A. 1999. *Aum Shinrikyō and Japanese Youth.* Lanham, N.Y.; and Oxford: University Press of America.

Minami Jikisai. 1998. *Kataru zensō.* Tokyo: Asahi Shinbunsha.

Minowa Kenryō. 1999. *Chūsei shoki Nanto kairitsu fukkō no kenkyū.* Kyoto: Hōzōkan.

Minsō.com. http://www.minso.com/sougi/m-kaimyo.htm.

Mitsunaga, Kakudō. 1996. *Sennichi kaihōgyō.* Tokyo: Shunshūsha.

Mizutani, Kōshō, ed. 1996. *Bukkyō to tāminaru kea.* Kyoto: Hōzōkan.

Monbukagakushō, ed. 2002. *Monbukagakuhakushō (Heisei 13 nendo).* Tokyo: Zaimushō.

Morinaga Matsushin. 1980. "Bukkyōsha no shakai fukushi katsudō." In *Gendai Bukkyō wo shiru daijiten,* edited by Gendai Bukkyō wo Shiru Daijiten Henshū Iinkai. Tokyo: Kinkasha.

Morioka, Kiyomi. 1994. "Attacks on the New Religions: Risshō Kōseikai and the 'Yomiuri Affair'" *Japanese Journal of Religious Studies* 21 (2–3): 281–310.

———, ed. 1986. *Kingendai ni okeru "ie" no henshitsu to shūkyō.* Tokyo: Shinchi Shobō.

Mukhopadhyaya, Ranjana. 2001. "The Brighter Society Movement of Risshō Kōsekai: A New Application of the Bodhisattva Way." *Asian Cultural Studies* 27:19–34.

Murakami Senjō, Tsuji Zennosuke, and Washio Junkyō, eds. 1926–1929. *Meiji ishin shinbutsu bunri shiryō.* Tokyo: Tōhō Shoin.

Murakami Shigeyoshi and Yasumaru Yoshio, eds. 1971. *Minshūshūkyō no shisō.* Vol. 67: *Nihon shisō taikei.* Tokyo: Iwanami Shoten.

Murata Yasuo. 1999. *Shinbutsu bunri no chihōteki tenkai.* Tokyo: Yoshikawa Kōbunkan.

Nadolski, Thomas Peter. 1975. "The Socio-Political Background of the 1921 and 1935 Ōmoto Suppressions in Japan." Ph.D. dissertation, University of Pennsylvania.

Nagao Saburō. 2002. *Mōkorita (jō).* Tokyo: Kōdansha.

Nakamura, Kyōko. 1997. "The Religious Consciousness and Activities of Contemporary Japanese Women." *Japanese Journal of Religious Studies* 24 (1–2): 87–120.

Nara Yasuaki. 1980. "Haisen kara konnichi made no bukkyōkai no ugoki: kisei kyōdan." In *Gendai bukkyō wo shiru daijiten.* Tokyo: Kinkasha.

NHK. 1990. *Tera ga kieru.* Video.Tokyo: NHKService Center.

Nichan neru. http://mentai.2ch.net/soc/kako/972/972443085.html.

Nihon Shūkyō Daihyōsha Kaigi. 1987. *Hieizan shūkyō samitto: sekai shūkyōsha heiwa no inori no tsudoi*. Ōtsu, Shiga: Nihon Shūkyō Daihyōsha Kaigi.

O'Brien, David M., and Yasuo Ohkoshi. 1996. *To Dream of Dreams: Religious Freedom and Constitutional Politics in Postwar Japan*. Honolulu: University of Hawai'i Press.

Oguri Junko and Nakamura Hajime. 1972. *Kindai Bukkyō: seiji to shūkyō to minshū*, edited by Nakamura Hajime, Kasahara Kazuo and Kanaoka Shūyū. Vol. 8: *Ajia bukkyōshi nihon hen*. Tokyo: Kōsei Shuppan.

Okubo Ryōshun. 2000. "Tendai." In *Nihon bukkyō no kenkyū hō: rekishi to tenbōm*, edited by Nihon Bukkyō kenkyūkai. Kyoto: Hōzōkan.

Ōno Tatsunosuke. 1961. *Nihon no Bukkyō*. Tokyo: Shinbundō.

Ooms, Emily Groszos. 1993. *Women and Millenarian Protest in Meiji Japan: Deguchi Nao and Ōmotokyō*. Ithaca, N.Y.: East Asia Program, Cornell University.

Osōshiki Puraza Sekise. http://www.osoushiki-plaza.com/library/index-data.html.

Otera netto. http://www.otera.net.

Reader, Ian. 2000. *Religious Violence in Contemporary Japan: The Case of Aum Shinrikyō*. Honolulu: University of Hawai'i Press.

———. 1996. *A Poisonous Cocktail? Aum Shinrikyō's Path to Violence*. Denmark: Nordic Institute of Asian Studies.

———. 1995. "Social Action and Personal Benefits in Contemporary Japanese Buddhism." *Buddhist-Christian Studies* 15: 3–17.

———. 1993a. "Buddhism as a Religion of the Family: Contemporary Images in Sōtō Zen Religion and Society in Modern Japan." In *Religion and Society in Modern Japan*, edited by Mark R. Mullins, Shimazono Susumu, and Paul L. Swanson. Berkeley: Asian Humanities Press.

———. 1993b. "Recent Japanese Publications on the New Religions: The Work of Shimazono Susumu." *Japanese Journal of Religious Studies* 20 (2–3): 229–248.

———. 1991a. *Religion in Contemporary Japan*. Honolulu: University of Hawai'i Press.

———. 1991b. "What Constitutes Religious Activity (II)?" *Japanese Journal of Religious Studies* 18 (4): 373–376.

———. 1987a. "Back to the Future: Images of Nostalgia and Renewal in a Japanese Religious Context." *Japanese Journal of Religious Studies* 14 (4): 287–303.

———. 1987b. "From Asceticism to the Package Tour: The Pilgrim's Progress in Japan." *Religion* 17 (2): 133–148.

———. 1983. "Contemporary Thought in Sōtō Zen Buddhism." Ph.D. dissertation, University of Leeds.

Reader, Ian, and George Tanabe. 1998. *Practically Religious: Worldly Benefits and the Common Religion of Japan*. Honolulu: University of Hawai'i Press.

Reader, Ian, and Paul L. Swanson, eds. 1997. *Japanese Journal of Religious Studies: Pilgrimage in Japan* 24 (3–4).

Riggs, Diane. 2004. Fukudenkai: Sewing the Buddha's Robe in Contemporary Japanese Buddhist Practice. *Japanese Journal of Religious Studies* 31 (2): 311–356.

Roberts, Glenda S. 1996. "Careers and Commitment: Azumi's Blue-Collar Women." In *Re-Imagining Japanese Women*, edited by Anne E. Imamura. Berkeley: University of California Press.

Rowe, Mark. 2003. "Grave Changes: Scattering Ashes in Contemporary Japan."
Japanese Journal of Religious Studies 30 (1–2): 85–118.

———. 2000. "Stickers for Nails: The Ongoing Transformation of Roles, Rites, and
Symbols in Japanese Funerals." *Japanese Journal of Religious Studies* 27 (3–4): 353–378.

Saga Shimbun. http://www.saga-s.co.jp.

Sakagami Masao. 1997. "Jiritsu to Jihi Kyūzai." *Bukkyō fukushi*, no. 1:147–154.

Sakurai, Joji. 1999. "Afterlife Names Are Worth a Bundle to Buddhist Priests." *San
Diego Union-Tribune*. April 4, A-31.

Sayre, C. Franklin. 1986. "Cultural Property Laws in India and Japan." *UCLA Law
Review* 33 (3): 851–890.

Schopen, Gregory. 1997. *Bones, Stones, and Buddhist Monks: Collected Papers on the
Archaeology, Epigraphy, and Texts of Monastic Buddhism in India*. Honolulu:
University of Hawai'i Press.

Sekizawa Mayumi. 2002. "Chiiki kyōdotai to shiseikan." Paper presented at Nihonjin
no shiseikan no yukue: jinseigirei wa nao yūkōka? Taisho University, Tokyo,
March 16.

Seno Misa. 1999. "Aru zendera no kazoku no shōzō." In *Bukkyō to jendā*, edited by Josei
to Bukkyō Tōkai-Kantō Nettowāku. Osaka: Toki Shobō.

Setouchi Jakuchō. 1998. *Jakuchō: Aozora seppō*. Tokyo: Kōbunsha.

Shanti Volunteer Association. http://www.jca.apc.org/sva/index/html.

Shimada Hiromi. 1994. *Kaimyō: naze shigo ni namae wo kaeru no ka*. Kyoto: Hōzōkan.

Shimazono, Susumu. 1998. "The Commercialization of the Sacred: The Structural
Evolution of Religious Communities in Japan." *Social Science Japan Journal* 1 (2):
181–198.

———. 1992. *Gendai kyūsai shūkyōron*. Tokyo: Seikyūsha.

———. 1981. "Religious Influences on Japan's Modernization." *Japanese Journal of
Religious Studies* 8 (3–4): 207–222.

Shuppan Nenkan Henshūbu, eds. 2000. Shuppan nenkan 2000: Shiryō, meibō hen.
Tokyo: Shuppan Ryūzusha.

Sizemore, Russell F., and Donald K. Swearer, eds. 1990. *Ethics, Wealth, and Salvation:
A Study in Buddhist Social Ethics*. Columbia: University of South Carolina Press.

Smith, Robert J. 1974. *Ancestor Worship in Contemporary Japan*. Stanford: Stanford
University Press.

Sōma Kazuko. 2000. "Bukkyōsha ni yoru jidō hogo no rekishi." In *Fukushi to Bukkyō:
sukui to kyōsei no tame ni*, edited by Ikeda Eishun, Kiba Akashi, Sueki Fumihiko,
Serikawa Hiromichi, and Tanaka Kyōshō. Tokyo: Heibonsha.

Sōsai Manna-:Manna-Q&Asōshiki.
http://ekitan.com/biz/handbook/data/10110400.htm.

Sōtōshū Kyōka Kenkyūjo Sōritsu Nijū Shūnen Kinenkai, ed. 1975. *Shūkyō shūdan no
konnichi to asu*. Tokyo: Kinkasha.

Sōtōshū Shūsei Chōsa Iinkai, ed. 1984. *Shūkyō shūdan no asu he no kadai*. Tokyo:
Sōtōshū Shūmuchō.

Staggs, Kathleen M. 1983. "'Defend the Nation and Love the Truth': Inoue Enryō and
the Revival of Meiji Buddhism." *Monumenta Nipponica* 38 (3): 251–281.

Stone, Jacqueline I. 1999. *Original Enlightenment and the Transformation of Medieval Japanese Buddhism*. Kuroda Institute Studies in East Asian Buddhism, 12. Honolulu: University of Hawaiʻi Press.

———. 1995. "Medieval Tendai Hongaku Thought and the New Kamakura Buddhism: A Reconsideration." *Japanese Journal of Religious Studies* 22 (1–2): 17–48.

———. 1990. "A Vast and Grave Task: Interwar Buddhist Studies as an Expression of Japan's Envisioned Global Role." In *Culture and Identity: Japanese Intellectuals during the Interwar Years*, edited by J. Thomas Rimer. Princeton, N.J.: Princeton University Press.

Sugawara Jūsei. 2002 "Dentō Bukkyō to sōsai girei." Paper presented at Nihonjin no shiseikan no yukue: jinsei girei wa nao yūkōka? Taishō University, Tokyo, March 16.

Sugitani Gijun. 1980. "Bukkyō undō wa yomigaetta ka: sengo bukkyō seinen undō shōshi." In *Gendai bukkyō wo shiru daijiten*, edited by Gendai Bukkyō wo Shiru Daijiten Henshū Iinkai. Tokyo: Kinkasha.

Taira Masayuki. 1994. "Kamakura bukkyōron." In *Iwanami kōza: Nihon tsushi dai-hachikan*. Tokyo: Iwanami Shoten.

Taishō Daigaku Gojūnenshi Hensan Iinkai, ed. 1976. *Taishō daigaku gojūnen ryakushi*. Tokyo: Taishō Daigaku Gojūnenshi Hensan Iinkai.

Takahashi, Yumi. 2005. "Being Old in an Aging Society: The Meaning of Old Age in Contemporary Japan." Master's thesis, Comparative Religion, Western Michigan University, Kalamazoo.

Takemura Makio. 1981. "Sōdai seido no hensen ni tsuite." In *Shūkyōhō kenkyū II*, edited by Ryūkoku Daigaku Shūkyōhō Kenkyūkai. Kyoto: Hōritsu Bunkasha.

Takigawa Zenkai. 1998. "Gendai ni okeru tsuizen no kadai to igi." In *Jiin no genzai*, edited by Hokushindō. Tokyo: Hokushindō.

Tamamuro Fumio. 2000. "Henka suru jiin no yakuwari to danka seido." *Shūkyō to gendai*. February. http://www.kamakura-net.co.jp/002interview.html.

———. 1999. *Sōshiki to danka*. Rekishi bunka raiburari, 70. Tokyo: Yoshikawa Kōbunkan.

———. 1987. *Nihon bukkyōshi: kinsei*. Tokyo: Yoshikawa Kōbunkan.

———. 1971. *Edo bakufu no shūkyō tōsei*. Nihonjin no kōdō to shisō, 16. Tokyo: Hyōronsha.

Tamamuro Taijō. 1963. *Sōshiki Bukkyō*. Tokyo: Daihōrinkaku.

———. 1967. *Nihon bukkyōshi: kinsei kindai hen*. Kyoto: Hōzōkan.

Tamura, Noriyoshi. 1979. "The Problem of Secularization: A Preliminary Analysis." *Japanese Journal of Religious Studies* 6 (1–2): 89–113.

Tamura Yoshirō. 2000. *Japanese Buddhism: A Cultural History*. Tokyo: Kōsei Publishing Co.

Tanabe, George Jr. 2004. "Popular Buddhist Orthodoxy in Contemporary Japan." *Japanese Journal of Religious Studies* 31 (2): 289–310.

———. 1995. "Sounds and Silences: A Counterresponse." *Japanese Journal of Religious Studies* 22 (1–2): 197–200.

Tashiro Shunkō. 1999. *Bukkō to bihāra undo: Shiseigaku nyūmon*. Kyoto: Hōzōkan.

Tendai Bukkyō Seinen Renmei. http://www2t.biglobe.ne.jp/~tendai/cgi_qa/renlst.cgi (currently, www.tendai-yba.com).

Tendai Koyomi Kangōkai, ed. 1983. *Tendai koyomi hōwashū*. Tokyo: Tendai Koyomi Kankōkai.

Tendaishū. http://www.tendai.or.jp

Tendaishū Jiteifujin Rengōkai. 1997. *Jiteifujin techō*.

(*Tendaishū*) *Tsūjō shūgikai giji hōkoku*. 1986–2000.

Thelle, Notto R. 1987. *Buddhism and Christianity in Japan: From Conflict to Dialogue, 1854–1899*. Honolulu: University of Hawai'i Press.

Tokuzū Betsuin. http://www.d1.dion.ne.jp/~tokuzo/text/94con.txt; also http://www.nichiren.net/tokuzoji.

Tsuji Zennosuke. 1942. *Nihon Bukkyōshi no kenkyū*. 3d ed. Tokyo: Kinkōdō Shoseki.

Tsushima Michihito et al. 1979. "The Vitalistic Conception of Salvation in Japanese New Religions: An Aspect of Modern Religious Consciousness." *Japanese Journal of Religious Studies* 6 (1–2): 139–161.

Ueda Noriyuki. 2004. *Ganbare Bukkyō! Otera runesansu no jidai*. NHK Books, 1004. Tokyo: Nihon Hōsō Shuppan Kyōkai.

Uko Kikuko. 1999. "Tera ni ikiru onna no ibasho to seido: Shinran no tsuma to musume wa nan to miru." In *Bukkyō to jendā*, edited by Josei to Bukkyō Tōkai-Kantō Nettowāku. Osaka: Toki Shobō.

Umehara, Motōo and Hasegawa Masatoshi. 2000. "Senzen-sengo no shihō fukushi no rekishi." In *Fukushi to Bukkyō: sukui to kyōsei no tame ni*, edited by Ikeda Eishun, Kiba Akashi, Sueki Fumihiko, Serikawa Hiromichi, and Tanaka Kyōshō. Tokyo: Heibonsha.

Uno, Kathleen S. 1991. "Women and Changes in the Household Division of Labor." In *Recreating Japanese Women, 1600–1945*, edited by G. L. Bernstein. Berkeley: University of California Press.

Upham, Frank K. 1987. *Law and Social Change in Postwar Japan*. Cambridge, Mass.: Harvard University Press.

Vesey, Alexander. 2003. "The Buddhist Clergy and Village Society in Modern Japan." Ph.D. dissertation, Princeton University.

Victoria, Brian A. 1997. *Zen at War*. New York: Weatherhill.

Wakahara Shigeru. 1981. "Hanrei ni arawareta shūkyōhōjin no shinja no chii." In *Shūkyōhō kenkyū II*, edited by Ryōkoku Daigaku Shūkyōhō Kenkyūkai. Kyoto: Hōritsu Bunkasha.

Watanabe Noriko. 1999. "Josei sōryo no tanjō: Nishihonganji ni okeru sono rekishi." In *Bukkyō to jendā*, edited by Josei to Bukkyō Tōkai-Kantō Nettowāku. Osaka: Toki Shobō.

Watanabe Shujun. 1998. *Hieizan Enryakuji: sekai bunka isan*. Tokyo: Yoshikawa Kōbunkan.

Watanabe, Shōkō. 1964. *Japanese Buddhism: A Critical Appraisal*. Tokyo: Kokusai Bunka Shinkokai.

Watt, Paul B. 1984. "Jiun Sonja (1719–1804): A Response to Confucianism within the Context of Buddhist Reform." In *Confucianism and Tokugawa Culture*, edited by Peter Nosco. Princeton, N.J.: Princeton University Press.

Werblowsky, R. J. Zwi. 1991. "Mizuko Kuyō: Notulae on the Most Important 'New Religion' of Japan." *Japanese Journal of Religious Studies* 18 (4): 295–354.

Wijayaratna, Mohan. 1990. *Buddhist Monastic Life: According to the Texts of the Theravada Tradition*. Translated by Cluade Grangier and Steven Collins. Cambridge: Cambridge University Press.

Williams, Duncan Ryuken. 2000. "Representations of Zen: An Institutional and Social History of Sōtō Zen Buddhism in Edo Japan." Ph.D. dissertation, Harvard University.

Wilson, Liz. 1996. *Charming Cadavers: Horrific Figurations of the Feminine in Indian Buddhist Hagiographic Literature*. Chicago: University of Chicago Press.

Wöss, Fleur. 1993. "Pokkuri-Temples and Aging: Rituals for Approaching Death." In *Religion and Society in Modern Japan*, edited by Mark R. Mullins, Shimazono Susumu, and Paul L. Swanson. Berkeley: Asian Humanities Press.

Xian Jian. 1980. "Sengo jiin no shakaiteki-keizaiteki hendō: hōseiteki sokumen kara." In *Gendai Bukkyō wo shiru daijiten*, edited by Gendai Bukkyō wo Shiru Daijiten Henshū Iinkai. Tokyo: Kinkasha.

Yamaori Tetsuo, Kakehashi Jitsuen, and Sasaki Shōten. 1993. *Tera wo kataru, sō wo kataru*. Kyoto: Nagadabunshōdō.

Yasumaru Yoshio. 1979. *Kamigami no Meiji ishin*. Tokyo: Iwanami Shoten.

———. 1974. *Nihon no kindaika to minshū shisō*. Tokyo: Aoki Shoten.

———. 1979. "Jūshoku no hōteki chii." In *Shūkyōhō kenkyū I*, edited by Ryūkoku Daigaku Shūkyōhō Kenkyūkai. Kyoto: Hōritsu Bunkasha.

Yazawa Chōdō. 1980. "Gendai ni okeru jiin no jittai wo miru: sengo no jiin wa donna yō ni ikiteiruka." In *Gendai Bukkyō wo shiru daijiten*, edited by Gendai Bukkyō wo Shiru Daijiten Henshū Iinkai. Tokyo: Kinkasha.

Yōkōzan Kisshōji. http://www.dokidoki.ne.jp/home2/kisyoji/index.htm.

Yoneda, Soei, and Hoshino Koei. 1982. *Zen Vegetarian Cooking*. Tokyo: Kodansha International.

Yoshida Kyūichi. 2000. "Nihon no Bukkyō fukushi." In *Fukushi to Bukkyō: sukui to kyōsei no tame ni*, edited by Ikeda Eishun, Kiba Akashi, Sueki Fumihiko, Serikawa Hiromichi, and Tanaka Kyōshō. Tokyo: Heibonsha.

Yoshida Kyūichi and Hasegawa Masatoshi. 2001. *Nihon Bukkyō fukushi shisōshi*. Kyoto: Hōzōkan.

Zen'nihon Bukkyō Seinenkai, ed. 2003. *Sōshiki Bukkyō wa shinai: seinensō ga eigaku nyu-buddizumu*. Tokyo: Hakubasha.

Index

activist-priests, 47
afterlife, 174, 176, 188, 235n. 35
amulet, 154, 157
ancestor, 25, 26, 28, 37, 39, 53, 60, 87,
102, 103, 117, 122, 125, 145, 169, 173,
175, 176, 179, 189, 197, 204n. 24,
211n. 40; bonds, 37; veneration, 28,
54, 78, 175, 181, 193
Anesaki Masaharu, 12
anshin. See peace of mind
Arai, Paula, 124, 167, 223n. 43
ascetic, 2, 21, 22
Aum Shinrikyō, 86, 92, 140, 152,
218n. 97, 228n. 1
austerity, 42, 78, 86, 87

begging, 147–148
Bihara Undō, 101
board of directors, 32, 85, 129, 150, 179,
206n. 40
Boke yoke Jizō, 102
bone-lifting ceremony. See *honeage*
bozu marumōke, 74
Buddhist associations, 28
Buddhist Child-care Association, 99
Buddhist hymns. See *goeika*
Buddhist Studies, 4, 47, 151, 196, 200n. 7,
224n. 50
Buddhist youth association, 104, 107
Bukkyō Hoiku Kyōkai. *See* Buddhist
Child-care Association
Bukkyō Kakushū Rengōkai. *See*
Federation of Buddhist Schools
Buraku Kaihō Dōmei. *See* Buraku
Liberation League
Buraku Liberation League, 176, 177
busseinenkai. See Buddhist youth
association
bylaws, 100, 107; and Light Up Your

Corner Movement, 48, 209n. 15; and
Religious Juridical Persons Law, 34,
149, 150; and taxes, 152; and temple
wives, 111–115, 118, 121, 122, 126,
137, 138, 223n. 32, 227n. 109

celibacy, 20, 22, 75, 131, 132, 136
cemeteries, 17
Chih-i (538–597), 11, 20, 90
chingo kokka. See state protecting
Christianity, 31, 66, 68, 99, 100, 191,
207n. 63, 213nn. 28, 30, 214n. 30,
219n. 17, 237n. 67
civic center, 35
civic groups, 7
clerical marriage, 8–10, 65, 79, 81, 82,
110, 111, 117, 118, 124, 126, 129, 137,
192–196, 215n. 55, 222nn. 6, 8,
237n. 58
commercialization, 141, 155, 160–162,
170, 185
Committee for the Promotion of
Harmony, 178
commodity, 38, 39, 60, 161, 162, 169,
183–196, 233n. 65
confraternities, 7, 143, 144, 195
consumerism, 51, 53, 183
convention, 47, 48, 55, 59–61, 106,
211n. 50
conventional morality. See *tsūzoku
dōkotu*
conversion, 60
corrupt Buddhism, 86
corruption, 1, 3, 7, 9–18, 42, 63, 83, 86,
104, 108, 141, 151, 159, 160, 181, 188,
193, 203nn. 6, 15, 205n. 33. *See also*
degeneration: theory, 11, 14, 18,
201nn. 11, 27
Cultural Assets Preservation Law, 162

Danjo Koyō Kikai Kintōhō. *See* Equal
  Employment Opportunity Law
danka: member system, 7, 15, 23–30, 42,
  63, 78, 188, 193; representative, 23,
  27, 33, 178, 179, 205n. 33
daraku bukkyō. *See* corrupt Buddhism
defending the temple, 83
degeneration, 10–12, 15, 17–19, 22, 32,
  167, 171, 200n. 13. *See also* corruption
Dengyō Daishi, 48, 50, 56, 72, 116, 119,
  149. *See also* Saichō
dentō bukkyō. *See* traditional Buddhism
destroy Buddhism and throw out
  Shakyamuni, 66
dharma-relatives, 127, 195
Disaster Countermeasures Division, 106
discrimination, 8, 10, 17, 18, 168–171,
  176–179, 183, 189, 236n. 45
doctrines, 4, 7, 8, 10, 11, 15, 61, 64, 71,
  77, 80, 88, 92, 96, 120, 134, 136, 152,
  154, 155, 167, 169, 177, 206n. 41
dokujukai. *See* sutra-reading-group
Donate a Meal Campaign, 210n. 29

ease of mind, 163
education mothers, 114, 224n. 50
Eizan Gakuin, 92, 93, 130
Enryakuji, 67, 93, 118, 141
Equal Employment Opportunity Law, 113
established Buddhism, 4, 7

family, 33, 90, 94, 175, 186, 187, 197,
  199n. 4, 203n. 9, 224n. 50; and clerical
  marriage, 79, 109, 125–129, 141–142,
  210n. 35; and graves, 146; and
  inherited temples, 82, 83; and Light
  Up Your Corner Movement, 44, 54,
  58, 60, 61; and posthumous precept
  names, 169, 171, 179–181
Federation of Buddhist Schools, 68
fire ritual. *See goma*
fuda. *See* talisman
Fuji Kōgen, 105, 114, 223n. 37
funeral Buddhism, 9, 16, 22, 38, 46, 63,
  89, 95, 104, 153, 165, 167, 171, 193

funeral company, 35, 36, 147. *See also*
  funeral industry
funeral industry, 30, 35. *See also* funeral
  company

gakureki shakai, 224n. 50
Gakuryō, 93, 218n. 4
Gathering to Pray for World Peace, 191,
  192
genze riyaku. *See* this-worldly benefits
Ginkakuji, 159
goeika, 58, 111
goma, 2, 42, 231n. 34
good wives and wise mothers, 114, 137,
  196, 222n. 27
grave, 35, 37, 43, 60, 61, 124, 146, 153,
  165, 171, 172, 175, 177, 186, 196,
  203n. 13, 204nn. 23, 28, 205n. 34,
  208n. 3, 217n. 90
Gyōin, 93, 129, 130

Hagami Shōchō, 11
haibutsu kishaku. *See* destroy Buddhism
  and throw out Shakyamuni
Hardacre, Helen, 54, 116, 208n. 1
Hasegawa Ryōshin, 99
Hiro Sachiya, 40, 57, 58
Hō no Hana, 207n. 59
honeage, 206n. 46
hōrui. *See* dharma-relatives
Hosokawa Keiichi, 103
household shrine, 149

Ichigū Wo Terasu Undō. *See* Light Up
  Your Corner Movement
Ienaga Saburō, 13, 18, 19
Imperial Japan Wartime Religious
  National Devotion Association, 100
industrialization, 98
inheritance of temples, 82, 92, 94, 95,
  193
Inoue Enryō, 95, 219n. 17
inukuyō, 229n. 17
ishiya, 146, 196, 230n. 28

Japan Buddhist Federation, 167, 173, 181, 187, 234n. 8
jigyōketa, 178
jiin chūshin shugi. See temple centrism
Jisan Myōryū (1636–1690), 75
jiteifujin tokudo. See temple wife ordination
Jiun Sonja (1718–1804), 74
Josei to Bukkyō Tōkai/Kantō Netowāku. *See* Tōkai/Kantō Network for Women and Buddhism
jūzenkai. See Ten Good Precepts

kaihōgyō, 22, 41, 78, 143, 207n. 67
kairitsu fukkō undō. See precept revitalization movement
kamidana. See household shrine
kanchō system, 69, 213nn. 27, 30
Kawahashi Noriko, 117, 118, 121
kechien kanjo, 134
kindergarten, 100, 101, 114, 220n. 42, 229n. 20
king's law–Buddha's law, 64, 65, 74
Kinkakuji, 164
kisei bukkyō. See established Buddhism
Kiuchi Gyōo, 200n. 11
Kiyomizu Temple, 158
ko sodate kannon, 118
kōeki hōjin. See public interest juridical person
Kōgen Ryōkū (1653–1739), 75
Kokuzeichō. *See* National Tax Agency
Kōno Jikō, 209n. 22
koseki system, 26
Kuroda Toshio, 142
kyōdōshoku system, 67
kyōiku mama. See education mothers
Kyoto Buddhist Association, 155, 156, 158
Kyōto Bukkyōkai. *See* Kyoto Buddhist Association
Kyoto City Old Capital Support and Preservation Tax Regulation, 156
Kyōtoshi koto hozon kyōryokuzai jōrei. See Kyoto City Old Capital Support and Preservation Tax Regulation

land reform, 8, 30, 31, 115
lay Buddhist societies, 27, 28
lay-priest, 88
legal codes, 7
liability insurance, 148
Light Up Your Corner Movement, 43–61, 96, 100, 102, 104, 106, 107, 138, 139, 192, 194, 208n. 5, 221n. 57, 231n. 33, 238n. 4

magic, 11–13, 17, 174
mail-order-priest, 10
master-disciple relationship, 91, 92, 95
meat eating, 67, 70, 75, 76. *See also* vegetarianism
Mibu Shōjun, 71, 72
Minami Jikisai, 121, 128
minshū kyōdan. See people's organization
Mitsunaga Kakudō, 11, 210n. 40
mizuko kuyō, 43, 143, 167, 229n. 19
Mizutani Kōshō, 171
modernization, 12–14, 18, 19, 55, 68, 80, 206n. 46
mōkorita, 52
monasticism, 4, 131
moral, 45, 51, 79, 181, 186, 193; crisis, 58, 60

national devotion armies. *See* national devotion groups
national devotion groups, 70
National Tax Agency, 153
natural funerals, 37, 186, 187, 189, 195, 206n. 49
New Buddhism, 18, 19
new new religions, 4, 7, 39, 61, 86, 87, 92, 108, 188, 199n. 4, 207n. 63
new religions, 4, 7, 10, 13, 14, 27–30, 39–41, 44, 46, 51, 54, 59–61, 68, 69, 86, 92, 114, 117, 140, 153, 195, 196, 199nn. 3, 4, 211n. 53, 214n. 30, 238n. 2
next-worldly benefits, 22
Nishioka Ryōkō, 73, 105, 129
Niwano Nikkyō, 51, 192

Nonprofit Organization Law, 100
nonprofit organizations (NPOs), 101

ōbō-buppō. See king's law–Buddha's law
Ōmotokyō, 28, 204n. 22
ordination, 8, 10, 64, 75, 82, 85, 89, 121, 125, 128, 129, 131, 215n. 45, 217n. 95, 218n. 6, 226n. 95; temple wife ordination 110, 122, 138, 192, 194

peace of mind, 120, 157, 158, 174
people's organization, 44
petto kuyō, 43
pilgrimage, 143
pokkuri-dera, 102
precept, 4, 20, 62, 63, 71, 72, 74, 75, 77, 79, 89, 97, 108, 110, 122, 132, 134, 137, 165, 169, 171, 173, 176, 181–183, 187, 196, 200n. 7, 205n. 32, 223n. 33, 227n. 103, 237n. 55
precept revitalization movement, 74
priestly recruitment, 8. See also recruit
Prince Shōtoku (574–622), 96, 97, 219n. 22
privatization, 34, 123–125, 138, 141, 151, 194, 195
professionalization, 18, 73, 141
proselytizing, 5, 38, 115, 123, 135, 136, 141, 143, 189
public interest juridical person, 152

Reader, Ian, 14, 41, 102, 154, 157, 231n. 43
recruit, 63, 90, 92, 94, 95, 108
recycle, 50, 51
Religions Bill: 1927, 27, 69
religious affiliation, 8
Religious Juridical Persons Law, 7, 27, 30, 33, 34, 103, 140, 150, 151, 153, 184, 200n. 8, 205n. 40, 207n. 58
Religious Organizations Law, 27, 69, 199n. 5, 200n. 8, 205n. 40
renunciation, 2, 9, 10, 17, 19, 43, 84, 92, 124, 139, 192, 194

responsible officer, 34, 85, 150
Risshō Kōseikai, 29, 51, 59, 114, 192, 204n. 22, 209n. 25, 210n. 29, 218n. 96
rokuza nenbutsu, 229n. 17
ropparamitsu. See six pāramita
Russo-Japanese War (1904–1905), 68
ryōsai kenbo. See good wives and wise mothers

sabetsu kaimyō, 176
Sakai Yūsai, 11, 58, 78
Saichō, 11, 12, 46, 49–52, 56, 62, 64, 74, 75, 80, 91, 96, 97, 151, 200n. 8, 208n. 16, 212n. 1, 215n. 45, 238n. 3
scholar-priests, 47, 154
sectarian studies, 11, 80
secularization, 11, 18, 108, 123, 131, 137, 139, 171, 193, 195, 201n. 25
seimeishugi. See vitalistic salvation
sekinin yakuin. See responsible officer
Sensōji, 67, 72, 143
Setouchi Jakuchō, 11, 124
Shanti Volunteer Association, 220n. 40. See also Sōtō Volunteer Association (SVA)
Shigain, 67
Shikoin, 96, 97
Shimazono Susumu, 13, 38, 54, 55, 161, 200n. 4, 201nn. 8, 9
shinbukkyō. See New Buddhism
Shinkōbukkyō Seinen Dōmei. See Youth Alliance for New Buddhism
shizensō. See natural funerals
shōmyō, 56
shūgaku. See sectarian studies
shūkyō hōjin hō. See Religious Juridical Persons Law
shūkyōdantai hō. See Religious Organizations Law
shūkyōhōan. See Religions Bill
Sino-Japanese War (1894–1895), 68
six pāramita, 230n. 23
social engagement campaign, 8, 44, 96, 103, 104, 108, 194

social welfare, 45, 48, 95, 96, 99, 101, 102, 107, 148, 163, 187, 188, 193, 195, 207n. 67, 231n. 33
sōdai, 29, 34, 37, 38, 47, 85, 124, 129, 205n. 40. See also danka representative
Sōka Gakkai, 8, 29, 30, 206n. 41
sōshiki bukkyō. See funeral Buddhism
Sōtō Volunteer Association (SVA), 100, 220n. 40
Special Committee to Study the Temple Successors Problem, 137
state protecting, 64
state-religion relationships, 64
stonecutter firm. See ishiya
Sugitani Gijun, 72, 105, 218n. 2, 224n. 52
sutra-reading-group, 55, 56

Taishō University, 69, 70, 72, 92, 99, 129, 130, 153
Takahashi Shinkai, 177
Taki Eishin, 121, 122
talisman, 2, 41
Tamamuro Fumio, 17, 26, 37, 203nn. 6, 11
Tamamuro Taijō, 16, 203n. 13
Tanabe, George, 14, 41, 154, 157, 231n. 43
Tani Genshō, 209nn. 9, 13
temple centrism, 83
Temple Family Information Center, 132
temple registration system, 7, 16, 24–26, 28, 60, 65, 98, 166, 177
temple representative, 36, 85, 125, 159
temple's board of directors, 27
temple wife ordination, 10, 133–137, 194
Ten Good Precepts, 74, 75, 133
Tendai ikka, 94
Tendai Sect Comprehensive Research Center, 107
Tendai Sect Temple Wives Federation, 114, 118, 119, 120, 122, 134, 138
Tendai Seishōnen Hieizan no Tsudoi. See Tendai Youth Gathering on Mount Hiei

Tendai Young Buddhist Association, 104, 105, 228n. 3
Tendai Youth Gathering on Mount Hiei, 191
Tendaishū Bukkyō Seinen Renmei. See Tendai Young Buddhist Association
Tendaishū Dōwa Suishin Iinkai. See Committee for the Promotion of Harmony
Tendaishū Jiteifujin Rengōkai. See Tendai Sect Temple Wives Federation
Tendaishū Sōgō Kenkyū Sentā. See Tendai Sect Comprehensive Research Center
terauke seido. See temple registration system
thaumaturge, 21
this-worldly benefits, 14, 18, 43, 157, 202n. 30, 231n. 43
three practices, 50, 58, 60
Tōkai/Kantō Network for Women and Buddhism, 121
Tokyo International Buddhist School, 88
tomo ni ikiru, 116
tradition, 7, 61, 63, 81, 82, 89, 102, 103, 110, 122, 128, 141, 162, 164, 188–190, 193, 195, 204n. 24, 222n. 27
traditional Buddhism, 4, 7
traditional family, 50, 53, 139, 194. See also family
Tsuji Zennosuke, 14, 15, 17, 201n. 14
tsūzoku dōtoku, 54

urbanization, 29, 32, 37, 43, 223n. 35

vacant temple, 84, 85
values, 46, 49, 51, 53, 57, 61, 66, 104, 117, 189, 199n. 4, 223n. 35, 235n. 32; crisis, 44, 54
Vatican, 73, 191, 192
vegetarianism, 21, 76, 78, 144, 229n. 20
Vietnam War, 44, 105
Vihara Movement. See Bihara Undō
vitalistic salvation, 13
volunteer, 48, 52, 58, 106

Watanabe Shōkō, 15
Weber, Max, 11, 12
World Religion Summit on Mt. Hiei, 105
worldview, 54, 55, 60, 61, 138, 199n. 4

Yamada Etai, 70, 71, 77, 183, 192,
   214n. 34
Yamaori Tetsuo, 103

Yasumaru Yoshio, 13, 54, 55, 201n. 8
Yomeirazu Kannon, 102
Youth Alliance for New Buddhism, 71

zaike sōryo. See lay-priest
Zennihon Bukkyōkai. *See* Japan Buddhist
   Federation
Zōjōji, 67

About the Author

Stephen G. Covell is currently an assistant professor in the Department of Comparative Religion at Western Michigan University. He received his Ph.D. from Princeton University in 2001. For ten years he lived in Japan where he conducted fieldwork in Buddhist temples; conducted research at Tokyo University, Taishō University, and International Christian University; lectured; worked as a translator; and taught English. He is currently working on a biography of Yamada Etai, the 253d head priest of the Tendai sect.

Production Notes for
Covell / *JAPANESE TEMPLE BUDDHISM*

Text in Goudy, with display type in
Hiroshige Book

Composition by Lucille C. Aono

Printing and binding by The Maple-Vail
Book Manufacturing Group

Printed on 60# Sebago Eggshell, 420 ppi